GENEROSITY AND THE CHRISTIAN FUTURE

Stacy

All best wishes

Princeton 2005

GENEROSITY AND THE CHRISTIAN FUTURE

GEORGE NEWLANDS

First published in Great Britain 1997
Society for Promoting Christain Knowledge
Holy Trinity Church
Marylebone Road
London NW1 4DU

British Library Cataloguing-in-Publication Data.
A catalogue record of this book is available from
the British Library.

ISBN 0-281-05018-X

Typeset by Bibliocraft, Dundee.
Printed in Great Britain by
Redwood Books, Trowbridge, Wiltshire.

CONTENTS

PREFACE

Generosity and the Christian Future arose out of Henson Lectures delivered in Oxford in the spring of 1995. The official subject of the lectures is the appeal to history in Christian apologetic. It struck me forcibly that the history of Christianity may have far more in front of it than behind it, and that the future is every bit as important to the Christian tradition as the past. I decided to consider the Christian future and the problems which appeared likely to face Christianity both in its internal development in theology and Church and in its relation to public issues. It became clear that a recital of the possible problems was not satisfying without an attempt to develop a systematic Christian response. In reflecting on the huge potential for future conflict in polarized cultures, cultures with religious differences and divisions between the religious and the non-religious, concepts of generosity commended themselves as having the potential to lead to constructive rather than destructive tensions. I have attempted to spell out some of these dimensions of generosity as a suggestion for Christian response to the future.

Generosity has been a reality of experience as well as a subject of reflection in the construction of these chapters. I am grateful to the Electors of the Henson Lectureship for the opportunity to try out some of these ideas before a live audience, and especially to Keith and Marian Ward with whom I stayed in Christ Church. I want to thank Trinity Hall, Cambridge for its continuing welcome to a former fellow; President Gillespie and his colleagues at the Center of Theological Inquiry at Princeton and at Princeton Theological Seminary for a delightful and profitable visit there (not least Ross McDonald and student friends), and Duncan Forrester, then in Princeton, for hospitality and valuable comment on the material in draft form. I am grateful to President Campbell and colleagues at McCormick Theological Seminary in Chicago, to Don and Carol Browning and colleagues in the Divinity School there, to Matthew and Betsy Dickie-Gebhard, to Brian Gerrish and Dawn de Vries. My thanks too to the Faculty of Divinity at Glasgow University for study leave, to the British Academy and the Faculty for very welcome funding, to Alex Wright and SPCK for taking on this project, and to my wife Elizabeth and family for their generous support.

INTRODUCTION

The theme of this book is the Christian future, and the development of a theology of generosity in response to the challenges likely to face Christian faith in the twenty-first century. Different concepts are used in Christian theology at different times to express the central elements of the gospel within different cultures. I find that concepts of generosity help me to articulate a view of the priorities facing theology and Church in the immediate future. In particular I want to explore the suggestion that Jesus Christ is the generosity of God for us. This leads me to concentrate on the contribution of Christian doctrine to public issues, and especially the relation of Christology to human rights. It has always seemed to me that if Christian faith is relevant to any of us it is relevant to all humanity. I am centrally concerned that faith should remain in the public square, and that the circle of faith should always be outwards facing. The theology sketched here is both liberal and pluralist in intention. Of course those who speak of love, or generosity, are not necessarily more loving or generous than those who do not, but this need not deter us from trying to think through the implications of these central concepts of the human imagination for faith. I also want to encourage us to attempt some imaginative leaps of faith into the Christian future, not as a form of prophecy but as a way of inviting us to try to look at some basic issues from less familiar angles.

The Christian future

Some initial markers on the Christian future within which generosity may be reconceived. The Henson Lectures which I delivered in Oxford in 1995 represented an attempt to imagine the challenges facing the Christian faith during and after the period of unprecedented and accelerated change which awaits society over the next few decades. We cannot see the future. One might be tempted to call these lectures 'Walking on the waters'. But we can make a concentrated effort to assess the likely effects of the evolution and removal of many of the factors now largely determinative in the

1

shaping of theology and Church. We may reflect on the possibilities for change, on conservative and liberal reactions, on shifting patterns of pluralism and integration within cultures, religions and ideological identities. We can reflect on the past, looking at Christian responses to cultural change in history. We may then consider some appropriate responses to massive cumulative change, intellectual and social, from the perspective of Christian theology.

There has been a spate of books recently on the Christian future. Robert Wuthnow's *Christianity in the 21st Century-Reflections on the Challenges Ahead* is in my view one of the best. In his introduction he makes an important point about the nature of such reflection. 'We miss the whole point of the future when we approach it as something to predict. Then we become forecasters, trying to guess tomorrow's weather so that we can carry umbrellas or sunglasses. The real reason we reflect on the future, I suspect, is not to control it, but to give ourselves room in the present to think about what we are doing'.

What sort of future do we want to see for Christianity, for the churches and for Christian theology? There is much to be found in Christianity today which gives grounds for hope. But there is much too which gives grounds for concern. In the face of a pluralist world culture the churches appear to be increasingly defensive, on the retreat, unattractive to thinking people. How are we to break out of the constraints which often make the churches either dull or exciting only in reaction? Is it possible to try to think ourselves out of contentment with a diminished and diminishing faith, and to consider the future of faith in a world which faces accelerating change?

This is a study of the future of Christian faith and Christian community. Of course, there is an important sense in which the future is always closed to us. Neither horoscopes nor science fiction will open it for our generation, any more than oracles, horoscopes and clairvoyance could open it in the past. In many ways it is perhaps just as well, we may think, that we cannot see into the future. Even more important than the future, it may seem, is a sense of the past. Awareness of history gives us perspective, saves us from being blinded by contemporary perceptions. Knowledge of an ancient civilization can produce a humane perspective on the present, as classical scholars have often been aware. Tradition is a key word for Christian community, which lives through the handing down of the gospel through the ages.

And yet. And yet tradition can also be the means of hallowing all kinds of errors, misconceptions and prejudices, over generations and over centuries. It can also fossilize our imagination, making it impossible to think beyond the tramlines of our conventional expectations. It may be that we can never jump out of our cultural skins. Our science fiction can never reflect anything but the present, however far into the future we date the episodes, and in whatever galaxies. But we can at least take conscious cognizance of the possibility that human history may only be beginning, that future developments may well be much more significant for the course of human flourishing than past developments, that the pace of change may well accelerate. The significance of discovery in the natural sciences for theology will always remain a matter of debate. One theme of recent cosmology which appears to me to be significant for my present purpose is the recognition that the future of the history of the universe as we know it may be much longer than the past, and that what is yet to be discovered will probably shed much new light on what we already know.

It is perhaps an essential element of the human condition that we often imagine ourselves in every generation to be civilized, humane and sophisticated, to have at last a reasonable approximation to a true picture of the way things are in our universe. Yet all previous perspectives have been shown to be provisional, and capable of revision, often substantial revision. Our present pictures can be no exception, and they are certainly not protected by attempting somehow to project them into a future context. But we can at least try, on occasion, to think about an open future, which is shaped but not entirely dictated by previous tradition and convention. Such thoughts will also be provisional, partial, incomplete. However, they might in principle at least be ways of moving towards that future. If we do not seek, we shall certainly not find. Like archaeologists, we may expect to have much better tools for analysis in the future. But perhaps we can at least save some sites from destruction in the present.

Different people in our highly pluralist societies look at the history of Christianity in very different ways. I shall suggest that there is much in Christian history for which we have to repent, though there is also much that is good. There is no reason to think that people in the past were more or less good than in the present. Different cultures have looked at ideas and actions in different ways.

3

Perspectives have changed and will change. We may hope that there is progress of civilization, as dogmatic attitudes soften and humanity learns to cease exploiting its fellow human beings. Yet anyone who hoped for such a civilized progress at the beginning of the twentieth century would have been shocked by the sequel. The replacement of authoritarian religious ideologies by authoritarian secular ideologies was definitely no improvement, as the fate of millions in the course of the century swiftly demonstrated. Civilization is not always easily achieved, maintained or enhanced.

Part I of this book looks at various possible developments in society and Church in the immediate and longer-term future. The first three chapters attempt to set out the problem. The fourth considers some contemporary responses, and the last two propose some solutions.

In the first instance we consider the future on the basis of the present, and in the light of an imaginary shapshot of the tasks facing a future Christian community, at the start of an ecumenical council, Vatican X. Within Christianity, perspectives on faith and theology may be radically shaken, notably by ecumenical and feminist theology. This will have a comprehensive effect on the expression of the Christian Faith. Technological development will produce new conditions for human life, especially through the physical and life sciences and in communications. There may be greater tolerance and understanding of differences, militant cultural fundamentalisms, religious wars. Renewal of faith will require inter-religious dialogue, reconsideration of human values, reappropriation of a sense of the presence of God. Corporate expression of Christian faith changes with changes in ecclesial structures. Ethical values are reshaped and reaffirmed under the pressure of political events. Faith in God may contribute to a new intellectual framework for life in reconciled diversity. We shall have to assess the phenomenon of the postmodern, and consider the response of theology and of the churches to social and cultural changes, especially since the nineteenth century. It will be central to our enterprise to reassess the phenomenon of pluralism, both in the humanities and in the natural sciences.

As far as the humanities are concerned, examination of convergence and divergence in a wide spectrum of contemporary American theological programmes should lead us to produce models for construction out of sharply differing proposals. In the natural sciences, I shall suggest that the development of theory in cosmology may assist in the understanding of faith, illuminating problems in anthropological narrowing of concepts of God and in the use of naive scientific realism in theology. Interdisciplinary study of the structure of faith may have much unrealised potential for the future.

The future contains the potential for radical transformation in theology and community. Changes in the perception of ecclesial, social and physical realities will sharply alter our notions of the conceivable. Freedom from current plausibility criteria will bring new constraints and possibilities, illuminating contemporary Christian social ethics, creating new perspectives in the assessment of Christian tradition, forcing reappraisal of the theory and practice of faith. Perception of the methods and the substantial content of theology changes in correspondence with the evolution of faith in Christian worship, service and dialogue. Metatheological reflection will continue to develop in relation to fundamental and ecclesial theology. Suggestions for future paradigms will be offered, in response to a changed future context, and with reference in the present to Tracy and Jüngel, Lindbeck and Küng. The concept of God and the shape of Christology in a future confession of faith will be explored.

Theoretical developments in the social sciences, in psychology and politics in particular, will continue to cast new light on the emergence of ecclesial structures and on faith's expression in communal practice. Critical analysis of the work of Drewermann, Schillebeeckx and Troeltsch may point us to the requirements for a paradigm for theory and practice.

The text of a future theology must remain unwritten. A conjectural subtext is possible, and may serve to focus the attention of theology in the journey towards the future of the Christian faith. Faith expects that the Spirit of the self-giving love of God, creator and reconciler of the physical cosmos, will continue in the long-term future to be ceaselessly active in the physical cosmos, in strange transformation and invitation to radical and specific forms of Christian discipleship.

In the present, a proposal for the way ahead, around the focus of generosity, is both possible and in my view desirable. Part II is the construction of a specific programme. First, then, some initial markers on generosity. Generosity, according to the Oxford

English Dictionary, comes from the Latin *generosus*. It means: (1) Nobility of birth or lineage (*gener*). This use is now only archaic. (2) High spirit, nobility of conduct. Now only: willingness to forgive injuries (1623). (3) Liberality in giving, munificence (1677). (4). Generosities (rare), instances of generosity (1647). In the adjectival form, it can also mean furnished liberally, hence abundant, ample, used of diet, colour, of wine. Its use in English goes back at least to Shakespeare: 'Most generous, sir. This is not generous, not gentle.'

Generosity suggests going beyond the bounds of what is strictly required in giving, abundant and ample provision. It suggests justice tempered with mercy, and the ability to bypass the strictly appropriate in order to reach out to the other.[1]

There is a less positive side. 'He was himself generous as a giver, parting, indeed, with that which did not altogether belong to himself' (1882). No concept is incapable of inappropriate use. Love, honour, justice, all have been used in the exploitation of humanity, and generosity is not exempt from danger. Those of us who use the language of generosity are not necessarily more generous than those who do not. Generosity can be patronizing, indicating a use of power which can amount to moral blackmail. There is a clear and important link between generosity and justice. Not every concept of generosity will be just, and not every theory of justice will be reconciled easily with the basic requirements of generosity. Generosity can mask a refusal to grant statutory rights and privileges to oppressed communities, and may inhibit the development of self-reliance. Apparent generosity can be a device to avoid the necessity of facing up to the unpleasant realities of injustice, conflict and the need to oppose oppression openly. From this it emerges that effective generosity will be anything but sentimental, may call for hard choices and a considerable measure of sacrifice.[2]

What of Generosity in the biblical narratives? At first glance there seem to be hardly any instances. Grace and generosity appear often to be synonymous, for example in 2 Corinthians 8.1, in the N.E.B., the generosity which God has given to our congregations in Macedonia. Certainly generosity has the character of spontaneous compassion which is basic to grace. But grace, we said earlier, is not a substance but God's mode of presence with us. I want to suggest that generosity is another way of describing that presence, and that it may communicate the heart of the matter in the public square in a way that grace may not so easily do. A Christian understanding of generosity is the generosity of God in Jesus Christ. As such it encompasses love, compassion, forgiveness, reconciliation, hospitality – the whole range of gifts of the spirit of Christlikeness. All that can be said of God's action love and grace in the Bible, and of human response in love, can be seen as dimensions of generosity. In this sense we can see numerous biblical narratives, the narratives of Exodus, of covenant commitment, instances of human faithfulness – Ruth and Naomi, David and Jonathan – the parables of the Good Samaritan and the Prodigal Son, the growth of the churches in mutual sharing, and above all the life, death and resurrection of Jesus in solidarity with the vulnerable, as paradigms of divine generosity and appropriate human response.

Generosity in Corinthians – magnanimity – and in Christian writing is often related to open-handed financial contribution to the funds available for distribution by the community. It is clearly right that generosity should often involve finance. Finance is crucially necessary. But in itself it is not sufficient. It is this wider agenda of generosity which springs from the generous love of God in incarnation and reconciliation, and which may be a stimulus to imaginative Christian thought and action.

It may seem that the history of the Church is in many respects a history of profound lack of generosity, both in internal and in external affairs. Why does the religious dimension in human life so often lead to conflict, bitterness and war? Here the tradition, in and beyond the biblical period, can be counter-revelatory, showing us how God does not want things to be, inviting us to repent, believe and respond to the gospel. We shall have occasion to look at generosity in the tradition of the gospel, both in theory and in practice. Stress will be laid on the importance, indeed the urgent necessity, of generosity by example in the churches. Here there is also a positive side to the tradition, which may help us with the future.

Generosity is closely related to other concepts which often occur in theological and philosophical reflection – notably compassion and altruism, but also justice, forgiveness reconciliation, hospitality. These too may have positive and also negative aspects. Corporate generosity may not be quite the same as corporate hospitality. Considerations of generosity may overlap with all or any of these. In his *Acts of Compassion* Robert Wuthnow has produced a remarkable empirical account of the scope and sources of compassion in American religion. There may develop in society a sense that supporting other people is a mutually beneficial process which is in the ultimate interest of all the members of that society. This can become a self-fulfilling and self-reinforcing movement, which is the more effective the wider the net is cast. Much of this support develops through the work of small groups. These too may be more inward looking or more outward looking. They may reflect the best, or the worst, depending on your perspective, of liberal and communitarian visions, of effort directed mainly towards the common good or to the witness and self-understanding of more particular interest groups.

Generosity is related to altruism, to concern for the welfare of others with at least a measure of personal disinterest, to at least a determination to privilege the best interests of the other. It is related to forgiveness, for it seeks to provide support despite the presence of obstacles including where necessary wrong actions by the recipient of generosity. It is related to reconciliation in that it is concerned for the building up of relationship in community, overcoming a tradition of suspicion and mutual misunderstanding.

It would be possible to build a complete systematic theology around the theme of generosity. I do not propose to do this, partly because I have recently set out a such a systematic account in *God in Christian Perspective*, and partly because I understand generosity as arising particularly out of one area of the Christian reality, the self-giving of God in cross and resurrection. Out of this engagement comes new creation, and a cosmic significance of generosity as a fruit of the Spirit.

God's generosity is understood by faith especially as a theology of the cross, tracing the rainbow through the rain, though it is given permanent effectiveness through the resurrection. As such it may then be seen as the hidden force of God's creative action. It springs from the vulnerability of God, God in the public square, crucified under Pontius Pilate, God for the public square, for all humanity. Generosity is the force which may break up the log-jam of incompatible belief systems and ideologies, but it is always a non-violent force, a force effective in nourishing authenticity in the other. The language of generosity may be powerful, but the reality of the generosity of God will take us beyond the language to further reflection on the substance of the divine reality.

I find it helpful to start from the centre of the gospel as the source and basis of God's generosity, in the vulnerability of the reality of incarnation. Beyond this it then becomes natural to see much in the biblical narratives and in the tradition of the Church as encapsulating generosity. The most familiar of the parables to most people, the Good Samaritan and the Prodigal Son, have been reconceived in thousands of ways, and may be conceived as parables of the generosity of God. All that can be said of the grace of God and the divine love in the Old Testament and the New can be illuminated by thinking of this as an expression of the divine generosity. Part of the aim of this study is to anchor these themes in the fabric of the basic issues facing Church and theology in the society of the future, a task which springs from a rich continuing tradition but which has to be to be reimagined afresh in every generation.

Sometimes this can be done by focusing deliberately on the language and conceptuality of generosity as such. At other times it is necessary to concentrate on problems and agendas in which the concept of generosity is absent or at at best only implicit. Only later will it be appropriate to reintroduce the theme of generosity as a contribution towards a Christian perspective on the issues. I shall not concentrate explicitly on the language of generosity in Part I of this study, in order to try to avoid the danger that problems may be masked in a premature rhetoric of generosity. I do not wish to suggest for a moment, either, that only Christians are generous, or more generous than others. What I am proposing is that generosity may be one of those bridge concepts which enable the effective communication of Christian faith within the realities of public life. To have any hope of achieving this it will be necessary to take a hard and focused look at possible futures, desirable and undesirable, pleasant and unpleasant, in Church and society, with specific reference throughout to a perspective of generosity. This will include exploration of generosity, Christology (and especially the vulnerability of Christ) and human rights. We shall have to reconsider the theological tradition in the light of generosity, the role of power and pressure in Church and community, the relation of religion to the public square in past and present. In the light of this analysis we must attempt to construct a strategy for generosity. Central will be concepts of Christian agonistic liberalism, for which I am much indebted to the work of Sir Isaiah Berlin.

PART I

The Christian future

1

FAITH AND THE

HUMAN FUTURE

Faith shaking the perspectives

Future shock. Open theology. Secular Christianity. Radical Church. Liberal approach. Liberation praxis. Humanization of mankind. Paradigm shift. Faith and freedom. The wind of the Spirit. Reconstruction, renewal, reshaping. The churches are not short of advice on change and renewal. Indeed the words relating to change and transition are so much used that they threaten to become meaningless. We have developed such a jargon of language relating to change that it becomes increasingly difficult to take the need for change seriously. More difficult, theologians and churches have long succeeded in building into their operating structures a kind of immunity to the prospect of change. The language of change is easily assimilated and repeated, at a stroke cutting out the need for any real reassessment or reconstruction.[1]

Most people realize that change for its own sake is rarely a good idea. The demolition of one set of ideas or structures often leads to a kind of mirror image in another style. The task is not to interpret the world but to change it. Bitter experience has shown that it is much more important to understand the world as it is before changing it, than to rush into disastrous change, bringing suffering to millions. Attempts to impose utopia in history have usually led to misery. But with all due caution, it is still important to attempt to think beyond the plausibility structures of the moment. Simply to forget nothing and to learn nothing is not enough. We must at least try to look forward. In the case of Christianity, this seems to me to be an urgent and pressing task. I should like to raise the question of the effects of massive cultural change. We cannot know how this will proceed, but we may expect that it will continue at an accelerating pace.

I should like us to consider here, imaginatively but as far as possible soberly, some possible and likely states of the Christian community in the long-term future. This is impossible, the stuff

13

of science fiction, not a serious enterprise. In one sense, of course, we must grant the objection. Yet philosophers spend time considering conditions in a number of possible worlds, and theoretical physicists do similar things. Different imaginative constructs can serve to widen the horizon of our imaginations, as it were, and challenge us to deepen our thinking.

Let us consider a possible future scenario. It is entirely possible that by the year 2500 Christian unity will have been achieved, at least by the major denominations. It is possible that the leader, perhaps a representative leader elected for a fixed term of office, might be a woman. Such a person might well be the Pope, in continuity with the historical papacy, not necessarily from the former Roman Catholic tradition or indeed from Europe. Consider the possibility of such a person, we may call her Pope Flora, and think of her as a former Baptist by tradition. If we had such a person as the nominal head of the Church, that might have tremendous implications for the future of our faith.

Consider the possibility that the Pope is advised by a Christian Council, and that the Council has called a new General Council of the Church. What sort of consequences would the resolutions of such a council have for the churches and for theology? What would be the implications of such a prospect for development in the churches in the interval between now and then? For the possibilities of the future certainly have implications for present action, as Moltmann and Pannenberg in particular have reminded us in twentieth-century theology.

We may also assume that technological development will continue in the scientific field, in the human sciences, the physical sciences and the life sciences, at the very least at the pace of the last hundred years. The consequences in medicine and in the world of communication alone are likely to have thrown up many new possibilities and many new issues. We must now turn to some of these new possibilities.

If we ask ourselves what sort of contributions to human flourishing we would like the churches to make, then one of the most important for most of us would be a contribution to the achievement of world peace, a peace which embodied, as the current phrase has it, justice, peace and the integrity of creation. Conflict often arises from fear, which is in turn fuelled by insecurity, prejudice and intolerance. Religions, and not least the Christian religion, have contributed to prejudice and intolerance through the ages, though they have sometimes also been instrumental in helping to break through prejudice, to open closed doors. Clearly, a united Church would have opportunities far greater than are available at present to make a real impact on the factors which make for tension in our world, and are to some extent at least the legacy of historical conflict between different Christian traditions.

It is also clear that a significant contribution to justice and peace will also require much greater co-operation and discussion between adherents of the major world religions than has been possible in the present, and will have to take account of the perhaps increasing proportion of humanity who have no religious adherence at all, but who are still concerned for the development of a humane future for the planet.

Against the possibility of greater communication, and against the typically modern presupposition of an increasingly liberal approach to other traditions must be placed the reality of different sorts of militant fundamentalism as a response to radical pluralism in the modern world.[2] We see this in Christian fundamentalism, Protestant, Roman Catholic and Orthodox. We see it in Marxist fundamentalism, for example in China and in North Korea. We see it classically in European liberal values which themselves are often intolerant of those who adhere to different cultures and their interpretations of society. Where there is radical difference coupled with radical intolerance, conflicts are likely to increase. There is no guarantee that we are moving towards a future of justice and peace. On the contrary, unless we take positive action to move in one direction, we may find ourselves sliding towards a future which will bring little joy to future generations. As we have suggested, few people at the end of the nineteenth century could have imagined the benefits which the twentieth century has brought to mankind, but even fewer could have imagined the catalogue of horrors which have also unfolded. We may find that Christian communities mushroom and collapse more frequently than in the past, due to the influence of mass media, rather in the way that Marxism grew hugely and then collapsed in the twentieth century.

Faith and communication for a new world

Faith in the Judaeo-Christian tradition has developed in different ways over many centuries. I have described faith in the present as faith after faith, faith in the God of Jesus Christ continuing to direct people's lives as a reality in the midst of accelerating change, from the religious to the secular and back again to a variety of global religious experiences, from monolithic to pluralistic cultures, within cultures which contain elements of the modern, the anti-modern and the postmodern in varying combinations. If we are to think of faith for a new world, we can afford neither to lose the heart of the Christian gospel in the quest for modernity, nor to obscure the centre of the gospel in the packaging of an age that no longer addressed us where we are. To operate successfully within these tensions is the perennial task of theology.

God is love, love characterized precisely in the self-giving of God in the events concerning Jesus of Nazareth. This is the centre of Christian faith, at one level entirely simple, and at another level susceptible of all the theoretical reflection which we can possibly bring to bear on it. To develop this theme is always to enter into dialogue in the continuing stream of modern theology. I make no apology for turning at this point to some fundamental issues in contemporary theological research.

We theologians are inevitably children of our age, with all the limitations that this imposes. Most serious contemporary systematic theology continues to pursue the legacy of the European Enlightenment. Some pursue the great tradition from Kant through Schleiermacher to appeal to religious experience. Others follow the designs of Barth, much indebted to Hegel, towards what is termed postmodernism and appears to critics to be a kind of communitarian fideism. Anglo-American scholars tend to pursue more empirical and pragmatic philosophical theologies, which are less easily related to biblical studies than continental systematics, though there is a branch of empirical philosophy, with strong links to the philosophy of science, which flourishes in conservative churches, untainted by the corrosive influence of the social sciences. There remains a huge conservative evangelical theological community, which concentrates on conservative biblical studies and is largely fundamentalist. To it correspond remarkably similar conservative groupings based on a fundamentalist approach to church tradition, in Roman Catholicism and Orthodoxy.

Nineteenth-century liberal theology believed that its own sort of rational argument would eventually prevail, because it would be seen to be intellectually superior to the alternatives. This has not been the case. Much more conservative theologies could be intellectually sophisticated and could continue to appeal to the academic mind. Sociological, cultural and political factors could encourage various sorts of fundamentalism, not least in an age of increasing religious and ideological purism. The socialism of the Weimar Republic is replaced by Nazi autocracy. The liberal Marxism of the twenties is replaced by Stalinism. Various sorts of religious fundamentalist state have been a feature of the modern world. It is entirely possible that varieties of religious fundamentalism will increase in popularity in the future, and in time come to dominate the main-line churches, driving out more liberal options.

It is all too easy to imagine a situation in which fundamentalist versions of the major world faiths could initiate and consolidate wars of attrition, in which each side believed that it has a God-given task to subdue the other side – rather like the ideology which fuelled the medieval Crusades. While pessimism is rarely helpful, it is important to remember that unpleasant developments occur in human history with considerable frequency. It may be of course that fundamentalist religious beliefs are bound in time to collapse under the weight of their own inherent improbability. But if we may take Marxism-Leninism as a comparable belief system, it persisted in purist form for a very long time, as an intellectual as much as a social option. In Ireland, that most religious of countries, both in the North and in the South, we may see the fruits of religious intolerance. That then is one of the possibilities for the future. Against it we may place the reflection that to be religious is to value all human beings, to defend their freedom to flourish, and to be religious or not religious. To be tolerant in the face of intolerance, affirming in the face of negation, is a basic Christian virtue, and indeed this is true of all the major religions. This is not profound, we may say. But it may be profoundly important for human survival.

The last decades have seen the attempt to develop new paradigms of the relationship of knowledge to social structures,

17

notably in the work of Jürgen Habermas. The phenomenon of the postmodern in its various manifestations has taught us about fragmentation and its value, about the importance of disentangling privileged majority or dominant viewpoints from suppressed or overlooked minority viewpoints. It has taught us a hermeneutics of suspicion.

In theory, therefore, the postmodern ought to be of enormous assistance in ecumenical dialogue, exposing the use of privileged positions and illegitimate claims to power for what they are. In practice, however, in our various denominations we have continued to defend our inherited positions, to the disadvantage, intellectual or indeed physical, of those in less privileged states. Indeed the insistence on radical pluralism which is part of the postmodern, far from leading to more mutual tolerance, may lead us to suggest that each interest group has the right to make up its own rules and operate them without regard to others. If my view of, say, human rights does not correspond to that of an organization like Amnesty International, then I may carry on a policy of genocide or whatever, according to my own system of ethics.

How does one do theology in the present? A recent and to my mind particularly imaginative approach to the problem of a postmodern theology is taken by Peter Hodgson in *Winds of the Spirit*. Hodgson takes up (from Hal Foster) a useful distinction between 'the postmodernism of reaction', found among neo-conservatives who denounce the secularity and liberalism of modern culture, and a 'postmodernism of resistance', which 'arises as a counter-practice not only to the official culture of modernism but also to the "false normativity" of a reactionary postmodernism' (55). I am in sympathy with Hodgson's view that 'the postmodern does not cancel the essential gains of modernity – rationality, freedom, human rights, subjectivity, dialogue etc. – but rather appropriates and reconfigures these modes of thought and action in new circumstances, often quite radically' (55). The new challenge to theology is characterized as a quest in three dimensions: emancipatory, ecological and dialogical. The first has to do with oppression, liberation and the freedom of God, in civil rights and black-power movements, in feminist and womanist, gay and lesbian theologies, among the physically challenged and the elderly. 'Liberation theology has become the ecumenical and global theology of our time' (67). God is absent when justice is not done to the poor, the dispossessed and the exploited. Asian theology and black African American theology are good examples of this perspective. 'The black spirituals make it clear that Christ was experienced as present precisely in the slave community, clearing a space of freedom in the midst of bondage and brutality' (76). Feminist theology documents the exploitation of women. The ecological quest engages with postmodern science and the new cosmology. The dialogical is linked to the emancipatory, pressing towards communicative practices which have freedom as their goal.

Hodgson stresses the relation in all good theology between theory and praxis. 'Theory without praxis is mere ideology; praxis without theory is mere technique' (33). Therefore the freedom of the Gospel is a challenge to expressions of idolatry in ideologies – helists racism, sexism, classism, naturism, homophobia, xenophobia – and in injustice, expressed in political, social, economic and environmental oppression. What is needed is an incarnate praxis, focused on the cross as the shape of empowering love. 'God is at risk and suffers in the world, but also rejoices in the emergence of everything that is good' (323).

I have to say that on the whole I am very much in sympathy with Professor Hodgson's approach to theology, in general and in particular. I shall perhaps come back to areas where we might marginally disagree. Beyond this, however, there are perhaps some major questions which we might look at. For example, after the social justice for which Hodgson is striving has been achieved, where does the cutting edge of theology then lie? It may of course be thought that the human predicament is such that one injustice is always succeeded by another, and so the task of achieving justice and the service of God in worship is a never ending one till God brings in his Kingdom. It may also be thought that beyond Hodgson's synthesis there are still fundamental enquiries to be held, for example into (1) the nature of God's generosity, (2) the relation between word and sacrament in the articulation of God's presence in creation, (3) the Christian contribution to a theology of world religions and (4) the Christian contribution to a workable programme for the protection and support of universal human rights. I return to Hodgson's understanding of God. Here he lays down a number of considerations which are germane to talk of

God. But perhaps he has difficulty in pulling these together into an integrated thesis.

However conceptually unsatisfactory for us, there is, it seems, a paradox at the heart of our understanding of God. God is infinitely beyond our full comprehension, not a being but the ground of being, beyond the concepts of the religions, as Nicholas of Cues long ago recognized. He is also, Christians continue to believe, fully and definitively expressed for us in Jesus Christ, in whom he was incarnate, through life, death and resurrection, in vulnerability and self-abandonment This is the contribution which Christians bring to the dialogues of the future, in trust and humility, not knowing where these will lead us, but trusting in the God of Jesus Christ to use them as instruments of his love.

Faith and renewal in theology

I come back to theology. Theology is about God and about humanity. At different times it is necessary to stress God or people. Theology is about God. In a sense it is always the same, about the same God. It is Catholic, it is apostolic.

Simply saying that theology is about God will not necessarily help us. It is not about our private or institutional or tribal concept of God. Indeed we need to have a certain humility about our personal concept of God. Restoration of catholicity should mean freedom from our local institutional and organizational prejudices, to reflect on God's presence as appropriated in different ways in different traditions. Historically, a divergence of religious beliefs has often led to increased hatred and bitterness. We must turn to a new awareness of the dangers of exclusivism. Triumphalistic self-assertion, though it may be intellectually exciting, appears to lead to frequent human tragedy. Theology is about human beings. There is no competition between true concern for God and true concern for humanity. To be religious is to value all human beings, and to defend their freedom to flourish. Theology is for people. It has to be done appropriately to its subject matter and to its recipients. It is about God, who is love. It has to convey the excitement and the surprise of that love. It has to challenge people with God's love, and to overcome a history in which it has threatened people with God's wrath.

In the face of endless theological debate, it is not surprising that a certain disenchantment with the theoretical side of theology sometimes sets in. In recent years, coming originally from the more liberal wings of the Church, there has been a call for praxis rather than metaphysics, social action rather than academic speculation. But this can lead to an anti-intellectualism, producing a decisive shift towards church communities which are simply orientated towards management, and a consolidation of theological fundamentalism.

More promising in some ways are such movements as the Celtic Christianity movement, green and environmentally friendly, though the Celtic lands have scarcely been models of religious tolerance over the centuries, with their intoxicating blends of religious and national fervour. We may reflect that one of the very few issues uniting religious opponents in Ireland in recent years has been the banning of family-planning clinics, North and South. This cause has been espoused not only by bigots but by people of charm, intelligence and integrity.

The corruption of the best is indeed the worst of all. We ought, one might think, to be able to look back on a more liberal theological tradition and be proud. Yet liberal Christians, among whom I count myself, in their reaction to alternative proposals through the centuries have often been as arrogant, dogmatic and intolerant as those whom they have opposed. They too have engaged in unpleasant party politics, and they have systematically excluded those whom they have regarded as less than 100 per cent committed to the party line of the day. The politically correct have been every bit as brittle, triumphalistic and myopic as their opponents. Indeed, the historian might reflect that the weaknesses of the liberals have provided ample justification for excesses of the traditionalists, as vice versa. No wonder Pascal said that Jesus will be in suffering to the end of the world. We shall return to see what can be learned from liberal failures.

How does theological renewal take place? The question of authority is central here. An important issue is the role of the Bible. Here fundamentalism is rife, but there is also movement among those who would still regard themselves as evangelicals. Let us think of a proposition on the authority of the Bible. 'The Bible is the rule of faith. It is not the centre of faith itself. But it is the best guide to ensure that all the central structuring elements of the gospel are represented to us appropriately.' It seems to me that many modern evangelicals would be willing to agree to such a position, and that there are ways to consensus here. From a pluralist perspective, it could of course be argued that the whole idea of a prioritization of the Judaeo-Christian tradition is fundamentally triumphalistic. Either we have a library of sacred books of the world, all on a par with one another, it could be argued, or we abandon the whole notion of central texts and concentrate on adoration of God as the ultimate central mystery. But there is nothing wrong with difference of opinion, provided that it is accompanied by respect for other people's perspectives – unless these perspectives themselves involve exploitation of others.

Any significant future reflection on the role of the Bible will have to take account of feminist criticism. It will recognize the patriarchal framework within which much of the text is created. Paradoxically, a decisive shift away from biblical fundamentalism would also free more people to appreciate the strong points of evangelical Christianity.

Theology in the future will have to take fresh account in every generation of the Bible. It will also have to take fresh account of the issue of a theology of world religions. In such dialogue and co-operation something like a principle of subsidiarity may emerge, allowing the major faiths to work together in every way that they can, without overruling the appropriate authorities of any one particular faith. But such co-operation is easier to advocate than to implement. The horrors of the Holocaust, and the crimes against Muslims in the former Yugoslavia, are examples on different scales, but equally unacceptable. The whole issue of tolerance is complicated by internal persecution within the major religions, where minority groups continue to be persecuted by majorities. Tensions are clearly inevitable, but the difference between constructive and destructive tensions remains crucial.

The nature of theology, the authority of the Bible, inter-religious dialogue – another central issue for the future remains the nature of salvation, the human future in God's purpose. Christian theologians in the future will doubtless consider as they have done in the past the cosmic dimension of salvation through Jesus Christ. The problems of the interrelation of the divine and the human will remain. Doubtless in the future we shall know infinitely more about the nature of the human than we do now, if only through advances in the life sciences. Yet we may guess that the delicate balance between unique personal character and cultural determination will remain a puzzle, not least in the light of continuing intensive genetic engineering.

Salvation means participation in the peace of God. Peace with God and with each other is part of the goal of salvation, and of the more perfect humanization of humanity. Future writers may like the general thrust towards a definition of salvation as involving the peace of God. They will make their own contribution, adding to the anthropomorphic limitation of human perception a dimension which, though it did not come close to the vision of God, at least corresponds in practice somewhat to the extra dimension which St Thomas has theoretically sketched out for the angels. Salvation in the Eastern tradition, they note, has been closely tied to a vision of pure union with God in mystical contemplation, in retreat from this world towards alignment with God. In the Western, Augustinian tradition it has been seen most often in terms of rescue from the sins of the flesh, a salvation of human biology.

Salvation raises always the question of the shape of the human. Human beings, we shall doubtless continue to believe, are created in the image of God, and sustained and directed by God towards fulfilment. Human beings may be produced in the future in all sorts of different ways. In some respects a separation of procreation from human sexuality might begin to untie some of the knots on personal relationships into which church traditions have tangled themselves for centuries. In all cases it will be important to reaffirm the basic Christian perspective, of God's initiative and God's sustaining care. 'For Christians, Jesus Christ is the basic form of humanity.' This can be a divisive statement. But when Christology is seen always as inclusive, always to be read in a charitable light in relation to non-Christians, always to be used in a non-triumphalist context, areas of the tradition which have sometimes been discredited may be rediscovered and again appropriated, with profound implications. For Christians, Christ as vulnerable, as human, as fragile, as unconditionally self-giving will always play a role in the search for human flourishing.

A fundamental question remains. How do we develop our understanding of God? The nature of God will probably remain as mysterious as it has always done for Christians. Three millennia of faith in Christ are nothing compared with the time scales which are dealt with in contemporary astrophysics. We can say that the God in whom we trust today is the creator of the physical universe, and is revealed as cosmic self-giving love in the events concerning Jesus, his life, his death, his resurrection. But beyond this we can use only the imagination of faith. Our blueprints for the risen Christ are no more descriptions of ultimate spiritual reality than the cosmologists' red anti-quarks are descriptions of physical reality.

However one approaches the matter, there is a most important residual element of mystery in God. In his recent *Mystery and Promise, A Theology of Revelation*, Professor John Haight, of Georgetown University, argues that revelation comes in the form of a divine promise which is God's own self-donation to the world. Revelation is the gift of divine humanity, which renders reality intelligible in an unprecedented way. This image, presented explicitly in the crucifixion of Jesus, illuminates the mystery that surrounds us, the cosmos out of which we have evolved, the tortuous history of humanity and the ambiguities of personal existence. John Haight emphasizes that we must seek to understand revelation in terms of contemporary cosmology and the environmental crisis, as well as from the context of a religiously plural world. The image of revelation given to us by God is of the vulnerability of God, the divine kenosis. Kenosis is then related to mystery and promise, vision and hope. Mystery is about the limits of experience and enquiry, and points to God's self-limitation in self-giving. The humility of God should lead us to sensitivity about other religions in speaking of revelation. The mystery is of promise and hope, and points to the self-humbling of God in the life, death and resurrection of Jesus.

This revelation is to be understood not only anthropologically but cosmologically. Creation is the product of the non-obtrusive love of a self-emptying God, and the universe is itself a story grounded in promise. Human history is itself a gift of divine revelation, within which a human self-understanding can be reached, in which a critical consciousness is combined with trust in God.

Fundamental theology as I see it is concerned with the imaginative description of a God who is infinitely transcendent and all-compassionate. Because it is a description which uses the whole scope of human conceptuality it has no preferred epistemology, no single correct method. That way it differs from numerous ideologies which have thought themselves more rigorous and scientific by adoption of an exclusive line of argument, e.g. traditional

Thomism and traditional Marxism. Theology operates by analogy from the human to the divine. But for Christian theologians it gains a basis in divine reality through the revelation of God in the events concerning Jesus Christ, events which indicate the nature and character of God.

There remains a significant flaw in much theology in this area. God, we said, is self-giving, self-affirming love. But because of its own imperfect praxis, traditional theology has found it impossible to express the dynamic creativity of divine love. It has been unable to take this compassionate creativity as the cornerstone of its fundamental theology. This is, perhaps, a basic human flaw, which is unable to match principle with actualization practice.

One of the most decisive breakthroughs in the understanding of God may come, we suggested, through the feminist movement. It is not that feminist concepts of God as such have replaced the tradition. The position is rather this. The affirmation that God is neither male nor female does raise in the sharpest possible form a question about the use of two of the most important traditional grounds for the doctrine of God, the Bible and the tradition of St Thomas, underlining that God is always infinitely greater than our human thoughts, even the most venerated human thoughts. In this way the feminist movement may act as a catalyst for a radical reassessment of the tradition, on God, on the human, on the understanding of the Church and of ethics.

God is in God's own nature self-giving love. Only God is capable of total self-giving, which is God's way of opening up relations between the divine and the human, between human beings and between us and any other beings in the universe.

What are we to say about God? That is certainly the question. All the prolegomena are nothing but the wrapping. It's the substance that matters. We may feel that if only the academics of the past had been less intoxicated with their own designer-sculpted epistemological passwords and nostrums, there might have been faster progress in the theological enterprise. There is little point in avoiding naive realism only to wallow in critical obfuscation. Whatever you do, there are problems. But at least you have to try to weigh up the advantages and disadvantages of different approaches, and make a choice. When you've made it, you have to try to minimize the disadvantages and maximize the advantages.

There is, I suppose, an argument for taking on board formally a counter to the male hijacking of the faith which lasted for so long. God is clearly not masculine. But God is not feminine either. God is God. That is something that we find difficult to grasp, however closely we grind the wheels of analysis. It is perhaps worth recalling that in the ancient languages of the Church nouns were masculine, feminine and neuter almost by accident, and in fact didn't carry any gender connotation unless you wanted to include it. So when the ancients said 'Deus est caritas', they didn't perhaps imply that God is a male lover any more than that God is a female lover. They just meant that God is love. *Deus*, God, happened to have a so-called masculine ending, just as *mensa*, table, happens to have a feminine ending. God is God. God is love. God is infinitely loving, enduring, accompanying, being present, affirming.

I turn to the notion of revelation, the grounds on which we can make the positive affirmations that we make. Theology has spent a considerable time on this theme, for it provided a kind of instant test of the state of the art of current theological trends. Discussion of revelation also has ecumenical significance. The old anathemas between the denominations has gone, but there is still a slightly disreputable tendency to grind old denominational axes under the polite guise of methodological programmes, notably in relation to revelation. The phenomenon is not, of course, new.

Revelation is linked, as it has always been, to Scripture and Church, to text and word, community and sacrament. We are back to the issue of authority. There is stress in modern theology on presence, on the inspirational divine presence in the community, Christian and non-Christian, in various ways. Through the ages there have been periods of stress on word, on sacrament, on text, on myth and on narrative, on history and on story. Each of these motifs has highlighted distinctive strands of the understanding of revelation. I come back to the nature of presence, a concept much criticized in the tradition, especially the tradition of the theology of the Word. The presence remains a hidden presence, but it is not a diffuse presence, for it is always the presence of the spirit of Jesus Christ. This is how God makes himself known throughout the universe. Yet it is not an exclusive presence, for Christ involves the divine relationship to other religions on earth, though the nature of this engagement is understood differently by Christians and non-Christians.[3]

The relation of the Holy Spirit to Christology has been one of the focal points of recent Christian thought. Ralph Del Colle has recently examined the possibility of a new Roman Catholic Spirit Christology. Though he devotes much space to twentieth century authors, the distinctive contribution of this book is to link recent work to a much older scholastic tradition of reflection on Christology and Trinity, and ask how the tradition can enrich the contemporary search. *Christ and the Spirit – Spirit Christology in Trinitarian Perspective* has six main chapters. The first, on pneumatological Christology in the Orthodox tradition, sets out from Lossky's critique of Latin Trinitarian models, based on a reading of Palamite theology, and considers possible defences of Latin thought in Rahner and in Latin scholastic Trinitarian categories. Critical is the relation between the two missions of Christ and the Spirit, and the development of a pneumatological Christology as well as an incarnational Christology. This leads into discussion of Spirit – Christology in the neo-scholastic tradition, notably in the work of Matthias Scheeben, Emile Mersch and Maurice de la Taille. The relation between grace and presence in Trinitarian self-communication is central. How to maintain the distinctiveness of the three Trinitarian hypostases while developing a Spirit – Christology of the divine presence remains the Catholic objective. This is now exemplified in the work of the Australian theologian David Coffey. The Holy Spirit is the love bestowed by the Father on the Son and vice versa. The bestowal of the Spirit is central to the process of incarnation. Incarnational and Spirit Christology are two aspects of the Trinitarian interrelationship. The presence of the Spirit actualises the presence of Christ in human life.

There have indeed been historical indications of a sense of the presence of God through the Spirit of Christ, notably in various charismatic movements. But here, often, the spirit is apprehended as guaranteeing an individualist piety, a centre of strength which too easily falls over into a sense of infinite moral superiority. But the kenosis of God in incarnation led to a fulfilment in the kenosis of the Spirit. This is not an impoverishment. It meant that the Spirit is always given to be given away, and its presence is manifest in mutual support and concern. Such an understanding of Spirit, as the giver of peace, may assist the dialogue of religions to make progress in recent decades. It also allows a reappropriation of the Bible and the tradition of the Church which bridges the old gap between the spirit and the letter, affirming the centrality of Jesus Christ while avoiding the imprisonment of praxis in an often inhumane culture.

Projections of the future

I should like now to consider again the value of imaginative projections of the future, especially in the light of recent discussion on modern/postmodern attitudes to culture. My own example from Vatican X was clearly culture-bound in all sorts of ways. We have noted that there will be different and developing futures for Christian faith in different parts of the world, reflecting combinations of cultural shifts. Provided that we remember that these will change in different ways, one sketch may stand as an example, indicating priorities as I see them and stressing that there will undoubtedly be major changes from the present, in whatever directions these occur.

In the future it will be important to appreciate and respect the visions of others, while seeking to engage with others in supporting personal and social values which we ourselves regard as central to human well-being.

The need to recognize and appreciate difference, alterability in some postmodern writing, was well put by Clifford Geertz in the introduction to *Local Knowledge*:

> To see ourselves as others see us can be eye-opening. To see others as sharing a nature with ourselves is the merest decency. But it is from the far more difficult achievement of seeing ourselves among others, as a local example of the forms human life has locally taken, a case among cases, a world among worlds, that the largeness of mind, without which objectivity is self-congratulation and tolerance a sham, comes. If interpretive anthropology has any general office in the world it is to keep teaching this fugitive truth.(16)

Christians believe that humanity is created by God, to be respected in diversity and in a relationship of mutuality which was classically demonstrated and made possible by Jesus Christ. They may rejoice to find this echoed in any area of society, without upstaging, correcting or in any way hijacking the affirmation.

POSTMODERN FUTURITY

This brings us back to the basic issue of how to commend a Christian perspective while respecting the integrity of those who adhere to alternative perspectives. It will be useful at this point to return to the discourse about modernity/postmodernity. I have already indicated a certain unease with theologians who rush too quickly to postmodernism as a way of retrieving the ground thought to be lost to unbelief through modernity. In reply it may be argued that I have simply adopted a modern world view without taking account of the objections. Some account of this issue must now be taken.[4]

The last decades have seen the attempt to develop new paradigms of the relationship of knowledge to social structures, notably in the work of Jürgen Habermas. Central here has been the debate about the foundations of knowledge, the roles of particular traditions and of universal canons of rationality, between Habermas and Gadamer. This debate has taken place largely within the framework of continental philosophy. Its sociological and philosophical presuppositions have by no means always been acceptable for example in the Anglo-Saxon world, in which all general theories of meaning, of society and of the nature of humanity have met with rigorous criticism. Here too the textual work associated with deconstruction has often been met with scepticism, rather as the existentialist and Marxist philosophies of earlier decades of the century proved highly vulnerable to sceptical analysis.

An excellent initiation into the issues raised by modernism/postmodernism for theology was provided by David Tracy's *Plurality and Ambiguity*. Whether or not we agree with his own programme, his description of the fluidity of historical perspective and the variety of textual hermeneutics is brilliant and highly persuasive. Tracy is acutely aware of the ambiguities in the Enlightenment inheritance. Yet for him, as for Habermas, there is still hope.

> We can continue to give ourselves over to the great hope of Western reason. But that hope is now a more modest one as a result of the plurality of both language and knowledge and the ambiguities of all histories, including the history of reason itself. And yet that hope of reason – a hope expressed, for Westerners, in the models of conversation and argument still

created by the Greeks – still lives through any honest fidelity to the classic Socratic imperative, 'The unreflective life is not worth living.' (113)

In his deservedly popular *The Condition of Postmodernity*, David Harvey analysed the transition from the modern to the postmodern in the understanding of workers in various fields, notably architecture and the arts generally, but also and most perceptively in their relation to economic and political movements, and to conceptions of philosophy, and of time and space. He pinpointed clearly the advantages and disadvantages of the modern, the advantages and disadvantages which have accrued to humanity from the Enlightenment quest for rationality in all things. Harvey argues that the postmodern is in most respects not a different movement from the modern, but rather a series of developments within modern culture. I agree in large part with this analysis, and with his observation that there are advantages and disadvantages both in the stress on the universal which characterizes the modern, and in the stress on the particular which characterizes the postmodern. These features have a pervasive influence in many dimensions of culture and society, from the economic to the aesthetic.

Harvey's study is an ever-important reminder of the need for intellectual argument to relate to the many layers of complexity involved in considering questions of the shape of society – actual or desirable. It has been taken up in a theological context in Colin Gunton's most interesting 1992 Bampton Lectures in Oxford, published as *The One, the Three and the Many*. Professor Gunton underlines the highly problematic nature of the modern programme, deriving in large part from a deficient understanding of God as creator and reconciler. His response is a reaffirmation of the classical doctrine of the Trinity, as the revealed clue to God's nature and the quality of relationships which God intends for humanity, in their personal, ecclesial and social dimensions.

All Christians would share with Colin Gunton in finding much amiss in the human predicament at all stages in its history, and in seeing the answer to human fulfilment in a proper Christian understanding of God. *Cor nostrum est inquietum donec requiescat in te.* I should find it less easy to share entirely in his analysis of the modern or in his particular Trinitarian response. It is indeed true, as Adorno and others have repeated, that the world of enlightened reason led in our time to the death camps of the Third Reich, and to the murders of millions with the aid of sophisticated modern technology and logistics in Russia and in China. The concentration camps were supervised in part at least by doctors of philosophy. Yet the abuse does not take away the proper use, and the failures of modern society are not a sufficient reason to despair of it.

There is a fine line to be drawn beween cynicism and optimism concerning the human condition. In considering the failures of the modern we should not forget the massive advantages brought by modern medicine, and as Professor Gunton himself recognizes, there is much to be said for liberal democracy. In our justified disappointment about the inequities of the modern world, between rich and poor, we should not romanticize past solutions, theological, social or political. In the days when they were widely accepted, life for most people was nasty, brutish and short.

The Christian community itself has of course been a massive force for good in humanity, through its worship and its pastoral care. But it has also been a force of social control and social divisiveness of a kind which has done great injury, and we have a duty not to forget the uncomfortable dimensions of our tradition. The question of paradigm shifts in modern consciousness, and their dimensions throughout the 'thick' culture of our societies, has been perceptively explored by Richard Bernstein in *The New Constellation: The Ethical-political Horizons of Modernity/Postmodernity*. Bernstein sums up succinctly the issues at stake in the critique of the legacy of Heidegger, Foucault, Derrida, Gadamer, Habermas and Rorty. The debate about liberalism in modern thought is well set out in the discussion of Rorty, and the appropriation of text within the particularity of a concrete social context is focused by the analysis of Gadamer and Habermas. Bernstein's view of Habermas as an important mediating figure between the search for universality and the need to affirm the particular is one which I would emphatically endorse. In this respect it seems to me that Habermas' work provides an important bridge towards the overcoming of the problems of a Cartesian understanding of reason as the cultivation of individual self-consciousness through the development of the language of communicative action.

On the specific area of justice, Francis Fiorenza has noted that Habermas marks a notable advance on Rawls.

31

Rawls distinguishes between justice as a basic political theory of society and a full theory of the good within moralm theory. For Habermas, the primacy of justice means that justice specifies, delineates and determines one's concept of the good. His ethic brings together questions of the good life with those of justice and discusses them as questions of justice within a discourse about justice that takes into account interests and needs. (Fiorenza in *Habermas, Modernity and Public Theology*, ed. Browning/Fiorenza, 66f.)

However, Rawls has since modified his position somewhat, and we shall return to this subject in chapter 9. The search for an appropriate mode of communicative action is not easy. Christian faith is not simply about individualism, though it respects individuals as individual others. It is not simply political theology, though it is deeply concerned about the shape of justice, which involves social justice. Faith is concerned with every sphere of mutuality, and this may raise hard questions about power and pressure which cannot be resolved at a party political level. This point has been made cogently by Christopher Rowland in his paper, *Reflections on the Politics of the Gospel.*

For most of us the political is of little direct impact in the way in which we conduct ourselves. But those interactions between individuals and in small groups, remote as they might seem from formal political processes, deserve the description political. Not only are they shot through with the influences of the formal social setting, but in themselves they manifest the exercises of power, the subordination and the impoverishment of human beings in the struggle for the maintenance and extension of individual interests . . . The narratives of Jesus' action portray a challenge to convention and imply different standards of human relating. (*The Kingdom of God and Human Society*, ed. R. S. Barbour, 239–40)

Addressing contemporary pluralism, Bernstein makes distinctions which I find helpful. He notes the dangers of a fragmenting pluralism, a flabby pluralism, a polemical pluralism and a defensive pluralism, before coming down in favour of what he terms 'an engaged fallibilist pluralism.'

Such a pluralistic ethos places new responsibilities upon each of us. For it means taking our own fallibility seriously – resolving that however much we are commited to our own styles of thinking, we are willing to listen to others without attempting to deny the otherness of the other. (336)[5]

The stress in Habermas on mutuality, which was, we may reflect, anticipated in many areas of the development of philosophy, e.g. in Theunissen's *Zwischenmenschlichkeit* or in Voegelin's *To Metaxu*, will be seen in a Christian context as deriving ultimately from the creation of humanity as co-humanity, and as paradigmatically shown in the self-giving love of God in the vulnerability of Jesus Christ. In an American context mutuality has been developed in Don Browning's *A Strategic Practical Theology*. I do not think it appropriate here to offer a parallel discussion to the ground so excellently covered by Bernstein and others. I do however want to say something about the critique of liberal values which has been the focus of so much debate in politics, philosophy and theology, notably in discussion of the nature of justice, e.g. between MacIntyre and Rawls, and in theology in the writings of Hauerwas. As in the case of most important debates in philosophy and theology, there is much that can be said on both sides, and any solution must take account of the substantive points raised. For myself I am happy to affirm the centrality of a liberal viewpoint, in theology and in politics. It is true that liberal notions of justice, in the political and the economic sphere, have been selective and often oppressive. It is true that liberal theology has often reduced the Christian gospel to something which was hardly worth disbelieving, not to speak of believing. For these reasons the critique of liberalism has often been salutary. But it seems to me that what it needed is an improved version of liberal values, not a replacement by other perspectives. The alternatives in history so far appear to me to have been on balance much worse, and the critique of liberalism has often had a dark side, directly or indirectly encouraging oppression. I agree with David Tracy that liberal theology is the best way to communication and dialogue. But it is clearly a programme in need of intensive further development. In this respect it is helpful to recall the title of an essay by Helmut Peukert, 'Enlightenment and Theology as Unfinished Projects', in the Browning/Fiorenza volume (43ff).

Comments useful for this discussion on fundamentalism and postmodernism are made by Ernest Gellner in his *Postmodernism, Reason and Religion*. Gellner traces the rise and the spread in the modern world of Islamic fundamentalism, in a largely sympathetic characterization. He stresses the development of Islamic law in the modern world. 'A socially and politically transcendent standard of rectitude was ever accessible, beyond the reach of manipulation by political authority, and available for condemning the *de facto* authority if it sinned against it' (7). He notes the universalization of the application of Islamic law in a modern technocratic society, and the importance of martyrdom within the tradition. 'A puritan and scripturalist world religion does not seem necessarily doomed to erosion by modern conditions. It may on the contrary be favoured by them' (22). With this objective perspective he compares unfavourably the wholesale cultural relativism of postmodernism. 'Objective truth is to be replaced by hermeneutic truth' (35). It is really a form of subjectivism, which is practised as a form of expiation for the sins of colonialism (Geertz). Gellner himself prefers a third option which he describes as 'Enlightenment rationalist fundamentalism', which refuses to absolutize substantive convictions but does absolutize some procedural principles of enquiry – in fact, the modernist programme of the Enlightenment. It seems to me that Gellner is most illuminating in the first section of his book, in explaining the strength of Islamic fundamentalism in the modern world. There are obvious affinities to Wuthnow's account of Christian fundamentalism in the American religious Right.

It is clear from recent analyses of fundamentalism that this development is not, as is often thought, a phenomenon necessarily associated with comparatively primitive cultures and ill-educated people. On the contrary, the development of unified social structures, centralization, the influence of cultures by the mass media and other technological developments may greatly strengthen both the attractiveness and the effectiveness of fundamentalism. The possibility of a world society dominated by religious fundamentalism in the long-term future is an entirely viable possibility, though it is emphatically not a possibility that I myself would welcome.

RECONCILED DIVERSITY

How are we to achieve mutual respect and encouragement on our planet among a multiplicity of religions and ideologies in the future? That remains a central question. On the one hand, we have to recognize and respect diversity. We must try to avoid judging others by our own criteria and failing to consider their criteria. On the other hand, there needs to be genuine development towards mutuality. Communicative action has to replace mutual incomprehension, fear and hostility. These are issues as old as humanity itself. They appear in different forms at different times and places. Christians see God as the creator and reconciler of all humanity. They see the basic clue to understanding and action in God's participation in humanity in the life, death and resurrection of Jesus Christ. Here is the answer to the human question of its future. It is an answer which respects both the mystery of God and the mystery of man. It does not prescribe any fixed form of interaction or lifestyle. But its shape is definitive, as the shape of unconditional love. Central to the theme of our project is the notion of reconciled diversity, of mutuality with respect for the voices of particularity. We shall come across an impressive assessment of reconciled diversity in Hans Frei's characterization of types of theology. There is a somewhat similar assessment of different theological styles, in this case those of Barth, Holmer, Phillips, Lindbeck and F.S. Fiorenza, in Martin Cook's *The Open Circle*. Cook searches for an open confessional method of doing theology which will combine particularity with the ability to learn from and interact with other confessions, and he finds an open model in Niebuhr rather than Lindbeck.

Openness, as we saw from Geertz, has to be openness to others at all levels of their cultures, and not simply an intellectual acceptance. This is stressed by Kenneth Leech in his book *The Eye of the Storm: Spiritual Resources for the Pursuit of Justice*, which emphasizes the urgency, and the difficulty, of genuine openness to minority communities of the oppressed. The gospel speaks directly about visiting prisoners – a litmus test of the community's generosity towards those at the bottom of its scale of priorities (cf. Andrew Coyle, *Inside – Rethinking Scotland's Prisons*). It is possible that recent emphasis on the social dynamics of community in biblical interpretation may alert us again to the challenges which Christianity poses to our assumptions about social interaction (cf. H. C. Kee, *Knowing the Truth – A Sociological Approach to New Testament Interpretation*). Werner Jeanrond has called for a new critical hermeneutics which involves communal action in response to the reading of the biblical text (*Theological Hermeneutics*, 180), and Hans Frei in his posthumous collection *Theology and Narrative* has left us a fascinating discussion of the role of sociology in relation to interpretation ('Theology and the Interpretation of Narrative'). I have the impression of vast areas here still to be explored in the Christian future, rather than of a field almost completely exhausted.[6]

Much ground-breaking work on the relation of religion to culture and society was of course done by Max Weber and his friend and colleague Ernst Troeltsch. They made mistakes, in part because what was attempted was often new and complex. Anyone who has read Drescher's biography of Troeltsch, sympathetic as it is, will be in no doubt of the mistakes and the real dangers, not least in Troeltsch's exclusive romantic nationalism. The more positive aspects of the road from Schleiermacher to have been well signposted again recently in Brian Gerrish's *Continuing the Reformation*. The new answers are in many ways less satisfactory than the old answers, of the Reformation and the early Church. But that is the common path of research and development, and it may be that we need a little patience. At the same time, awareness of the value of diversity may lead us to appreciate a cross-fertilization of traditions of theology, spirituality and praxis which would never have suggested themselves to Weber and Troeltsch.

One might perhaps reflect in conclusion, on behalf of reconciled diversity, that when particular programmes, methods and doctrines cease to be prescriptive they become more attractive as imaginative invitations. An example, suitably from a quite different source, might be the Trinity in Catherine Lacugna's recent *God for Us*. Here Trinitarian reflection is helpful, not indeed in absolutizing in God the social conventions which we currently prefer, but in suggesting more sensitive understandings of human interaction.

> The communion of persons in the Spirit does not entail a leveling to the lowest common denominator. Koinonia does not swallow up the individual, nor obscure his or her uniqueness and unique contribution, nor take away individual freedom by assimilating it into a collective will. The goal of Christian community, constituted by the spirit in union with Jesus Christ, is to provide a place in which everyone is accepted as an ineffable, unique, and unrepeatable image of God, irrespective of how the dignity of a person might otherwise be determined: level

of intelligence, political correctness, physical beauty, monetary value. (299).

If the future brings new problems for us to wrestle with, it also promises new possibilities. I like this.

2

FAITH AT VATICAN X

Since I have suggested chapters on the Christian future, we might as well plunge in at the deep end. This section is set in the year 2517 C.E., and I've given it the title

Vatican X – an imaginary snapshot

(It is of course quite impossible for us to jump out of our cultural skins, as it were, and the following bears all the hallmarks of 1997, if not 1967, but I hope it may challenge you to think of possible futures for yourselves – precisely where you think my own sketch breaks down.)[1]

The Pope stepped down from her portable exercise machine, a rather smart contraption made of elasticene (a new metal, particularly useful to travellers, which conveniently folded away to fit into one's hand luggage), and unplugged it from the mains. At least the voltage in Oxford, England, was the same these days as it had been in Cambridge, Massachusetts. It had been an odd choice to have the Council here in Britain this time, rather than in the Theocratic States of America. But it was the 1,000th anniversary of the Reformation, and Oxford had featured pretty largely in the original events, given too that the last council had been in Worms. It was also the Anglicans' turn to host the council, even if the present Pope was herself an American Baptist. Yesterday had been a rather curious day. They had got to chapter 13 of the draft document, and had at last agreed the entire text of a chapter without endless debate. It was about equality, a blanket declaration renouncing all forms of discrimination on religious, sexual, racial or other grounds, and it had gone through without question.

These were issues that might have torn the Church apart 500 years ago, as people had burned each other at the stake over views on the Eucharist 500 years before that. The certainties of one age, the unshakeable certainties, had become unthinkable to the next. Truly the Church is a most amazing institution, thought Flora.

It was time, she reflected, to set down her own private account of the proceedings, before the details became too obscure. What was needed was a sketch, decree by decree, of the main events and of the opinions which accompanied them. There had been ten main areas for discussion, each for two days of debate. As she thought of the pattern, she pressed the green button on her thought transmitter, and a text flowed crisply out of the small grey box on the corner of her desk.

The first schema of the new Council involved the foundations of theology. This was itself a surprise to those who had thought that the praxis of the Church should be the initial focus. But there would be much change necessary in our praxis, and it was thought wise not to attempt to change the world, or at least the Church in the world, before we had some understanding of it. How these debates still echoed the battles of long ago! Twentieth-century debates on realist and antirealist philosophical theories had echoed their medieval predecessors, but now with a new twist. Now in the twenty-sixth century the old words would appear again in the discussion, but the context was different yet again. You can't jump into the same river twice, as they'd said long ago. The text itself was very short. This was to be a feature of this Council. *Non est hoc aliud quam nova formatio ecclesiae,* was written as a sort of motto across the top of the document. It was, she reflected, regrettable that even the *periti* here could no longer get their Latin right. Even worse that their style imitated the rhythms of the pop group, rediscovered in the twenty-second century, which copied the text of that earlier children's horror, *Winnie Ille Pooh.* She recalled the order on the first page of the document before her. (1) *On fundamental theology.* (2) *On God.* (3) *On revelation, Scripture and Church* (4) *On salvation* (5) *On the human* (6) *On the Church* (7) *On society* (8) *On ethics* (9) *On the religions* (10) *On the universes.* The order itself had not greatly changed in a thousand years. But the contents were definitely not what they were.

De theologia fundamentale. It was remarkable, Pope Flora reflected, how theology had changed since the twenty-first century. How many essays had she produced as a college student on church history from the nineteenth to the twenty-third century? One cannot of course blame previous generations for not seeing what they could not see. Vision is always 20/20 with the benefit of hindsight. Then as now, different sorts of Christians did what they could, most of the time honestly and sincerely. Like us in the twenty-sixth century, they were very much children of their age, with all the limitations that this imposes. In those days they were still arguing about the legacy of the systematic theologies of the European Enlightenment. Rather to the surprise of liberal thinkers, it had taken three further centuries for theological fundamentalism in the major world religions to crumble under the weight of its own improbabilities, and even today, in 2517, there was still a wide spectrum of theological opinion. This diversity was, however, now welcomed on all sides. The various attempts by the Nation and Church committee, in its various shapes over the twenty-second century, to produce a uniform national perspective by enriching the water supply with suitably politically correct additives had not improved the state of the nation.

De theologia fundamentale. Sapientia omnia, Dei et hominis cognitio. I suppose they got the idea from the 900th anniversary celebration for Calvin's Institutes, mused Flora. Theology is about God, she reflected. Theology is about humanity. Theology is about God and human beings. Theology is about people and God. At various times it was necessary to stress God or us, or the combination in different ways, to correct imbalance and point to what is necessary in a particular situation.

Theology is about the God of all human beings. The recent repetition of the dark biblical paradox of the slaughter of the innocents had at least led to a new understanding and reassessment between the members of the major world religions. This was indeed strange, for it might well have led to a deepening of hatred and bitterness all round. But instead there was a surprising awareness of the dangers of exclusivism. Triumphalistic self-assertion, though it may be quite justified intellectually, appeared still to lead to inevitable human tragedy. The recent formation of the secretariat of the Society for the Propagation of Religious Unity was something which may be 500 years overdue, but which could in one sense not have come at a better time.

Theology is about human beings. To be concerned for God is to be concerned for humanity in and for itself. There is no competition between true concern for God and true concern for humanity. This was not a new idea. She remembered the paper she had written on the early European theologian Karl Rahner for a history of doctrine class. To be religious is to value all human beings, and to defend their freedom to flourish, and to be religious or not religious. To be tolerant in the face of intolerance is a basic Christian virtue. She thought of David Hume, and wondered if he would appreciate the thought. Theology is for people. It has to be done appropriately to its subject matter and to its recipients. It is about God, who is love. It has to convey the excitement and the surprise of that love. It has to challenge people with God's love, and to overcome a history in which it has threatened people with God's wrath.

A blinding white light flashed before her window. Flora pressed a button and the perma-plastic pane slid into the floor. Her sister stepped in and dropped her heli-pack in the corner of the study. They had coffee, and then Marcia flew off to the local megamarket to pick up some new spacesuits – constructed of the most fashionable material – which she had ordered the previous week. Marcia was sometimes concerned about her appearance, Her Holiness reflected, though she had always looked good. Cultures change out of recognition, it sometimes seems, and yet lots of human characteristics had perhaps not changed so very much in the last couple of thousand years or so. But, mused Flora, anyone who thought Marcia was just interested in shopping would be gravely mistaken. Despite her conventional L.A. upbringing, Marcia had had a very close relationship with her Scots great-grandmother, who had lived to the age of 176, and had learned from her never to take things entirely at face value, and at the same time to make up her own mind about everything. That mind, Flora reflected, was not the pontifical mind when it came to matters of religion – another indication of the continuing variety of responsible opinion in these matters – and a confirmation, if it were needed, of the decision not to programme the Council in such a way as to produce uniform 'assured results' at the end of the meeting.[2]

The bulk of the conciliar document on the Bible was not particularly controversial. It recognized unanimously the patriarchal cultural framework in which much of the text was written. The battle for women's rights in the Church had long since been won, decisively helped, it had to be conceded, by the comprehensive implementation of respect for all human rights which had followed the end of the Great Disaster, the last fling, please God, of all fascism, moral, political, economic and religious, two hundred years before. It was remarkable that the most ardent progressives were now the Orthodox, who at one time had been the most intransigent of all – led by Her Eminence the Metropolitan of Minsk.

The documents also recognized the decisive nature of the historical and theological affirmations in that framework which were so central to the Evangelical platform. The disappearance of fundamentalism meant that even the liberals now recognized that the attractions of Evangelical Christianity were not simply to be put down to immaturity in the young and senility in the old. After all, even the fundamentalists had captured the Church by democratic means originally. In a sea of uncertainty people always look, considered Flora, for strong, simple answers. Even if there aren't any, the Pope reflected, they often prefer what they can get to an anarchism which is often more clever than sound. In any case, inter-faith dialogue had put the internal Christian agenda into a quite new perspective.

As Flora saw it, there was nothing in this document which might not have made sense to some of the American Catholic bishops who participated in Vatican II way back in the twentieth century. The only remarkable thing was that it had taken 500 years to get comprehensive agreement on it in the Church. As usual, delay meant that another almost more urgent problem, which might have been solved by now, was probably still 500 years away from solution. But that was the next section.

Another light flashed, this time green, in a control panel against the door. She pressed a button and a hologram of her spouse appeared full size in the centre of the study, boasting a large 'H' initial on its forehead. 'How are you surviving the Synod this afternoon?', it enquired solicitously. 'I hope things are going more smoothly there than they are down here this week? But I expect we'll get the wards straightened out in time to come along to the final session.' Being the Pope's husband was not always an easy task. People expected him to be a constant source of support, benevolence and compassionate love. But sometimes what was most needed, for staff and patients alike, was a compassionate kick in the pants, or firm reorganization of management procedures.

Hassan worried about the balance between leadership and inefficiency. Unlike Flora he was an Anglican, from a Yemeni background, and she teased him about the foibles of his tradition. If Baptists were loud and Presbyterians dull, Anglicans were universally famed for being patronizing, and they all more or less recognized themselves in their caricatures. Last week's refurbishment of the intensive-care wards with aluminium shielding had played havoc with some of the new heart chips in the last batch. The reason for this was far from clear. Neither high-tech nor high culture could take the odd glitch out of the most carefully constructed health care.

It was just as well, Flora remembered, that the kids had gone off to college before she was elected to the four year term of the papacy, for they did not exactly have much time off these days. Just as well too that top-quality college education was readily available to all. She thought back to the 'good old days' of Vatican II, when racist prejudice and class discrimination were unconsciously universal even here in the civilized world of Oxford, and shuddered with distaste. Jenny would probably not have made it here, on any count. Now her daughter was flourishing and would probably graduate next year in macro-robotics. It wasn't that genuine excellence in education and in many other areas of life was hard to find: it was just that it had taken so long, and so much totally unnecessary conflict, for it to be shared by everybody. And this had come at a cost – one child per family. It was an amusing irony that her predecessor Pope Alexis, the energetic Metropolitan she used to play unreal tennis with, had been the inspiration and driving force behind the world parliament's final constitutional commitment to the centrality of contraception.

How did she ever come to be a priest, she wondered? Ministry is of the essence of the Church. It was interesting that hundreds of years ago, when all sorts of people had nurtured hidden agendas about the cruciality of their particular clerical traditions, they buried the juicy bits at the end of the text, after long chapters of blandly benevolent and reassuring verbiage. Now they had come to see that the essence of the Church is not to be served but to serve. Of course we have always said this, thought Flora, and centuries to come will see the major flaws in our most modern constructions. But at least we now recognize that Christianity is about self-giving, mutual respect and regard, not somewhere along the line but from the beginning. Pity it had taken a Third World War to learn this.

It had been, on reflection, a good idea to accept the central affirmations of all the major churches within the basis of the World Uniting Church. Flora did not really mind being infallible, even if only for a four-year term, and without prejudice to the quality of her tennis, aerobics workouts and other diverse leisure activities. What mattered was that the Church retained some confidence in God, and did not succumb to the trend to death by self-generated embarrassment. God was God, yesterday, today and tomorrow. The Christian gospel was as much the way, the truth and the life as it had ever been, and to that extent she was proud to symbolize and represent officially the element of trust in the faith.

Her infallibility, she reflected, was the infallibility of the service of self-giving love, than which nothing could be more basic to human life. Her infallibility reflected the infallibility of all Christians, but only when she acted appropriately. It was remarkable how the universalizing of the concept of infallibility had brought to the Church a much greater sense of responsibility. Dynamic re-imaging of self-giving love brought the possibility of actualization of service. This was nothing new, of course. But it is in part a matter of saying what has been said and what is to be said, and acting on its utterance – as has been said.

Yet it was quite a thought. She looked back to the idiocies of previous centuries, where thinking Christians had solemnly refused each other eucharistic fellowship, insisting on devaluing each other's ministries and drawing the appropriate consequences in all areas of church life. We must live with the pain of our divisions, they had solemnly intoned. With friends like these, she thought. By the middle of the following week most of the documents which she had agonized over had gone through the Council, the majority with surprisingly large majorities, at least two-thirds. This was encouraging, and of course much more encouraging than the massive majorities of yesteryear, when the Catholic Church had vied with Stalinist assemblies to produce majorities of 99 per cent for Councils and Synods at the drop of a hat.

Overkill, she reflected, was one of the best ways of ensuring the ultimate failure of autocratic management. Let them get on with it, and the absurdities may eventually collapse under the weight of their own improbability.

The peace which followed the Great Reaction had, it was hoped, brought a new maturity to the planet. (Though when did people not think they were mature!). This had a lot to do with the final achievement of the economic balance between North and South. No one 500 years ago could have begun to predict the bewildering changes in the world's population that were to follow. AIDS had decimated Africa and then had a much more detrimental effect on Asia. Bans on artificial contraception enforced by different religions during the Great Reaction had boosted the populations of North and South America, and of the Middle East, to unimagined levels. They had fed this multitude only by cancelling all foreign aid to those even worse off than themselves. The War had then almost destroyed the planet, and only fortuitous developments in medical technology had prevented the disappearance of humanity in its entirety. It had even been thought for a time that only a bunch of evil-looking, radiation-fattened cockroaches would be left to inherit the earth, and there was talk of inserting coded information into their DNA, in the hope of ensuring the survival of some human values in their chain of development in the future. But the risks of disaster were thought too great. Just as well, thought Flora, or we should perhaps be ruled by giant superintelligent cockroaches today.

Last week's Jolly Green Giant party at her and Hassan's friends the Musaks had been a remarkable indication of how far things had changed. People had turned up in an assortment of iridescent insect costumes, and they had piped in a vast dish of salmon *en croute* shaped like a gigantic cockroach. If her residual Baptist conscience suggested to her that she and Hassan had perhaps eaten and drunk a little too much, nevertheless she was delighted to recall the relaxed atmosphere in which people had lived now for almost 100 years, in the absence of many of the fears and tensions which had characterized so much human history. Perfect love casts out fear: that was as central to faith today as it had been from the beginning. Economic well-being for all had certainly brought about a notable increase in humour and a sense of fun, without the pomposity which had mimicked the economic stratification of the past. Pomposity, thought Flora, always accompanied triumphalism. Depompification had followed detriumphalization, to put it rather pompously.

There was, the Pope reflected, nothing like a better standard of living to make people feel more relaxed. Hassan would say that that was not quite true, for some of the wealthiest people had been notoriously edgy and ruthless, while extremely poor people, like his great-grandmother, had been sovereign over their circumstances. But when she considered the yawning gulf of social and economic inequalities which was the norm only four or five centuries ago, she could hardly blame those who had been angry and resentful then. It was, indeed, astonishing that they had been so tolerant.

Christian love must commend itself on the basis of its own intrinsic value to the rest of humanity, she had always said in her sermons. Well there had been a recent good example of this, in the episode of the abolition of prisons. One feature on both sides in the Great War had been the taking of considerable numbers of prisoners, who had been treated according to the the barbaric conventions of the Dark Ages in the twentieth century. There had been mass suicides, and peace brought a complete abandonment of imprisonment, progress made possible by developments in psychological medicine and in the Christian contribution to medical ethics. Last week Flora had visited the ghoulish chamber of horrors in Baker Street, London, a model of a twentieth-century British prison in a road said to be named after a typical Home Secretary of the time. She had been told that an organization, somewhat improbably calling itself called Amnesty International, had once documented prisons inifinitely worse even than this throughout the world. But that was a very far fetched notion indeed. And in any case, Amnesty was one of the first organizations to vanish without the tiniest remaining trace in the War, a testimony to the definitive power of modern technology.

The Parliament of Religions would meet next year, and the Council could only draft some guidelines for its representatives. One thing that pleased Flora greatly was the emphasis on the equality before God of all human beings, whether they be religious or non-religious. For too long interreligious dialogue had simply replaced one kind of imperialism with another. Now people were beginning to actualize what they had for some time conceded in principle. It had been the exclusivism of the religions, like the intolerance of Marxism long ago, which had lead to disaster, and internal and external collapse. 'Why had we clung on to our own traditions so fiercely and for so long?' thought Flora. Sociologists had explained this away long ago, but again the gap between imagination and actualization was formidable.

Part of the reason for the growing manifestation of tolerance was not of course due to the maturity of the human race at all. Perhaps there was something in the old fashioned dictum that whatever humanity can do, it cannot save itself. It is incorrigibly unable to see the wood for the trees. It was, literally, with the arrival on the planet of the Irokesen that an end to the War could first be imagined.

This brought Flora to the last and most intriguing of the schemata before her, *On the universes*. It had been the imminent possibility of the earth disintegrating in a nuclear holocaust on a scale liable to have consequences throughout the galaxy that prompted the Irokesen to intervene. Their delegation had travelled to earth at the speed of light, an achievement which *homo sapiens* could not yet begin to conceive. They had simply frozen all activity on the planet, and then defrosted people and things as they wished, to induce a measure of stability. The Church had assumed that such beings would be entirely unsympathetic to its message. But, astonishingly, they themselves followed a religion of cosmic love, which they related, in a way which is hard to imagine, to Jesus Christ as the centre of our Christian faith. However, the Irokesen had managed to actualize forgiveness and reconciliation as the centre of relationship, in a way which we had only imagined for millennia. They had had neither the textual tradition nor the philosophical tradition without which our own understanding would be inconceivable. But they had a sense of the presence of God which was not hard to recognize as what we understand as the sense of the presence of Christ. We have not, of course, been able yet to work out any of the consequences of this, thought Flora hastily. Nevertheless, she realized that a major reappraisal of the theological task was just around the corner, the results of which she would not live to see, but which would, she reckoned, have a liberating effect on the proclamation of the gospel in the future, and at the same time underline the centrality of some of its traditional affirmations.

Two weeks later Flora sat on the floor, with a bowl of kimshi in front of her, and the brazier charring the steaks nicely, in a reconstructed traditional restaurant in Seoul. It was a nice irony that her latest meeting should take place in a city of ultimate Christian conservatism. The original restaurant had long since vanished, on the day that the whole Pacific Rim boiled, flooded the Korean peninsula, and submerged the long-lost islands of Japan.

But the Irokesen had made the suggestion, and the Council assessors had thought it an appropriate gesture of reconciliation. Of course, as they had made it clear, their people would understand the schemata of Vatican X in their own way. 'But if we are to help you to bridge the gap you humans always talk about between possibility and actuality, then we need you to explain to us more clearly how you understand all this. What does it look like from the inside, to human brains? How do you understand your human perceptual deficit? How do you propose to tackle this? How can we help you best?'

Flora ordered some Gewürztraminerauslese to cheer up the first course. One of the things people had learned was to mix food and wine from different continents, by adding appropriate balancing agents. There had been protests, justified she had to admit, from the Real Food Campaign, but it had its advantages too, especially for papal jet-setters.

It was not easy to keep up with the intellectual rigour of the Irokesen. 'We appreciate the value of your analysis of the past,' they had said. 'But you have always been prisoners of your past, even of your sophisticated perceptions of the past. What we are really interested in is your programme for the future.'

They looked again at the schema on the nature of theology. Flora herself had instinctively looked at this in the light of the European tradition. But she had to remember that this was not the basic perception of the Irokesen, though of course they could plug in that dimension of consciousness at the touch of a button, and override their normal modes accordingly. In a nutshell, they reflected on God from a rather different section of the universe, close enough to ours for there to be some natural affinity of conception, far enough for there to be a corrective to every assumption. They viewed the connections of space and time rather differently, and the development of their astrophysics and biology had been correspondingly different fom ours.

But since they were also able to beam into our models, as well as others slightly further on the other side of the galaxy they had a rather larger view of God, Flora had to admit, than we had. With this is mind, it was desirable to seek to build bridges, even if imperfect bridges, towards what was clearly an intelligence of superior dimension to humanity's.

Flora was astonished when Mirc, the secretary from Iroks, said that he was happy to agree with this understanding. Iroks also regarded talk of God as imaginative effort to articulate the divine presence. It shared the understanding of the contingency of divine action through Jesus Christ, though it understood Jesus in relation to Iroks culture, and through an alternative narrative. After the crucifixion Jesus had spent some time, on a different time scale, in Iroks, where God had mysteriously transformed him into a spiritual body. Hence the Irokesen also affirmed the decisiveness of Jesus for cosmic reconciliation, but in their own way. But they felt that human understanding of the Christ event was too limited to cope with its wider significance.

After dinner the working group returned to the section. One of the most decisive breakthroughs in the understanding of God had come, she recalled, through the early modern feminist movement, to which, after all, she in some sense owed her place in the papacy. It was not that feminist concepts of God as such had replaced the tradition. The position was rather this. The affirmation that God was neither male nor female raised in the sharpest possible form a question about the use of two of the most important traditional grounds for the doctrine of God, the Bible and the tradition of St Thomas, underlining that God is always infinitely greater than our human thoughts of him (or her, or it), even the most venerated human thoughts. In this way, the feminist movement had acted as a catalyst for a radical reassessment of the tradition, on God, on the human, on the understanding of the Church and of ethics. It had taken several hundred years, especially after the Great Reaction, but the final results had been impressive.

The other great spur to revision, indeed to rediscovery of the breadth of the Christian vision of God, had of course been the presence on the planet of the Irokesen themselves. Though it had always been formally acknowledged that God was the God of more than planet earth, it needed the contact with superior beings, some of whom were able to affirm that they too worshipped God, to establish again the sense of the cosmic presence. It was, she reflected, something of an irony that it was only after the discrediting of the fundamentalists, who had tried in their own way to protect the greatness of God, that the scope of the gospel was again visible.

God, they had said in the schema, was in God's own nature self-giving love. Only God was capable of total self-giving, which was God's way of opening up relations between the divine and the human, between human beings and between us and any other beings in the universe. She was aware of echoes here of the great twentieth-century scholar Karl Rahner. Rahner had been an important influence way back in the days of Vatican II, but had

then, rather like St Thomas, been overwhelmed by condemna-
tions, in order to be rediscovered as a potent voice in the Church
centuries later.

The Moderator of the Indonesian Church's delegation was
suddenly interrupted here by a crash, as one of the local Korean
delegates slumped forward in his seat. Yung Lee Kim was already
120 years old, but there was still a Reformed tradition here of
having elder statesmen as representatives at council. An emergen-
cy pack was at once beamed up from the hotel reception, and Dr
Yung was instantly frozen solid. A colleague explained that his
new elasticene heart had been sending unusual signals through the
monitor on his wrist transmitter. A new chip was fitted in minutes,
and the delegate was soon in good form again. It was strange, he
remarked, how he had felt himself to be hovering in his ornithopter
over an old fashioned Korean Presbyterian choir of 500 voices in
pure white robes. Then the air grew cool, the white robes dimmed
and he fell asleep. Flora decided that this was a good time for a
natural break, and they agreed to meet again in the morning.

The Irokesen were particularly interested in the Council's
understanding of salvation. They had of course instant computer
access to the history of human doctrine on the subject, in micro
or macro perspective, with its twists and turns from incarnation to
atonement, its lighter moments of optimism, its darker attribution
of its own inadequacies to God, its struggle to see what might
be an appropriate gift for such a mixed-up species as humanity.
They liked the general thrust towards a definition of salvation as
involving the peace of God. They were slightly amazed that it
had taken so much war to get there. Again they made their own
contribution, adding to the anthropomorphic limitation of human
perception a dimension which, though it did not come close to the
vision of God, at least corresponded in practice somewhat to the
extra dimension which St Thomas had theoretically sketched out
for the angels. Salvation in the Eastern tradition, they noted, had
been closely tied to a vision of pure union with God in mystical
contemplation, in retreat from this world towards alignment with
God. In the Western, Augustinian tradition it had been seen most
often in terms of rescue from the sins of the flesh, sex in the Garden
of Eden, a salvation of human biology.

By the beginning of week three the Ethics section was finished
and the delegates were about to address the much more difficult

matter of the dialogue of world religions. Here there were continuing problems. Clearly it would not do to say simply that all were worshipping the same God. They might indeed be doing just that. But many of them had continuing different understandings and concepts of God, which were clearly incompatible with each other. One question was how far they could engage in combined worship and social action, despite their conceptual differences. The debate resolved itself into the old inner-Christian pattern of the actualization of reconciled diversity. It was agreed to do everything together that could be done together. It was agreed that nothing decided by the Parliament of Religions would take away the right of individual religious communities to decide their own affairs. It was decided, more controversially, to take the risk of sharing sacramental occasions wherever this was desired. This could indeed lead to confusion. But confusion was heaven, in comparison with the hell of the battle of the orthodoxies of the last century.

Flora reflected that one of the wisest observers of humanity in her family was her brother-in-law, who had long been a practising Buddhist. It had taken much longer than people today could imagine for the prejudices of the past to break down, and in the perverse way that history often seems to go, without the Great War we might perhaps have gone on for ever in the tunnel visions of the 1900s. Oddly, it had been the development of a Buddhist-based philosophy in the twenty-second century with the aid of tenth generation computer analysis which had made possible the growth of modern analytical philosophy. This in turn stimulated a creative reappropriation of the whole Christian tradition of the divine love. Ph.D. students still argued whether the hermeneutical revolution or the horrors of the Great War were the basis of the new theology of the twenty-fifth century. No doubt a little of both, as usual, she thought wryly.

Flora was glad at this point that she was not a twentieth-century theologian. For in that century she would have felt threatened, professionally insulted and bound to defend to the death her own original point of view. Instead she was delighted and surprised to see that things could be learned from other perspectives. She looked forward to the next session, which was to deal with the substantive issue of the nature of God. They returned to talk about salvation.

It was 2 a.m. and they were still arguing among themselves, unable to reach agreement on the Constitution of the ecumenical research project for the next decade. How does one resolve theological conflict, without engaging in an unproductive fudge? Fudge can be quite nutritious, and even valuable at times, she reflected. But that would not do. She excused herself and heli-beamed across to the Bodleian, which was open continuously, for a session of sustained reflection.

And there I will leave Flora, against the background of a future which will certainly be very different in some respects from the present, and therefore a challenge to our current certainties. Though we cannot know what these precise differences will be, it is in the light of that challenge that we must consider the nature of change and an appropriate Christian response.

3

FAITH AND THE MANAGEMENT
OF HISTORICAL CHANGE

The ongoing search for community

In this chapter I want to look at the response of theology and of the churches to social and cultural changes, especially since the nineteenth century. I come now to the traditional area of the Henson Lectures, the Appeal to History in Christian Apologetic. I suppose a more market orientated title nowadays would be Faith and the Management of Historical Change.

Interpretations of history fluctuate back and forth – this applies also to Christian history. History too will look different in the distant future. Our view of history is inevitably time-bound, as our view of the future is time-bound. We see Orwell's *1984* as the typical post-war vision of the 1940s that it was. But such visions still play a useful role in our assessment of the present. Among varieties of visions we may see unifying and diversifying visions. As is often said, Nicholas of Cusa had a vision of inter-religious harmony and dialogue – and admittedly it does not seem to have had much effect on European Christendom.[1]

Interpretations of church history develop with the cultures in which they are created – and are perhaps none the worse for this, provided that we understand their context. One thinks of the illumination of the tradition provided by the great German Protestant church historians – Harnack, Loofs, Campenhausen, etc. Ebeling looked at church history in the light of the dialectic between the law and the gospel, Bonhoeffer in the light of the similar distinction of man *contra mundum* and, *coram Deo-coram homine* etc. The debates between modern and postmodern interpretation have raised other issues.

When we look at history the first conclusion we may reach is that Christians have never been particularly good at anticipating future developments – from the embarrassing delay of the parousia on. The second reflection may be that there have always been and there will always be very different futures for Christianity in different places. Yet I think it is still the case that reflection on the future is still a prime driver to action in the present. In this chapter I want to concentrate on the past of the future, and the process of historical change in theology and Church. It is often by confronting and reflecting on its past that a society moves forward. Where it fails to do this, there is perceived to be an important missing dimension in its culture – one might instance the critique of modern Japanese society, in its reluctance to own any responsibility for the events of 1941–45.

Christianity is a religion deeply committed to history. Its understanding of God is crucially influenced by the events concerning Jesus, a man who lived at a particular time and in a particular place. Its strength has often lain in its presence as an unchanging constant in a world of turmoil and chaos. It is the richness of tradition which has attracted generations of thoughtful people, who find in its worship a larger perspective which helps them to keep the preoccupations and demands of the present moment in proportion, and to see human life in a wider framework. It is a tradition which provides the flexibility for confidence to change. A Christian community which loses the depth and variety of its tradition in a search for modernity rarely prospers.

Yet history has proved to be both a blessing and a curse to Christian faith. Enslavement to historical memory can be highly destructive. Vivid examples are usually seen in the historical antagonisms which have inflamed religious conflict in Northern Ireland and in the former Yugoslavia. The influence of the past on religious practice, for good and ill, is all-pervasive. Views on specific issues are enormously influenced by precedent and tradition, though they are sincerely and thoughtfully maintained in the present, whenever that present may be. St Thomas More sincerely believed that heretics should be punished by death. On grounds of the Bible and tradition men have long sincerely upheld capital punishment, slavery, the burning of witches and numerous other practices which most people today would consider highly undesirable.

How have we looked at the future in the past? When early Christians contemplated the future, they did not, it seems, expect it to be of long duration. They expected the end of the world to happen soon, when God would finally establish his kingdom. This state of affairs persisted up to comparatively recent times, and its recent alteration is an important mark of the coming of modernity. By the late eighteenth century there developed an expectation of a longer future, a future, by the grace of God, of human progress towards peace on earth. One may think of Kant's pamphlet *On Perpetual Peace.*

Within these constraints people naturally expected the continuation of their own ecclesiastical traditions and customs. In the Westminster Confession the Reformed expected Reformed life to continue, in births, marriages (with Reformed partners only) and in the structures of church courts. They did not anticipate radical change, and certainly not the degree of pluralism which characterizes the modern world. Christians lived in many respects insulated within the paradigms of their own faith community, which they expected to flourish in traditional ways. This applies as much to Schleiermacher's ideal community as to the builders of Gothic cathedrals. This insularity lasts surprisingly far into our own century. Thus when Ronald Gregor Smith in a series of books anticipated the coming of a secular Christianity, he appeared to see this as also about to be experienced *ubique, undique et ab omnibus.* The sense that very different things might happen at the same time in different places, with opposite trends, does not appear to have been significant for him. A situation of radical pluralism, at global and national level, appears to be a new feature of modern society. As such it demands perhaps a new theological response.

I should like at this point to raise another impossible question, and then to indicate a few possible indicators, if not to an answer at least perhaps to the shape of some of the issues involved in an answer. What will be the main characteristics of church history in the future, and what elements of the church histories of the future might surprise us in the present? We may be sure that there will be great differences. There have been great differences between the church histories of previous epochs. Eusebius saw all history as a providential process leading up to the establishment of Christian civilization by the Christian Emperor. Augustine saw the city of God enduring within the earthly city. The writers of the Magdeburg centuries saw a Christendom leading up to the Protestant Reformation. Nineteenth-century historians saw church growth and politics as intertwined, and their histories followed the pattern of secular histories by being largely constitutional histories. The twentieth century brought economic histories, and examination of the Church's role in the economic, social and cultural developments of nations – a process which still requires much elucidation.

We do not know what particular ecclesial interests will dominate the Church of the future. We may reasonably expect, however, that at some stage the main churches are likely to move towards a more united relationship. In this event they will probably seek to own all church history. This means that historians will be more concerned with the connections between the various denominational histories, and more likely to see the divisions within a more ecumenical perspective. It is likely too that the various minority interests who feel that the history of their ecclesial experience has been marginalized, reflecting their own marginalization, will have succeeded in forcing a radical reinterpretation. We have seen this strikingly in the recent reassessment of church history in America in the events succeeding 1492, and in the history of the black victims of oppression in the Caribbean.

If an important test of a community is the way in which it treats its minorities, then the churches have a great deal to repent for, in relation both to social minorities and to smaller Christian groups within areas dominated by larger denominations. Indeed it will have to be conceded that great tracts of church history have been the history of intolerant majorities persecuting minorities, on doctrinal and even on racial grounds. General acceptance of such a major reinterpretation of church history will presumably have an effect in changing further perspectives on current issues.

The issue of the role of the Church in history is part of the problem of the interrelation between the gospel and human culture in general. Sometimes the Church, in faithfulness to the gospel, has to oppose movements and practices in culture and politics, where these run counter to the basic elements of the faith, e.g. where there is exploitation of some human beings by others. But at other times the churches have to learn from those outside, when their vision has become limited and narrow. That is why there can be no fixed relationship betwen gospel and culture, and we can learn from different approaches.

History, it may be said, tells us nothing, does not repeat itself and does not provide moral lessons. Yet historical perspective has always been an important safeguard against short-sighted concentration on the immediate context of human problems. It submits the most compelling voices of the moment to the scrutiny of a comparative perspective from a distance. It also enables us to hear people whose voices were often silenced in their own time, due to the cultural or political constraints of the period. In the Church in Scotland I think particularly of Robert Leighton and John McLeod Campbell.[2]

Mine will be a consciously liberal and also pluralist interpretation of history.[3] In the pluralistic cultures of the Western world in the late twentieth century, women and men have responded to the challenges facing Christian faith and theology in different ways. Some have sought to consolidate communities through conservative strategies of different sorts. It is no accident that many of the most interesting theologies of this century have been consciously antimodern theologies, following Karl Barth in criticizing the accommodations made by theology to Enlightenment ideas. A faith evacuated of mystery and wonder becomes hardly worth disbelieving, not to mention believing. Yet it seems to me that a Christian theology orientated towards the future, and the massive cumulative change which this will bring, will need to take much more radical steps in reappraisal and reconstruction than has often been thought desirable up to now. Much postmodernism is simply antimodernism under another name. But I do think that the most likely result of failing to manage accelerating change will be continued rapid decline.

It was one of the lasting merits of Ernst Troeltsch's approach to theology that he appreciated fully the historical and social context of the discipline, and the implications of various sorts of relativity for theology. I want here to consider here some implications of the reading of history for the future of theology. I do not wish to do this in the framework of a purely theoretical analysis of the philosophy of history, but in examination of cases of the work of past theologians. Equally, I shall be not be discussing historical examples purely as an exercise in church history. For the whole book has an underlying argument, about the need for a reappraisal of Christian theology and practice which is advisedly both radical and liberal. It seems to me that there is a need for a reappropriation of the concept of God as unconditional, self-giving love, and that this has consequences throughout theology and Church, relating to justice and to human rights, in many different spheres.

I am inclined to think, rather unfashionably, that a liberal theological programme, of the sort largely pioneered in liberal Protestantism by Schleiermacher, is important for the Christian future. I shall begin by looking at Schleiermacher. Why is it that these programmes have proved unattractive to so many Christians up to now? Newman and the Oxford movement may be thought to have inspired a much more exciting and living Christian faith than Schleiermacher, and the same may be said of Barth *vis-à-vis* Troeltsch. In 1994 the Pope sold probably more copies of his books than all the liberal Christians in the world put together. I shall suggest that the richness of the Christian liturgical tradition is an essential element of a living community of faith, and that in different ways the liberal Protestant tradition has neglected this vital resource. God is to be loved and worshipped, with generosity responding to divine generosity, rather than simply acknowledged and rationally adhered to in some form of eviscerated spirituality. Beyond this, there has often been the perception that doctrinal reconstructions which take account of intellectual and cultural objections appear less religiously satisfying than more classical formulations. They seem to lack depth. They fail to provide rest for the restless soul in God. It remains a continuing task to maintain the profundity of the Christian gospel while being neither obscure nor intimidating to those who do not share the traditional perspectives.

How far can we see the past as a clue to the future? I want now to look at Schleiermacher, as a bridge between past and future, as an instance of the conflict between possible and actual worlds, and the task of the theologian within the given structural patterns of Church and society. Schleiermacher was followed by the Oxford Movement and Vatican I, and by theological retrenchment all round.[4] His achievement was to provide an effective vision of the ideal as a spur to the transformation of the actual, in the face of adverse trends in the immediate future. His central notion of freedom, learned largely from Kant, was important for understanding the structure of theology, Church and ethical action. There is a breakthrough in concepts in *The Christian Faith*, flawed and incomplete, but important for the future.

In the opening sections of *The Christian Faith* Schleiermacher displays a remarkable sense of theological balance, which makes it hard for us to classify him neatly in the traditional categories, as a pietist, a foundationalist, or whatever. He recognizes that theology has a particular social and cultural basis, within a specific religious community. But it must also be articulated in a comprehensible manner within the common framework, as he saw it, of academic thought. It has responsibilities both to the Church and to the academy, and only in this way can it be of service to the wider community.

Schleiermacher understood the objective experience of reality to be the sense of the presence of God, and his successors in the nineteenth century attempted to define this awareness more precisely. Impatience with this process led to the return to apparently harder perspectives, e.g. the Word of God in Barth. But it is not clear that the later imagery was more successful than the former. God's presence remains a hidden presence, centred in the events concerning Jesus, and all our language falls short of definition of the mystery.

When Schleiermacher considers the basic norms of theology he turns to the threefold basis of the religious experience of the individual, the Christian community as a check against individual eccentricity, and the Christ of proclamation. He stresses the inward rather than the outward, yet he is prepared to allow roles for the New Testament and the confessions of the Church as criteria for the assessment of the value of religious experience. On this basis he proceeded to create a bold reconstruction of Christian theology.

Today we take for granted much of what Schleiermacher proposed, somewhat as we take for granted the omnipresence of the motor car. Yet it is important to see how just imaginative his system was in its time. In some respects, his work is as far removed in ethos from that of traditional theology as the Levitical dietary laws are from modern nutritional science. And the change is equally important.

If we look at *The Christian Faith* in comparison with contemporary dogmatic textbooks, we see that Schleiermacher does not work from proof texts and schemes of plans of salvation. His account of the nature of the human, which is where he begins, emphasizes the corporate nature of sin, and abandons the notion of a mechanistic tradition of original sin. Unsurprising, we may think. Yet mechanistic doctrines of the transmission of original sin are still at the basis of much ethical teaching in church reports.

Schleiermacher's Christology offers a more convincing account of the humanity of Christ than of his divinity, and there are problems here too. But his account of reconciliation remains a powerful and persuasive exposition of the meaning of the Christ for human life, not least in the section in which the Spirit of the risen Christ is linked to the life of the Christian community, as the fruit of the resurrection.

Not everything in *The Christian Faith* works. The area of the relation of Christ to God, and the doctrine of God itself, are generally and I am sure rightly thought to be the least successful part of the reconstruction. The contrast between Evangelical and Catholic doctrine bears all the limitations of its cultural setting. But the work as a whole provides a glimpse into a new area of interpretation and an immensely fruitful paradigm shift. Jaspers has spoken of the different ages of human development, of Axial and pre-Axial ages and the like. Whatever we may think of the detail, he suggested there something of the achievement of breaking out of one hermeneutical circle into another. Sometimes these processes may take thousands of years, because they involve fundamental shifts in perception. I am suggesting that Schleiermacher came close to such a basic shift, and that this was in large measure not destructive of the tradition of the gospel, but an instrument of its renewal. This renewal also brought debate and argument: I include Karl Barth as part of the renewal process. I suggest that far from being complete, it is a process with a considerable future still to develop.

I begin, however, with a reminder of a warning. We shall not make progress in theology by any sort of simple repristination of the past. Schleiermacher's views in many areas of theology have not proved to be ways forward. His searches for a single key to theological method and a single overarching concept of piety have had disadvantages as well as advantages. His Christology emphasizes some areas well and is not so well equipped to deal with other areas. His idealised view of women lifted them up as a counter to male domination, but left them isolated on a pedestal which was not calculated to give them an equal and integrated stake in society. In common with most theologians up till quite recent times, the basic thrust of his thought was to emphasize the development of the relationship of the individual with God, rather than the engagement of the individual with God on behalf of his fellow-men in concern for social justice. But this does not mean that Schleiermacher's significance is somehow now exhausted.

This is where we come back to the significance of Schleiermacher and his work. Schleiermacher himself created a paradigm shift in theology by moving from the external to the internal, from concentration on the external observance of Bible and Church to the internal persuasion of the presence of God in the individual in the community. In doing so he classically defined a trend which was characteristic of the enlightenment. [5]

Beyond this Schleiermacher instantiates a much wider shift, the shift from the text-based to the person-based which is of basic significance. This was a shift fraught with problems. It is not surprising that some of the most acute minds in modern theology have been antimoderns. It is also not unconnected with the development of new readings of texts as texts in postmodern criticism. This concentration on the presence of God, of God as the self-giving God characterized through the love of Jesus Christ, has consequences which have hardly begun to work themselves out over the 200 years, and which are still to a large extent counterbalanced by the authoritative text and institution centred form which characterized Christianity over the previous 1800 years. This shift has the power to turn the impact of the gospel from a mainly church serving to a mainly human rights-serving community, whose influence on human development may well be of the most crucial signficance over the next 1,800 years. In this way Schleiermacher's influence could have, and already to some extent has had, a decisive influence not only in Protestant theology but also in Catholic and Orthodox thought. It will also be necessary to develop even further the critique of Schleiermacher, so that the dangers of his paradigm shift may be taken fully into account. Either way, it seems to me not unreasonable to predict that Schleiermacher will be a theologian of the future.

I have suggested that the theological programmes of Schleiermacher and Troeltsch had much of value to offer for the future understanding of religion, and for Christian faith in particular. Why then were they unable to commend themselves to the churches with greater effect? Part of the problem would appear to be this. Though Schleiermacher personally had a positive and exciting understanding of Christian faith, integrally related to worship and Christian life, his theology was often influential in a negative rather than a positive sense. It was clear what was not right in the tradition. The imaginative positive reappraisal was less clear. Christian faith needs more than logic or rationality. It needs a deep sense of the presence of God, colour and worship, and a strong dimension of social motivation. The liberal tradition in the person of Ritschl was often thought to be dull and gloomy. Hence it has been to Newman, Barth, Bonhoeffer and Rahner, rather than say to Schleiermacher, Troeltsch and Gilkey, that Christians have turned for inspiration in the modern world. It seems to me that any viable approach to the Christian future must include and substantially improve upon the central elements of each of these perspectives.

I'd like to emphasize the need for improvement rather than rejection here. A very significant part of modern theology and church history is the history of a reaction against Schleiermacher and all that he stood for. What went wrong? Perhaps, we could say, nothing went wrong. The history of theology and Church is rightly a history of debate, when one point of view provokes another. Life and thought move forward when ideas are debated, when different lifestyles interact, when variety produces creativity. Conflict can be creative. But conflict is often destructive, leading to tribalism, damage, loss and waste.

Schleiermacher was an important contributor to the philosophy of religion, to the rational task of working out theological procedures, differentiating the various strands of faith, and of theological thinking about the subject of faith, God. Many of his followers seemed, at least to their critics, to become so preoccupied with scientific theology, with critical rationalist and theological methodology, that they never got beyond this to discuss the substance and content of faith, God. There was a loss, it seemed, of the excitement, the profundity, the life-sustaining power of the Christian gospel. The means, it appeared, had become an end, and there was some danger of worshipping not God but a particular interpretation of theological method. Not a very satisfying pursuit at the best of times.

Where do we find authority in theology? Authority in theology is the authority of God. How is this authority mediated ? Through reason, revelation and experience. But God could be obscured, rather than illuminated, by too much rationalization. Revelation was another strand of the picture. For Protestants, the Bible as the primary source of revelation remained important. Many Protestants still hold a highly conservative view of the literal inspiration and authority of the Bible in all its verses. This seemed a much safer ground than the ever-shifting sand of academic theological opinion. Conservative Evangelical theology is still widely dominant in the Church not least in the Reformed tradition and in the 1990s. Bible-based religion has hit back. Hosea hammers Hillary Clinton, and so on. Evangelical movements were important in revitalizing the churches in Britain from the 1830s, and still are today. Most of the world's Catholics still hold a very conservative view of revelation based on the tradition of the Church. In the Anglican communion the Oxford Movement was to inspire Catholic revival in the Church. Modernism might be rational but it was dead boring.

There is of course a darker side to this – lots of little people suppressed by ecclesiastical power and authoritarian behaviour. But there is no doubt where the glamour lies. Where do we go from here? Back perhaps to Schleiermacher himself. What sold the *Speeches*, we may reflect, was the fact that this was not just another Enlightenment rationalist tract, but full of a warm affection for Christ the redeemer. Too Romantic for us? But at least we may note that for Schleiermacher there was a central connection between theology and worship. Theology was not to be worshipped, it led on to worship. It was not for nothing that he preached every Sunday for forty years, and sang in a church choir for a quarter of a century. Theology has to lead to worship, to encourage music and colour and prayer, not to inhibit it.

Schleiermacher was also aware of the connection between the service of God and the service of humanity. He was concerned for justice and fair treatment for people of other religions, for women, for human values outside the magic circle of the Church. Of course he expressed this concern in ways which today we think inadequate, dated and often completely wrong-headed. But he was aware that the Christian community is there to serve humanity and not to be just another self-seeking organization. These concerns, for service of God and worship and service of humanity in social justice and social engagement, were not always so prominent in at least some of his successors. And Schleiermacher was concerned with the substance as well as the methodology of theology. He wanted to say things about God, and not just thinking about thinking about God. What we can say about God remains important, when we have produced our methodologies and even when we have resolved our agendas on social justice.

I have laid stress, here as elsewhere, on the centrality of the sense of the presence of God, for Christians definitively established as the presence of the God who gave himself for humanity in Jesus Christ. More critical analysis of the sense of the presence of God must bring us back, in a contemporary mode, to Schleiermacher's concern for the nature of religion. I mentioned that Jaspers and others, notably Geering, have attempted to divide the development of religion into stages, such as the pre-Axial, the post-Axial and the modern. Such classifications have advantages and disadvantages, and are part of an ongoing appraisal rather than a definitive statement. But they have a significant role to play, in enabling us to reflect on the variety of relationships between religion and society which have appeared and disappeared through millennia. This should illuminate more critically the relationship between religion and culture in our own period.

What is religion, in a nutshell? W.P. Alston has suggested nine succinct characteristics. These are, (1) Belief in supernatural beings (gods); (2) a distinction between sacred and profane objects; (3) ritual acts focused on sacred objects; (4) a moral code believed to be sanctioned by the gods; (5) characteristically religious feelings (awe, sense of mystery, sense of guilt, adoration), which tend to be aroused in the presence of sacred objects and during the practice of ritual, and which are connected in idea with the gods; (6) prayer and other forms of communication with gods; (7) a world view, or general picture of the world as a whole and the place of the individual therein. This picture contains some specification of an overall purpose or point of the world and an indication of how the individual fits into it; (8) a more or less total organization of one's life based on a world view; (9) a social group bound together by the above.[6]

One might add that religions are always ambiguous in relation to human flourishing and also to the communication of the Christian gospel. When they are good they are very, very good, etc. Not all religions have all of these characteristics, and each religion will relocate these characteristics in different ways within its own self-understanding. A religion like Christianity which allows a significant role to revelation, and sees its centre as a gift from God, a discovery rather than an invention, will stress the transforming power of the presence of the love of God in the shaping of that religion. It is also clear that developments in the interaction

64

between religion and culture are not particularly susceptible to the influence of academic theology and analysis. Despite the growth of critical approaches to biblical studies and doctrinal criticism over the last two centuries, together with expansion of religious studies, there have been continuing waves of consolidation of pre-critical attitudes to religion. Even in the last two decades we have seen, for example in the reaction to Vatican II, a wider reversion to literalist readings of sacred texts, and to programmes of social and intellectual control within religious groups through authoritarian discipline. This need not be seen as a disincentive to engage in critical theology. But it has to be recognised that the process of critical development within the major world religions is likely to continue to be slow. Not everything in liberal Protestantism was desirable. Karl Barth was to be a necessary corrective to Emmanuel Hirsch. The decline of traditional Christian commitment might lead not to a Christian humanism, but to a sub-Christian religious ideology of a very unpleasant sort, of the kind sometimes seen in Northern Ireland.

The continuing importance of the anti-modern is a significant minor key, but disastrous as major key. Affirmation of unconditional grace, God as creator and reconciler, the life, death and resurrection of Jesus Christ, the life of the Spirit is important. But it needs to be related to the Church of the servant – Luther's *theologia crucis*, to the catalytic power of kenotic community.

Fundamentalism

We see too that the development of a more open, liberal approach to religion in society may often lead to the rise of a powerful religious backlash. It would be unwise to underestimate the power of fundamentalism in the present, and perhaps also in the future, in the major world religions. There is much to be said for fundamentalism.

In a confusing world of pluralistic culture and secularization, in the chance development of a vast universe, where is certainty to be found? In primal religions there is a sense of awe, a need to placate the gods. Great scriptural traditions arise in history. In Islam and in Christianity there is held to be a sacred text of inerrant truth. Most religious people are fundamentalists. Most Christians in the world today, it may be thought, believe implicitly in the Virgin

Birth and bodily assumption of the Blessed Virgin Mary, plus papal infallibility. It may seem to belong to human nature that we are all conceptual fundamentalists. We may think of movements for egalitarianism, the French Revolution, the Red Guard. There is a need for basic elements in Christian belief. Can we pick and mix? Do we not have to take all or nothing? In fact there is always a question of deciding on gospel priorities. It may be argued that certain sorts of basic beliefs are acceptable, provided they do not involve the exploitation of other people. There is a need for biblical authority, but also for historical criticism. What is indispensable?

THE FUNDAMENTALS

Characteristic of fundamentalism are doctrines of biblical inerrancy – verbal in the spiration and literal interpretation. These involve notions of historical truth, perhaps acceptable in sixteenth century but not to educated in a Western tradition today. James Barr sees fundamentalism as involving (*Fundamentalism*, 1) (a) the inerrancy of the Bible, (b) hostility to modern theology, (c) an assurance that those who do not share their religious viewpoint are not really 'true Christians' at all. The point may be made that, in the prophetic faiths, if there is one revealed text or one account of the life of a prophet as an exemplar, it is easier to be a fundamentalist and to sell a fundamentalist platform politically (cf. Nandy, in Whaling, ed., *The Samye Symposium*, 2).

George Marsden has traced American Protestant fundamentalism from the 1910 Presbyterian General Assembly with its five point declaration of 'essential doctrines' to *The Fundamentals* – 12 paperback volumes, 1910–15, and The World's Christian Fundamentals Association, 1919.

Fundamentalists are concerned with doctrine, also moral reform in the face of a sense of social crisis. We have seen the growth of fundamentalist cultures, with negative attitudes to women priests in most of Christendom, and the strengthening of negative attitudes to Judaism, Islam, slavery, capital punishment, sexuality. Marty and Appleby produced a kind of checklist of characteristics of fundamentalism, which may not apply to every group.[7]

It is important not to confuse fundamentalism, an essentially modern phenomenon, with (a) Evangelicalism (there is a good discussion in Reinhold Bernhardt's *Christianity Without Absolutes*) and (b) the classical tradition of Christian theology. The continuing value of the classical tradition, which often appears to be lost, with serious results, in Schleiermacher and Troeltsch, comes through in an essentially innovative manner in the work of Karl Rahner. In the liberal tradition it is often rejected as being inevitably accompanied by a repressive ecclesiology, and equally importantly, as being itself an authoritarian, exclusive and essentially intolerant conceptual framework. Neither of these conditions need be regarded as inevitable.

Genuine pluralism implies the willingness to learn from different traditions. The continuing value within a 'high' Christology and theology may be illustrated from a critical evaluation of the 1993 collection *The Christian Understanding of God Today* (ed. J.M. Byrne), a symposium to celebrate the quatercentenary of the founding of Trinity College, Dublin. Here Rowan Williams describes the Nicene Creed as 'a first step in the critical demythologising of Christian discourse' (45). The distinctive perspective of Reformation theology, according to Christoph Schwoebel, is that 'it interprets the doctrine of grace as the organising centre of all theological thought' (52). There remains need for self-critical interpretation. 'There is no room at all for the crypto-ideologies that must always lurk in these social Trinities which have not quite abjured all knowledge of the inner being of God' (J. Mackey, 74). It is not surprising that Troeltsch, who was struggling with the creation of a new perspective, was unable to see the classical tradition in a particularly positive light. 'Troeltsch was one of the few Christian theologians for whom the transience of Western culture and Western Christianity was so central' (Tracy, 147).

A new appropriation of liberal theology will need to maximize the advantages and minimize the limitations of the liberal heritage. It will to that extent be postmodern. It will be closer to the modern than the anti-modern in most of its significant characteristics. But it must be careful to cherish the legacy of the past for the benefit of the future, in order to avoid the intellectual vacuum of despair which is the spur to fundamentalism. The interpretation of history is itself a continually changing process.

POSTMODERN MEMORY – MODERN HOPE

We noted that the phenomenon of the postmodern in its various manifestations has taught us about fragmentation and its value, about the importance of disentangling privileged majority or dominant viewpoints from suppressed or overlooked minority viewpoints. It has taught us a hermeneutics of suspicion.

In theory, therefore, the postmodern ought to be of enormous assistance in ecumenical dialogue, exposing the use of privileged positions and illegitimate claims to power for what they are. In practice, however, in our various denominations we have continued to defend our inherited positions, to the disadvantage, intellectual or indeed physical, of those in less privileged states. Indeed the insistence on radical pluralism which is part of the postmodern, far from leading to more mutual tolerance, may lead us to suggest that each interest group has the right to make up its own rules and operate them without regard to others. If my view of, say, human rights does not correspond to that of an organization like Amnesty International, then I may carry on a policy of genocide or whatever, according to my own system of ethics.

In such circumstances the project of the modern may return to the centre of human concern. Bearing in mind the dangers of foundationalism, it will still be necessary to search for common human values which may be agreed in dialogue across cultural divides. Otherwise there is a considerable danger that we shall return to the sort of dialogue of the deaf which in numerous areas characterized the pre-modern age.

But the past is still a resource for shaping the future, not least to remind us of the element of necessary cultural relativism in many of our central concepts about the future of the human race. Let me take as an example the residual value for our thinking of the legacy of Greece and Rome. We are familiar with the stereotypical characterization of Graeco-Roman culture, supported on slavery, morally bankrupt and justified by a highly metaphysical, world-denying philosophy, leading to fascism. We must regret the institution of slavery, the élitism, the racial discrimination as much as we regret the exploitation of the Third World in the present. Yet one may suspect that some at least of the condemnation of classical civilization in the Christian tradition is based on some awareness of its attractions. We may feel infinitely superior to classical thinkers. But there were in ancient Greece and Rome at least some signals, pointers, markers to a humane and democratic view of civilisation of a sort which we have still not realised in the present. It is often said that the Greek legacy is a purely cerebral vision, an undue concentration on *logos*. Yet there was an equally important stress on *mythos*, and an attempt to construe human experience as an interactive engagement of reason with emotion and with imagination, of which the work of the great tragedians is an enduring monument, and which is continued in the greatest of the poets of Rome.

In the classical tradition there is a significant attempt to relate concepts of God to the central human concepts of mind, goodness, truth and justice. In recent writing H.-G. Gadamer's *Truth and Method* and Charles Taylor's *Sources of the Self – The Making of Modern Identity*, for example, have sought to appropriate the legacy of this tradition over the Christian era for our self-understanding. Both have been sensitive to the important additional dimension introduced to Western thought by the Christian tradition, Gadamer on incarnation and Taylor on *agape*. And it is true that the Christian concept of God, as a dynamic unity of Father, Son and Spirit is not to be found in the classical world. But there is much here which, in my view, remains of permanent value in the human search for truth and fulfilment.

Though this humanist tradition is familiar to us in a Western culture, there are analogous discussions of the highest moral values and their relation to transcendence in other highly developed cultures, e.g. in classical Chinese philosophy. In this study I am concerned with the development of a Christian theology in the future, rather than a philosophical synthesis of human core values in relation to transcendence, of the sort attempted by Karl Jaspers and others. But the value of this humane tradition for the critical theological imagination has constantly been demonstrated in modern theology, from Schleiermacher to Schillebeeckx.

Charles Taylor's *Sources of the Self. . .* is one of the best recent discussions of the historical development of human self-understanding. It is worth considering Taylor's basic argument. Part I deals with identity and the good, and the search for moral sources. We search for frameworks, within which to achieve a sense of moral identity. Different people identify and defend different 'hypergoods', and these often create threats for those who do not share them. We identify constitutive goods which then tell us what it is to be a good human being, and which generate injunctions aimed at this goal. In a negative sense these can degenerate into 'regimes of truth'. However we need moral visions, and we must aim to maximize the advantages and minimize the disadvantages of the values we espouse.

Part II is concerned with 'Inwardness'. Our modern notions of inner and outer are not shared by other cultures. For Plato, the source of order in things is not the inner self but the cosmos, on which the self may model itself. The steps here are then to Augustine and Descartes. For Plato man sees, for Augustine God opens the inward man to God by grace. For Descartes, the moral sources are not outside but within us. There follows the development of the modern view of the self, familiar enough to us, here traced through Locke, Montaigne and others.

Part III engages with 'The Affirmation of Ordinary Life'. Protestantism means that it is not only the life of the monastery, but also the daily tasks of everyday living, which are seen as pleasing to God and of ultimate significance. Here is the age of 'rationalized Christianity' and the moral-sense theory of Francis Hutcheson. Nature becomes a norm, and this is developed further in the culture of modernity, a society based on companionate marriage, a new demand for privacy and the development of a new romantic sensibility.

Part IV explores further 'The Voice of Nature'. Belief in God declines, religious practice declines. It is possible to have a spiritual understanding of the self without God. Horizons are fractured. We move to radical Enlightenment, to nature again, and to an expressivism inviting movement from division and opposition in history to a higher synthesis, notably in Marx.

Part V brings us round to the nineteenth century, and to 'Subtler Languages'. Moral sources are now ontologically diverse. Science battles with religion. Classicism battles with Romanticism. Dostoevsky and Nietzsche continue the process of internalizing moral goods. Modernism redefines subjectivity creating epiphanies of spiritual reality within a mechanistic world, sometimes forward looking, sometimes too immersed in 'the subjectivism of self-celebration'.

This brings us to 'The Conflicts of Modernity' (one might reflect that there is always conflict, but the closer the era under discussion, the more likely we are to reflect on the conflicts). Today there is controversy about the disengaged instrumentalist view of life which characterized the Enlightenment, and a sense of loss of meaning. This loss is not easily recovered, because it affects our entire culture. There is the question of sources of morality, to support commitments to benevolence and justice. A theistic perspective, rather than a naturalist humanism, may be valuable here. It may also be necessary to recognise a plurality of goods, and hence of conflicts, otherwise high ideals may be interwoven with exclusions and relations of domination. 'The great spiritual visions of human history have also been poisoned chalices' (519). But the abuse does not take away the proper use. Reviewing the tradition may help us with 'retrieval, an attempt to uncover buried goods through rearticulation and thereby to make these sources again empower' (520). There are dangers but also hope. 'It is a hope that I see implicit in Judaeo-Christian theism, (however terrible the record of its adherents in history), and in its central promise of a divine affirmation of the human, more total than humans can ever attain unaided' (521). We shall return later to the implications of Taylor for considering generosity in community. Here I want to note especially the complexity of social construction in the understanding of the self, combined with an emphasis on the value of residual moral values – factors often emphasized in a one-sided, either/or analysis.[8]

There is an excellent comprehensive discussion of the balance between secular and religious in the modern world in David Edwards' *Religion and Change*. In the quarter of a century since Edwards' study, the process of polarization and pluralization has continued at an accelerated rate. In the Christian West, Catholicism has become more conservative in Rome and more radical in the United States. In Britain and in Western Europe generally, church attendance has become sharply more marginal. Orthodoxy has scarcely changed. Protestantism has become more open to conservative Evangelicalism, as it suffers from the loss of its traditional power. Among the major world religions, the rise of Islamic fundamentalism has continued. The consequences are mirrored in the social upheavals of Iran, Egypt and Algeria, and in Western Europe, in the Salman Rushdie affair. That there has been little tangible progress is still being demonstrated at the time of writing by the condition of Bosnia, in which Christian and Muslim engage in relentless slaughter. At the end of his study Edwards expressed the hope that 'our children or their descendants, while not escaping either the burdens or the excitements of continuous change, may find a greater peace than has marked the religious life of our century so far'. It is true that the period saw a major step forward in the end of the Cold War. But the religious tensions, within Christianity, in inter-religious dialogue, and in human actions towards justice and peace, remain as great as ever. We cannot expect substantial progress without much more coordinated effort.

Edwards developed his theme further in *The Futures of Christianity*. Here he takes account of the different cultures in different parts of the world, and predicts different futures, some more secular, some more religious. The stress on diversity is important, as a guard against totalitarian tendencies. Yet it would also seem likely that development of mass communication and travel will accelerate the consciousness of belonging to a single global village in the future. In that case, mutuality, respect and understanding will be at a premium among the various futures as never before. Here the development of a theology of praxis in the so-called Third World may be an important complement to the more cerebral focus on rationality in European Christianity.

One central reflection on the last 150 years must be that the fruit of Schleiermacher's programme must issue in the social as well as the purely intellectual consequences of the gospel. I am happy to recall here, without implying the author's consent to any of what follows in my own text, some of the concluding words from Christopher Rowland's *Radical Christianity*.

> The struggle against *injustice* remains at the heart of those committed to the good news of Jesus Christ and that means the need to embark on a course of action, however inadequate it may seem, to remedy it. Those who refuse to remain spectators of the panorama of injustice or disputants about its cause and course will expect to be victims in conflicts with those who have most to lose in the removal of injustice. But it is they who will inherit the kingdom, for they were the ones to hold on to the dangerous vision . . . of the kingdom of justice which enables the suffering people to take off their bonds and keep moving along the road to liberation.

In that volume Christopher Rowland considered especially the struggle for justice in Latin America in the twentieth century. Yet if we consider the history of the Church here in Europe under the aspect of the consequences for justice and human rights of self-giving love, we see fairly rapidly that here too there has often been a history of victimization, in which the heart of the tradition itself, in incarnation and Trinity, has frequently been used in the service of oppression. As individuals and as denominations, Christians have been all too ready to use the gospel as a means of discrimination against others, as a way of exercising power, directly and indirectly, and of damaging many lives in the process. This conclusion is nothing new, of course. Yet perhaps we are more conscious of this today than in previous centuries, as we are more conscious of the subjection of women, or of the unacceptability of violence, than we were in the past. My suggestion will be that in the future we are likely to be even more inclined to read church history as a history with many good aspects, but also with numerous aspects for which we have to repent. In Scotland, for example, the heavy emphasis in the Reformed tradition on ecclesiastical discipline may be increasingly seen as a history largely of domination and social control, of the sort which Michel Foucault has enabled us to see. On a more positive note, the whole concept of tolerance and mutual respect has itself come largely out of a Christian perspective, well documented by Owen Chadwick in *The Secularisation of the European Mind*, and the need for an adequate correlation between the individual's search for knowledge and the knowledge which comes from the development of social relationships has remained at the heart of the often-criticized European philosophical tradition.

To develop further the theme of a future of complementarity between different theological perspectives I intend in the next chapter to call in the New World to redress the balance of the Old, and to turn to the Christian future in the United States.

Exploration of the connection between the Christian and the humane brings us back to Christology. Through Jesus Christ, God humanizes us. Here is the future of our religious past. We noted in Schleiermacher the characteristic emphasis on Christology, an emphasis which Troeltsch, despite considerable agonizing, found difficult to develop in a fruitful way.

The centre of Christianity is Jesus Christ, as he comes to us through word and sacrament. Christologies take up the various images which the Christian community has used in attempting to speak of Christ, and put them together to create larger patterns and perspectives. Incarnation and atonement are two of the most common categories. Though rightly subjected to critical scrutiny, especially when used in theories which appear to reduce the mystery to the tightly defined constructs of a particular time and place in the history of Christian thought, incarnation and atonement may still be helpful in the future.

In 500 years from now the ways in which we speak of God will reflect the tradition seen through the culture of an age very different from ours. How will the incarnation of God be conceived? If humanity is fortunate, it will be able to consider God from a much more naturally ecumenical perspective than we have available today. It will also be possible to think in rather different ways of the nature of humanity, not least because of the developments which we may reasonably anticipate in the life sciences and in the nature of society. The insights of groups which have up to now had only a marginal influence on Christian theology, such as feminism and Third World perspectives, will have come to a wider fruition, changing the entire landscape.

But all of this will be possible then as now, I suggest, by building on the reality of the presence of God. Christians believe that God is always the same, yesterday, today and tomorrow. In every generation there are things that help us to appreciate God's presence, and things that hinder. The Bible, the tradition and experience teach us that God was incarnate in a kenosis of self-giving love. The task is to respond to this love in an appropriately generous way in each generation.

The gospel of the resurrection includes a call for the transformation of lives, individual and corporate, after the pattern of the love of God. It is a challenge to look at all areas of society which remain untransformed, and to change them further. This could involve a new christological assessment of human rights, of prison conditions, of poverty, of economic and social balance on the planet.

4

FAITH AND

THEOLOGICAL PLURALISM

Constructive diversity

How is the Christian Faith to be expressed in a time of radical theological pluralism? This is, as they say, a very good question. I am going to consider this issue first in the context of the humanities, and especially of theology, and then in the context of the impact of the physical sciences on faith in the future.

If you had asked students of theology about the classic expression of contemporary theology, say in 1962, someone might have said, Bultmann's last book, or Tillich's. There were the great Bs – Barth, Bultmann, Bonhoeffer, Bornkamm – and Tillich. If you asked it in 1972 they might have mentioned Moltmann or Pannenberg or the so-called secular or death-of-God theologians. By 1982 all this has changed – we were now in the world of Margaret Hilda Thatcher. They would have thought of Gutierrez – not a German for once, not a European and not a Protestant. But they could have said Schillebeeckx, or Rahner, or John Hick and the Myth-of-God-Incarnate controversy nearer home, or Ninian Smart, or John Stott. After the era of secular Christianity, liberal academic theology was no longer in fashion. There is a new interest in comparative religion, in Hinduism and Buddhism, in the Maharishi Rashnish and his friends, in spirituality Christian and non-Christian, and there is a very sharp rise in interest in conservative theology, Protestant and Catholic. Outside professional theology, millions know of the Pope's views, while few have heard of the theologians. The circulation of the so-called quality press is nothing to the numbers reached by the ever more powerful mass media.

In the 1950s, we may think, there is still an orderly progression of waves of European theology. The 1960s brought secular theology, and people began to get worried. By the 1970s they had opted for a radical pluralism – every man for himself. By the 1970s God has also created woman, or at least the male theologians listened to women as theologians for the first time. They also had to listen to non-Europeans, the poor, the so-called Third World and other previously marginalized groups. There were so many voices, so many choices, the era of radical pluralism had dawned. The certainties of European Enlightenment philosophy have gone with everything else. Modernism is as dead as traditionalism. We were now postmodern, post-liberal, post early for Christmas.

The 1980s brought us choice and competition in theology as everywhere else. Market forces, the God of my choice at the place of my choice at the time of my choice. A new conservatism flourished. The tradition is in again, the Church, and a theology based on the tradition of the Church, is now radical chic. Narrative theology, telling the story of the tradition of the gospel in Scripture and Church, combined with stress on concentrated spiritual communities, became fashionable. Much Catholic theology, liberal in Vatican II, now became more conservative. In Protestant theology there is a sharp upsurge of conservative Evangelical theology and community. In America the moral majority asserted itself. In the World Council of Churches the Orthodox began to play a leading role. Orthodox Serbs and Catholic Croats, Orthodox Ukrainians and Catholic Ukrainians, in Scotland members of Action Christian Churches Together and of the Scottish Convention began to flex their muscles in new ways. Elsewhere in the world new fundamentalisms joined up with political movements, in India and Iran, in Libya and Iraq. By 1990, and certainly by 1996, anything is possible in theology.

That, of course, is a rather tendentious picture, as you will appreciate. No doubt people thought they were in a completely new ball game in 1896, and probably even in 895. But I hope you find the picture I've painted helpful in some ways, even if I don't expect you, or even recommend you, to believe everything I say. In any case, if you went to many theologians today, they would say that there is really only one dominant trend, which happens by a happy accident to be their own. Only my theology has really got what it takes!

Theology and the human sciences

I should like to develop my theme further with reference to a collection of essays on the latest in theology by a group of American theologians. Theology, we learned in Edinburgh as students, is created in Germany, corrected in Scotland and corrupted in America. And indeed in the 1960s my wife and I sat at the feet of the very aged Karl Barth and the very youthful Eberhard Jüngel. But the German creation is not perhaps what it was, and the Scottish correction has become strangely invisible, and so I pass on directly to the American corruption.

In every decade the American newspaper *The Christian Century* has charted currents of religious life and thought by asking prominent figures to reflect on 'How my Mind has Changed'. I want to look quickly at the articles for 1990 and 1991, collected and published by Eerdmans in 1991.[1] The most striking thing about these articles is, I think you may agree, their complete diversity.

The first is by the prominent Methodist theologian and writer on theological ethics, Stanley Hauerwas. For fourteen years he taught in the Catholic University of Notre Dame. Quote. 'I sat in uncharacteristic silence trying to figure out what it meant for me to be there as a Methodist. Suddenly I thought, "Hell, I'm not a Methodist". I went to Yale!' This story, he goes on (5) 'expressed the melancholy truth that for most of us theologians, where we went to graduate school informs our self-understanding more than our denominational identification does.' Yale gave him a sense of tradition and of the Church. He is concerned to write for non-theologians. 'In that respect I am trying to resist the professionalization of theology, which I consider a Babylonian captivity of theology by the Enlightenment university' (9). The influential Yale theologian, who also has an influence in England through exchange students, was Hans Frei, a fugitive from the Nazis who wrote little but is much respected, and is in many ways the father of so-called narrative theology, telling the story of the Bible and the Church as community.

The next article is radically different. According to the footnote the author, Carter Heyward, professor of theology at the Episcopal Divinity School in Massachusetts, is a lesbian feminist theologian of liberation – not quite the tradition of John Knox's wife, the impeccable Miss Bowes. Quote. '1980. The dawn of Nicaragua libre and the impending US presidency of Reagan, its ardent foe. I was studying black, feminist and Latin American liberation theologies, and was becoming convinced that a justice-making church could make a difference in the world.' (This, you may think, is the pistol in one hand and Peake's commentary in the other hand approach to doing the business.) 'Nicaragua shook my foundations' (11).

> I am learning the critical necessity of approaching our theological work the same way we do any authentic spirituality: through the particularities of our lives-in-relation. In a racist society, a black god/ess is not at all the same as a white god/ess. In a hetero/sexist situation, a goddess is different from a god. In a sex-negative culture, an erotically empowering spirit is utterly distinct from an asexual and erotophobic god who needs no friends. During these last ten years my understanding of god has been gyn/ecologized. I am learning that, as a process of liberation from either injustice or despair, healing is a process of finding, if need be creating, redemption in suffering. As we move into the 90s with an economic structure that is killing poor people, a war against drugs that is a racist war against the urban poor, and unapologetic 'post-feminist' contempt for women and girls and a mounting ecological crisis, we will need as much as ever to be able to create liberation in the midst of suffering.(19)

This may be thought to be a loud and angry voice, but it is also a real cry for our attention.

Our next voice is different again – Richard Mouw, President of the evangelical Fuller Theological Seminary in Pasadena. But he is a particular sort of Evangelical. He stresses that 'Evangelicals are more aware these days of the political dimensions of the gospel than they were twenty years ago. But it is also clear that they have much theological homework to do on social, political and economic questions.' He mentions J.B. Phillips' book *Your God is Too Small*, and he adds, 'If I had to choose the variation on Phillips' title that best captured my most recent exercise in corrective theology, it would be "your God is too fast" ' (24). Evangelicals sometimes see God as producing instant action on problems. But sometimes God likes to do things slowly. He remembers George Bush's call for a kinder gentler America, and he says 'I do hope that evangelicals will become a kinder, gentler people in the coming decade. Don't rush things. I am convinced that we have God's permission to take our time' (29). Here is a self-critical Evangelical, much more self-critical than the last contributor.

Next we have the famous Yale professor, George Lindbeck, best known for his 1984 book, *The Nature of Doctrine*, essentially a fairly conservative essay. He mentions his debt to his Yale colleague Hans Frei on narrative theology and, on canonical criticism, the Old Testament scholar Brevard Childs. 'More and more I have come to think that only the postcritical retrieval of such classic premodern hermeneutical strategies can give due weight to the abiding importance of Israel (including contemporary Judaism) and Israel's scripture for Christians' (35). If the 1960s were radical and liberal, the 1990s are postcritical and methodologically conservative, concerned with retrieving the tradition. God as National Trust Heritage Property?

Reflecting on his work he says, 'I began to look for Reformation Christianity self-consciously opposed to modern Protestantism in both its conservative and liberal forms. Its starting point is neither biblicistic nor experientialist but dogmatic. It commenced with the historic Christian communal confession of faith in Christ' (37). He adds that

> The four centuries of modernity are coming to an end. Its individualistic foundational rationalism, always wavering between sceptical relativism and totalitarian absolutism, is being replaced by an understanding of knowledge and belief as socially and linguistically rooted. Renewal depends, I have come to think, on the spread of proficiency in premodern yet postcritical Bible reading, on re-structuring the churches into something like pre-Constantinian organizational patterns, and on the development of an Israel-like understanding of the church. 1(39)

Premodern yet postcritical: having your cake and eating it, or being incredibly clever? He stressed the importance of small but committed communities, a bit like the oasis of sense in a desert of chaos in Alasdair MacIntyre's philosophical writings.

People are moving in every direction. Just a few pointers from the remaining essays to reinforce the point. Elizabeth Achtemaier, professor in Richmond, Virginia, writes on 'Renewed appreciation of an unchanging story': 'Our difficulty in America these days is that we want freedom without discipline, rights without responsibility, self-fulfillment without the necessity of committing ourselves (47).' We need to return to the Bible.

Richard Neuhaus, well known for *The Naked Public Square*, has moved from being a radical or liberal to being neo-conservative. The Enlightenment's autonomous 'way of the mind' is utterly wrong-headed. In late 1990 Neuhaus, a lifelong Lutheran, is received into full communion with the Roman Catholic Church. So it goes, as Vonnegut might have said.

But then Richard McCormick, a life-long Catholic and a Jesuit, writes this:

> Why is it that Rome generally only consults those who already agree with it? The coercive atmosphere established by the Holy See in the past decade provokes such questions about the honesty, and ultimately the credibility of the teaching office. In my earlier years I would have thought that love of the Church required benign silence on such issues. Now silence appears to me as betrayal (73).

The remarkable Elizabeth Schlusser Fiorenza, who wrote *In Memory of Her*, also talks about Catholic censorship, and stresses the need to articulate a feminist critical process for reading and evaluating androcentric biblical texts. On her own struggle she quotes Dorothy L. Sayers. 'Time and trouble will tame an advanced young woman, but an advanced old woman is uncontrollable by any earthly force.' She ends, 'It is gratifying not to have been tamed' (87).

David Tracy, well-known Chicago theologian, a liberal Catholic, searches for a way of speaking of God which is both mystical and prophetic, a new spirituality. Peter Berger, famous sociologist of religion, contributed 'Reflections of an Ecclesiastical Expatriate'. Once a Lutheran, now he finds the churches too wedded to particular cultures, and increasingly intolerant. Neither religious fundamentalism on the right nor what he calls left – liberal liberationist politics – will do. Yet one must hope. 'The church will survive until the Lord returns. In its worship today, even where that worship is weak and warped, the church participates in the eternal liturgy of all creation. Nothing can change this' (111). So God, yes: the Church, not today. Robert Bellah too looks for living traditions of religious life, and Thomas Oden of Drew University offers the title 'Then and Now, the Recovery of Patristic Wisdom', in an essay that could almost have been written by John Henry Newman in 1840.

Postmodern does not mean ultra-modern. The after-deconstructionist good news is that the disillusionments of the illusions of modernity are already being corrected by classical Christian teaching. While some imagine postmodern, palaeo-orthodox Christianity to be pre-critical, I view it as post-critical (131).

In total contrast again, Sallie MacFague of Vanderbilt calls for a new, ecologically sensitive 'creation spirituality'.

The last two major essays are rather different. Jüngel in Tübingen reflects on the legacy of his East German student days, under an oppressive regime. He sees the Trinity as a clue to developing a community of what he calls mutual otherness, in which the uniqueness of Christ is not diminished but in which different religious communities are equally respected. Under the heading 'Awakening from the Sleep of Inhumanity', Sobrino speaks of his work among the poor of El Salvador. 'The first thing we discovered in El Salvador is that this world is one gigantic cross for millions of innocent people who die at the hands of executioners. Father Ellacuria (murdered recently) referred to them as "entire crucified peoples".' He ends, 'I have learned that there is nothing as vital in order to live as a human being than to exercise mercy on behalf of a crucified people, and that nothing is more humanising than to believe in the God of Jesus Christ' (163). A short epilogue by William Placher emphasizes amid diversity the common theme of community, its risks and its hopes, and the need for constructive dialogue among people holding opposing viewpoints.

It does seem to me that a responsible Christian approach to theology just must take into account the radical pluralism of opinion and, equally important, of practice.[2] It is all the more necessary of course for us each to think out precisely where we stand on all of this. But we cannot simply shut our eyes and pretend, as we often did in the past, that we alone have the whole truth, and that all or at least most others are simply misguided. We have to combine precision and profundity with charity, not least a theoretical and methodological charity, and we have to look at other people, even these miserable theologians who don't see as crystal clearly as we see, with mercy. We need to be open, and tolerant. Blessed are the empty minded, for they shall inherit the earth. We also need to think, and to have a coherent view of our own. What you think I have no idea, and you are old enough to decide for yourselves.

In conclusion I want to say briefly what I think, not to offer you a blueprint but to annoy you into suggesting better alternatives.

It seems to me that neither total theories of theology, all-embracing systems, nor totally fragmented accounts, will do. In the future we shall still have variety, with some effective proposals more highly structured than others. Theology for me is likely to remain in some ways foundational. The foundations are not for disposal, and these include central structuring elements of the biblical narrative, the love of God, the understanding of God as creator and reconciler, the gospel message of forgiveness and reconciliation, the events concerning Jesus, his life and teaching in a particular situation of social and cultural conflict, his death and his resurrection. They also include, at an informal but still important level, at least some criteria of public truth, rationality and coherence.

Theology in my view is in other senses non-foundationalist. The foundations do not include particular philosophical and theological frameworks, whether of the ancient world, the Middle Ages, the Reformation, the Enlightenment or the twentieth century.

As I see it, the concept of the presence of the love of God to all God's creatures, a presence to be known eschatologically in all creation as the presence of Christ, remains central. How this presence, which potentially transforms all human life and relationship, and all cosmic structure, is to be understood and appropriated varies, dependent on critical engagement with prevailing local social, personal, economic, political and religious circumstances. This presence is made effective within God's framework of forgiveness and reconciliation, as the love which comes from God and goes to God, and is always focused on the events concerning Jesus, as the pattern for Christian reflection, service and worship.

Remaining with the American future, but intimately related to the European past, it seems to me that a paradigmatic step is taken towards the recognition of diversity while identifying convergence and divergence in Hans Frei's *Types of Christian Theology*. This is a remarkable analysis of different approaches to theology in the post-Enlightenment period. In the extant chapters, left incomplete at his death, Professor Frei analyses five types of modern theology, and shows how much modern discussion has centred on disputes about which of those types, methods and conclusions is the truth. It is worth setting out the skeleton of his argument.

In type one, 'theology is a philosophical discipline within the academy' and 'its character as such takes complete priority over communal religious self-description within the religious group'. Examples are Kant and Gordon Kaufman. The concept of 'God' is a human construct to describe the ultimate reference point for human cultural and moral concerns. Specific Christian concepts are given meaning by their inclusion in and contribution to a wider cultural heritage.

The second type also subsumes theology under a general philosophical *Wissenschaftslehre*, but seeks to correlate specific Christian with general cultural structures such as natural science to the 'spirit' of a cultural era. Examples are Bultmann, Pannenberg and Tracy, but also Carl Henry. Here more attention is paid to specific internal Christian concepts, but again the specifically Christian is subsumed under the general religious experience.

The third type also seeks to correlate theological data to universal criteria for valid thinking, but proposes no comprehensive structure for integrating them, only *ad hoc* examples, e.g. a broad appeal to the character of human experience. Examples are Schleiermacher and Tillich. Here the language of the Church is always specific to a particular religious community, and cannot be dissolved into a more general cultural or philosophical vocabulary. Theology is not founded on philosophy.

In the fourth type, the practical discipline of Christian self-description governs and limits the applicability of general criteria of meaning in knowledge, rather than vice versa. Christian doctrinal statements have a status similar to grammatical rules implicit in discourse. The typical example here is Karl Barth. The logic of faith, internally coherent, takes priority over any sort of correlation with culture.

In the fifth type, Christian theology is exclusively a matter of Christian self-description, as for example in the 'forms of life' approach of D. Z. Phillips. Here theology is entirely internal to religion, and functions in a personal way to help shape our religious consciousness and the behaviour which stems from this. What emerges from this superficially rather dry and theoretical discussion is that theology has learned different valuable things from each of these types, and also, to be fair, from the disputes between their proponents. In *Types of Christian Theology* Hans Frei succeeds in breaking through some of the traditional barriers to theological dialogue, to reveal the insights and merits of contrasting ways of thinking about God.[3]

It belongs to our human nature, we said in the last lecture, to look for certainties in life, above all in religion. We want certainties in the basic areas of Christian doctrine above all. 'Back to basics' is a notion with a universal appeal. To learn to appreciate other perspectives does not come naturally to us. We may sometimes find it easier to be reconciled with the citizens of another continent than with our nearest neighbours in our own church. What has this to do with theology tomorrow? Christianity today is often under threat in modern society, and naturally feels a need to be defensive. It produces new strategies to compensate for the loss of power, of traditional tribal bases, of external authority. Fortunately the gospel encourages us not to believe in theology but to have faith in God. This is perhaps a pointer to renewal. He that would lose his life shall find it. Christ is there in solidarity, in generosity, in affirmation. Christ is there in tolerance and mutuality, in reconciliation and in making peace. It is this substantial reality which has always invited human reflection on theology, and which will no doubt continue to encourage us beyond the bounds of our own conceptual hesitations.

But how? I suspect that theology will continue much as before, by trial and error, with some pursuing pure paths of conceptual economy, and others developing complex amalgamations of different traditions. It will always be necessary to criticize and argue, to discard and restart. For myself, I think that there is probably more to be gained from learning to bring together the strong points of different approaches than from concentrating everything on the exegesis of one particular model.

The natural sciences – perceptions of the universe

The discussion so far has been concerned almost exclusively with the world of the humanities. I turn now to quite a different area which seems to me to be of decisive significance for the human future, the area of the natural sciences. I am going to use the example of astronomy and cosmology. It may of course be said that the life sciences will have at least as much effect on our future as the physical sciences. But I want in the first instance to make the point that almost any of the natural sciences raises serious issues for the shape of the human future and the appropriate theological response to this. We may note that here too there is radical pluralism in interpretation, and pluralism in the issues raised by the different scientific disciplines.

What has theology to do with astronomy? Not a lot, you may think. Times have changed. For many people at least in the ancient world, planet Earth had a unique position in creation and a special relationship with its local God, a bit like the head of department in a university, there when you want him or her, not when you don't and usually vaguely benevolent.

By the nineteenth century at the latest, it was clear to most human beings that our planet is only a minor speck on the cosmic agenda. This realization brought a sharp loss of confidence in traditional religious beliefs. Who are we, insignificant in the mystery of the universe, to presume to any sort of relationship with the creator of the universe, of the sort indicated in the biblical narratives, which were clearly pre-scientific narratives? We have recently discovered classical laws of physics which reveal the elegant simplicity of the universe. The physical order is mechanically determined and predictable. It is essentially complete. It has accessible foundations. Unlike talk of God, it lends itself to controlled experiment. We are the masters now.

At the end of the twentieth century, the picture has shifted yet again. We see that the narratives in the Bible were never intended to be seen as pseudo-scientific accounts of physical cosmogony. We see that nature is enormously complex. There is much indeterminacy at the micro-level and unpredictability at the macro-level. When we think of the creation of life, for example, there is a complex interplay of chance and law, which is capable of many different explanations. Every passing year seems to bring more mysteries about the nature of biological evolution. There is no need to bring God into this. But Christians will see God as exploiting in continuing creation all these possibilities which he has made potentially available in the initial structure. John Polkinghorne put it like this: 'God does not fussily intervene to deliver us from all discomfort, but neither is he the impotent beholder of cosmic history. Patiently, subtly, with infinite respect for the creation with which he has to deal, he is at work within the flexibility of its process' (*Science and Providence*, 44).

Whatever we make of that, there is clearly a very great deal which we do not understand about the cosmos. The assumptions of one generation are speedily overturned by the next, as a comparison of the works of, for example, Sir James Jeans and Stephen Hawking will readily demonstrate. Revolutions in perspective take place. Sometimes it appears that hard won theories are all in the mind, and there is no way of telling which is more true. The theories are heavily underdetermined by the facts. Yet some theories last much longer than others, because they appear to more people to offer coherent and rational explanations.

It is not today insuperably difficult to think of God as working through the processes of development in nature. It is even possible to think of God as acting in highly unusual and specific ways at different times, in a somewhat similar way to the occurrence of surprising events, against expectation, in the cosmos. There remains on the human level the huge problem of disease, disaster and evil. But the possibility of various sorts of divine action, even if not in frameworks now conceivable to us, lies open.

It may seem improbable that a God who created the universe should be concerned for such an infinitesimal speck of it as the human race. Yet it is also the case that the fact that the universe can sustain human life at all required a structured balance between finely drawn constraints. That it is such a universe, constructed, it has seemed to some, on an anthropic principle, counts more for than against the notion of a creator with a purpose for humanity.

In the contingency of the physical cosmos there is much that is incomprehensible. Christians believe that God has accompanied us into our journey in the universe, in the events recorded in the New Testament, and has produced light in the human condition out of the dark areas of humanity. God is not an agent in the world of created agents. Engagement of God with the created order may be inconceivable, – we don't have the concepts, – but it is not unthinkable. Arthur Peacocke has suggested that God could be causally effective in a 'top-down' manner, bringing order through fluctuation, without abrogating the regularities and unpredictabilities that operate at the various levels of existence that constitute our 'world'. But since God is personal, this flow of 'information' is more appropriately described as a 'communication' by God in love to the world of his purposes and intentions through those levels of the hierarchy of complexity capable of receiving it.

What is clear is that we are still a long way from having a definitive picture of the cosmos. Indeed, different theories may usefully characterize different aspects of the cosmos as they are conceived by different people. And in any case, though we tend to see ourselves as sophisticated, we may still be at the beginning of a long history of exploration and understanding.

Let me come back to some of these themes. When we ask about the relationship between astronomy and theology, I suppose it is most natural for us to look at the area of cosmology. Here, in so far as I understand it, the attempt is made to look at the origin, evolution and structure of the universe as a single object of enquiry. We may look at the observable universe, with its different sorts of structures of matter. We may draw conclusions (e.g. from the microwave background radiation) to the effect that matter was first essentially homogeneous, and then became more differentiated. We may reflect that early in this process there may have been fairly sudden temperature shifts, hot dense phases of expansion followed by cooling, through which a complexity of structures had appeared.

What happened to start the process of creation, in the Big Bang or initial singularity or whatever, we do not appear to be able to say. We can only observe from our own fixed and limited perspective in the universe, making deductions about other parts of the universe but not able to be absolutely certain about phenomena beyond a certain distance. We are between the origin and the end point, and there may be a very long way still to go. We keep having to revise what we mean by cause, time, space and matter. We may even begin to think that there is an important interdisciplinary element in developing concepts like relationship, evolution, diversification, complementarity. There is an important role for the imagination in human thought, and it may help to try to harness all the areas of human conceptual capacity to focus upon what are often pretty complex issues. What is common to astronomy and theology may be something common to all academic subjects, namely thinking, asking ourselves what it is we think thinking is, thinking about thinking and then trying to think harder! It becomes possible for us to relate theological categories to cosmological categories, looking for cognitive resonance rather than cognitive dissonance. Ted Peters says this of the concept of continuing creation:

The idea of continuing creation may obtain a more profound meaning through Prigogine's use of the Second Law of Thermodynamics as it combines the irreversibility of time with the creation of order out of far-from-equilibrium chaos. Cosmic entropy is complemented by local creativity. What happens locally is that genuinely new things appear. The structures of reality are not reducible to, or fully pre-determined by, the existence of past material.

But can astronomy speak to theology? Cognitive resonance may be better than cognitive dissonance, swopping ideas is usually better than a dialogue of the deaf. On the other hand, there remains perhaps a crucial area of difference between the subject of theology, God, and the subject of astronomy, the physical cosmos. God for classical theology is the maker of heaven and earth, the creator of all that is. God is not a part of creation. The cosmos is God's creation. The God of Christian faith is not an object in the world of objects. God is affirmed to be the creator and sustainer of all that is, and to be in his essential nature personal, characterized by self-giving love, of the sort decisively revealed in the events concerning Jesus Christ. God is concerned for all creation and has a particular concern for humanity, indeed is uniquely present, as a hidden, supporting presence, to every human being who has been, is or shall be.

Such a God is not particularly suitable for presentation at mathematical gatherings. For talk of this God, of vulnerability and incarnation, or hiddenness and residual mystery, of rough edges of faith and paradox, is neither aesthetically pleasing nor elegant, nor simple, nor particularly coherent. And such a God is not guaranteed to 'make sense' of the universe.

So much the worse, you may well feel, for the God of classical Christianity. Hence the great desire, particularly since the European Enlightenment, for a God without all these awkward edges. We discover the God of deism, who winds up the universe like the archetypal watchmaker, and then lets it go on running without external intervention, until doubtless it runs out of energy. With such a concept we may perceive some sort of beauty and harmony of the universe, if not the eternal music of the spheres on their ceaseless round, at least something with a certain internal logic, symmetry, cohesion, mildly unpredictable but not entirely random causality.

Such a concept of deity would allow a suitable balance of freedom and determinism in nature and in human nature, a balance which could be tightened up or slackened off to taste, much as the present government deals with staff and students in our universities.

In such a scenario the laws of quantum mechanics or theories of relativity could be seen as arguments for or against the existence of such a God, depending on your own selection of data. There would be reasons for and against divine existence, and without valid reasons you easily slip into fideism, or blind credulity. Indeed, God could become the initial premise of an argument, the first cause, the ground for existence, the guard against final scepticism.

It is not surprising that theologians, philosophers, philosophers of science and scientists make frequent attempts to correlate the data of creation to creator. We need some sort of cognitive resonance between our beliefs about the personal and about the physical world. Sometimes these correlations are with Christianity, sometimes with other religions and ideologies. In Scotland Tom Torrance has sought vigorously to relate the scientific method as he sees it to Calvinist Christianity. Fritz Capra in America related Buddhism to physics. Marxist philosophers have found exact correlations between the nature of the universe and the doctrines of dialectical materialism.

A somewhat parallel case of retrenchment in the face of challenge is to be seen, in this case in relation to modern science, in John Polkinghorne's Gifford Lectures, *Science and Christian Belief – Theological Reflections of a Bottom-up Thinker*. I have learned a lot from Polkinghorne's imaginative integration of the insights of science and religion, notably in *Reason and Reality*. Here he contrives to produce a remarkable orthodox restatement of the Nicene Creed, illuminated from his earlier professional background in theoretical physics. Sometimes philosophers, especially logicians, produce rather conservative restatements of Christian doctrine, by a process of rational deduction which takes little account of the dimensions of historical complexity, cultural relativity and social setting in Christian theology. John Polkinghorne produces analogies from science of the acceptance of the unexpected, or the surprising nature of reality, and this enables him to accept positions without considering the whole range of the issues. This is perhaps most clear in the treatment of biblical interpretation, notably in the brisk accounts of Jesus' life and his resurrrection, where a rather positivist appeal to faith frequently solves the problems of historical evidence, and of the move from historical to theological deductions.

I have to confess to a certain unease about such close correlations. There may be too many happy accidents. This is not to say that 'magic-bullet' theories of everything to do with theology and science are without value. On the contrary, the enthusiasm with which they are sometimes pursued often turns up new ideas, stimulates discussion, creates surprises. Far better than a bored and lazy scepticism which can forget nothing, and learn nothing. Yet some caution is always in place. We still have a long way to go. Today's certainties, which may be perfectly justified certainties, become tomorrow's problematic areas.

In my view there are connections between the world of cosmology and astronomy and the world of theology. God in Christian faith is the maker of heaven and earth. God is responsible for creating and sustaining the universe as it is. God is also a personal God, who is in his essential nature love, and who is directly concerned for every human being. Modern science raises problems for such an understanding of God. How does this picture of providential care square with the complexity and immensity of the universe? We need to have some provisional answers at least, if our understanding of God is not to be isolated from our understanding of the rest of human knowledge. We can construct and invent new God-concepts, which can be adapted to new discoveries. But Christian faith at least is committed to affirmations about the character of God's love, revealed through Jesus Christ. Suffering and evil on our planet count against the belief in a loving God that the experience of love, on an individual or a community basis, counts for. A lot depends on how much weight you give to the historical existence of the Judaeo-Christian tradition, of worship and service to humanity as the service of this God, in a particular period of human history.

Christianity is committed to particularity. In other religions there is also a tradition of service to God, and in some periods of society a belief in transcendence, less defined. But God is in no sense a necessary postulate. It could well be that there is no God, and we don't need God as an explanation of anything. But some of us think that there are grounds for belief that God is there, and that God is love. We can't look up into the sky and see 'God is love' in illuminated signs in the Milky Way. We can look at the history of the community in the Judaeo-Christian tradition and see how people in every generation are able to identify with a sense of the presence of God, mediated through reflection on the tradition of the gospel, in the biblical narratives, and in the life, worship and service of the community. If there is such a God, then it is not unreasonable to understand the universe as the subject of God's creative and sustaining action. Some things count for, some against. Nothing of this can be proved by reason, but at least it can be shown to be not unreasonable.[4]

Towards a liberal critical perspective

The future will be a future shaped by all kinds of new scientific developments, and equally important, new perceptions of ourselves in the light of these developments. In assessing the possible impact of historical change on the Christian future it is of course desirable to take into account existing accounts of future scenarios. There is already a fairly considerable literature on Christianity in the twenty-first century. I have thought it best to build up an independent argument. But here it will be appropriate to mention a handful of representative examples. I have been arguing for a strengthened perspective of liberal Christianity. There is a good study of this subject in Donald Miller's *The Case for Liberal Christianity* of 1981, perhaps significantly not much noticed at the time. Miller argues for a reconstruction of a liberal Christian identity betweeen fundamentalism and secularism. He sees fundamentalism as the result of a process of reification. 'Reification is that process by which an abstraction or approximation comes to be treated as a concrete reality' (16). This has especially been the case with sacred texts and creeds. Miller argues that liberal Christians need to stress a distinctive agenda which has a positive approach to religion, transcendence, worship, the discipline of prayer, and a commitment to social action in community. His conclusion, with which I am in substantial agreement, is that 'We need a rebirth of liberalism as we move ahead into a world in which polarised thinking provides one of the greatest pitfalls' (152).

A rather more radical plea for change was made by Ewert Cousins in his *Christ of the 21st Century*. Cousins, like Geering, employs Jaspers's distinction between Axial and post-Axial religious consciousness. He finds a model for religion in what he terms the Second Axial Period in the work of Raimundo Panikkar and Teilhard de Chardin, leading to a Christic mysticism. 'This archetype of the cosmic person contains all the essentials of the fullness of the mystery of Christ, for it includes his life, death and resurrection as part of the redemptive Paschal mystery' (190).

Much more substantial and instructive in my view is Robert Wuthnow's *Christianity in the 21st Century – Reflections on the Challenges Ahead*.[5] We saw in his introduction an important point about the nature of such reflection.

> We miss the whole point of the future when we approach it as something to predict. Then we become forecasters, trying to guess tomorrow's weather so that we can carry umbrellas or sunglasses. The real reason we reflect on the future, I suspect, is not to control it, but to give ourselves room in the present to think about what we are doing. (4)

He too notes the continuing vitality of fundamentalism. 'Will fundamentalists set the agenda for American Christianity in the twenty-first century?' (9) He sees the main challenge facing liberals as whether they will continue to let the fundamentalists set the agenda for them. 'Or will they in some way be able to rise above the challenge presented from fundamentalists, charting an orthogonal course based on an independent vision of who they are and what they can be?' (10). He then looks at the underlying paradigms or frameworks of our thinking, considering first institutional challenges to religion, community, identity and the role of the Church. How can the Church sustain communities? The Church may be a kind of community of memory, and a source of support groups for various sections of society, but in order to do this, and to meet the ethical challenges of the modern world, they will have to provide role models, and appropriate stories for the community, while learning how to care. This is the subject of section two. Stories are important but they have to be lived out in action, as role models are. 'Models of compassion provide models of hope, of the selves we think it is possible to be' (95). Wuthnow then turns to doctrinal challenges to Christian faith – pluralism, polarity and the character of belief. There is an interesting section on the future of fundamentalism. Unlike parts of Europe, where religion was closely controlled by government in the nineteenth century, in America local citizens were free to develop religion in their own ways, and this gave society strong religious resources. Out of the uncertainties of the 1960s came the new concern for the moral order of the Eighties. Fundamentalism constructs a polarized world of light and darkness, rejecting modernity, but selectively. Liberals tend to let fundamentalists set the agenda (127). Instead they should seek to be a counterculture to secularism, a third way.

This leads to a consideration of faith and public affairs. There is in America an agreement to disagree. In this the religious right may have a future, supporting special purpose groups as the traditional denominations decline, bringing religious symbolism to the centre of politics.

The last section reconsiders the possibilities of faith for constructing personal lives. The quest for identity will always continue. The state of the middle class will remain important – continuing, one hopes, to develop the reality of service to the whole community. What is the relation between Christian conviction and critical thought? 'We might say that Christianity sacralises – makes sacred – the intellectual life. It gives the questions we struggle with in our work and in our lives a larger significance' (212). In conclusion Wuthnow suggests the importance for the society of the future of Christianity's central message of hope.

This is an eminently sane and penetrating account of the state of religion in America today, observed from a sociological perspective by an acknowledged expert. It does not come up with startlingly novel conclusions, predicting a future for religion in many ways like the recent past. Polarization in religion and politics appeals to us because it appears to be much more fun than the wearisome task of working towards compromises between entrenched positions. There is the exciting prospect of battle, of decisive victory and the routing of the enemy. But history would appear to suggest that what follows is often equally ambiguous, and that it may sometimes be better to nurture the fragile plants of mutuality, in a balanced ecological environment of diverse forms of spiritual life. Whether in the United Kingdom we shall follow more closely a model like that of Wuthnow's America, or, say, the French model of much more rapid secularization, is hard to tell. Either way, there will be advantages and disadvantages for Christian faith in community. It is up to us in the present to seek to make the task easier rather than more difficult for future generations.

A rather different approach to the social future, stressing diversity and complexity rather than large monochrome structures, and with a Christian background, is well illustrated in recent books by Charles Handy, in a recent of books, especially *The Age of Unreason* and *The Empty Raincoat*. Handy utilizes his expertise in management studies to reflect on the changing structures of society. He sees a combination of information technology and biotechnology changing the way we live. More people will live longer, and the over-75s will be a significant proportion of society. Work patterns will change with short-term contracts rather than life-long tenure, and job-sharing. There will be a further move away from labour-intensive industries, a move towards knowledge-based organizations, requiring new levels of education, and a further move towards service, as most of our needs are met by contracting out what we ourselves are not good at. 'A dramatic change in the economic climate may slow things down, but it will not stop them. The world of work has already changed. We need to take notice' (*The Age of Unreason*, 43).

The Age of Unreason considers the impact of change, not continuous change but discontinuous change, on the structures of society. He stresses the dangers of complacency. 'A frog, if put into cold water, will not bestir itself if that water is heated up slowly and gradually and will in the end let itself be boiled alive, too comfortable to realise that continuous change at some point becomes discontinuous and demands a change in behaviour' (7). He calls for 'creative upside-down thinking'. Looking at his own sphere, he notes that the world of work is changing rapidly because the organizational structures of work are changing. In the future there will be small cores of key workers, with a huge periphery of part-timers, on short-term contracts. Organizations will never be the same again. We shall have to shape work to suit our lives, create our own portfolios, change or be managed by change. Organizations will have to be more open to their staff, if they are not to stifle initiative (186f.). Handy's is an optimistic and a profoundly religious vision.

My hope is that our various religions and faiths will be more outward-looking than inward-looking, realising that to strive towards a heaven, or something like it, in this world, is the best guarantee of one in the next world, wherever and whatever that may be. Britain's countryside is dotted with ancient churches. They are important symbols, but they should be symbols not of spiritual escapism but of God's and man's involvement in the world around them. (212)

The Empty Raincoat begins from three pieces of sculpture.

> One of them, the dominant one, is a bronze raincoat, standing upright, with no one inside it. To me, that empty raincoat is the symbol of our most pressing paradox. We were not destined to be empty raincoats, nameless raw numbers on a payroll, role occupants, the raw material of economics or sociology, statistics in some government report . . . The challenge must be to prove that the paradox can be managed and that we, each one of us, can fill that empty raincoat. (2)

Handy suggests the need for innovation before current ideas run out of effectiveness, the need to develop space beyond the core of essential paid work in a future society, and the need to develop the art of compromise and mutual trust in dealing with other people. Handy emphasizes that the nature of work will change, creating free time both in daily hours and in large areas of life, especially after the age of 50.

> The demise of the traditional job, the re-chunking of time and the new areas of choice for would-be parents, combined with longer and healthier lifespans, mean that the traditional sequence of events – school, job, house, children, retirement – is no longer fixed. Flexilife is now the mode. (167)

Handy calls for a new sense of connection in social life, and he ends with a plea for the importance of local initiatives. 'Change comes from small initiatives which work, initiatives which, imitated, become the fashion. We cannot wait for great visions from great people, for they are in short supply at the end of history. It is up to us to light our own small fires in the darkness' (271).

Handy's is a benign and attractive vision. Yet of course developments in life patterns can also have sinister dimensions, as much science fiction and similar writing reminds us. We may recall John Wyndham's Midwich Cuckoos or P. D. James' novel about sterility to suggest the dangers of biotechnology. But of course despite the dangers, the abuse of concepts does not take away their proper use, as we have seen from Charles Taylor's sane and balanced study of the self.

In closing this section on developments in the business world we should perhaps mention an area which seems likely to have a major impact on large sections of society in the next decade or so, namely the development of information superhighways through computer networks, and ever easier access to the colossal amount of data parked on these highways. These facilities may have the opposite effects of making the world and its various cultures a much smaller, universally accessible place, and also enabling individuals to create for themselves a more private world of their own design and selection, through the data which they choose to access and to interact with.

On the one hand mass media may enable governments to distribute mass propaganda. On the other hand, they may enable people to make their own choices regardless of what their rulers advise. Much may depend on the capacity of technology to block off as well as to open up avenues of technology in the future.[6]

We have looked at a science-fiction snapshot of the Christian future, at an analysis of the snapshot, a glance at the history of our present condition, and at the plurality of currently available perspectives, through the development of the human and natural sciences, from which in part, at least, the future will develop. We must now attempt some positive suggestions for constructive moves in the as yet unknown theological future.

5

FAITH AND

TRANSFORMATION

Dialogue and change in perspective

Sometimes cosmological speculation is a way of avoiding the sheer intractability and complexity of local issues. It is sometimes easier to contemplate the aesthetic beauty of the universe than to tackle pressing cultural and social issues nearer home. But on the positive side cosmological paradigms may lead to an awareness of the importance of the longer-term future, of a time-scale in which most of the significant developments in theology and Church were seen to lie in the future and not in the past. Too often when the Church has the opportunity of considering possible imaginative developments for 500 years in the future, it has become obsessed with the customs and habits of 500 years in the past. One useful effect of twenty-fifth century educational programmes may be the development of a combination of a new critical perspective on historical development with an awareness of the genuinely enormous potential of the future.

We need not expect the theological future to be free from problems. Christians have never been promised an easy life in this world. Christian hope is a resurrection hope, which may be anticipated in our lives on earth but which always awaits eschatological fulfilment in another dimension after death. Neither modern social medicine nor modern politics has affected this perspective, though they have considerably increased life expectation and the quality of life for most people on the planet. The peace of God, fulfilment within God's love, is and remains an eschatological expectation.

Realism does not always mean pessimism. In the event, future Church Councils may well bring a series of pleasant surprises. All sorts of developments are at least logically conceivable, perhaps because there will be a thorough computer-aided exploration of the arguments of previous Councils, and exploration of the advantages and disadvantages of every angle. Perhaps even, however improbably, the presence of extraterrestrial life could remind earth-dwellers of the limited nature of their own existence and experience. Perhaps there will be the recollection that remembrance of the tradition is important, but only to enable us to look confidently at the shape of the future. Perhaps there will be a final melting of the intolerance which has been pretty uniformly spread around the various ecclesiastical parties for a thousand years. Whatever it is, future councils may end, not simply with a series of well-sounding platitudes for an ideal community but with a genuine programme for an exciting human future.

What could be achieved in the future, under what agenda could a line be drawn? The list is heartening in its comprehensiveness. As far as internal church relations are concerned, the three great Christian communions, Orthodox, Catholic, Protestant, could finally agree on a complete exchange of eucharistic fellowship, ministerial recognition and positive discrimination on behalf of all groups marginalized by the ecclesiastical tradition. Today such a consensus would be unthinkable. This has been in no small measure because some of the sharpest minds have embraced the most conservative positions, on ministerial order, eucharistic fellowship, population control and the like, bringing their arguments to new heights of sophistication. But of course the same could be said of Augustine, Thomas More and Aquinas, not to mention St Paul! Truly, a thousand years are but as a day in the sight of the ecclesiastical tradition, and 5,000 years just a long weekend.[1]

In the Churches' relation to other world religions, there could be a new covenant commitment to mutual respect and to co-operation on all social issues, as well as a permanent commission to explore theological study together. With regard to the Churches' relationship to society, there could be a reaffirmation of commitment to justice and peace, together with a comprehensive confession and commitment to repentance together with a new pledge to reassess the servant role of the Church in the world. Perhaps most important, and a framework for all the rest, there is a need to reassess the entire Christian tradition in the light of awareness of God as sacrament embedded in different dimensions of cosmic reality. This may be both an affirmation of and a questioning of local values and cultures, and a stimulus to a deeper vision of the depths of the divine love. Nothing in the central structuring elements of the Christian gospel has necessarily changed here. On the contrary, the basic dimensions can be strongly reaffirmed. In the same way, local religious identities may be reaffirmed. But a large residue of tribal prejudice could be finally jettisoned.

What will happen to Church Councils, traditionally the epitome of dissent and intrigue? Vatican X could be the first Council in which the priority of the future, long discussed in abstract, is at last made concrete as the determinative point for all theological and ecclesiological work. This could be the Council, too, at which the human participants finally take on board the consequences of their own cultural relativity, with its scope and its real limitations. It might be a kind of further hermeneutical retrieval of the consequences of the old sin of being *sicut Deus*. There has long been talk of conscientization. Here might be conscientization of conscientization. One of the consequences of new critical reflection might be a fresh realization of the guilt of religious communities, because of the damage they have done to their fellow human beings. Called to bring freedom, they created victims. Yet in another sense they have all been victims of societies without adequate education or motivation. On the other hand, they might recognise that the religious traditions have also brought about much that was good in society. The paradox lies, as always, in the contrasts. There has been such conscientization before. But guilt often brings mere hardening of attitudes, and new evasions of responsibility.

It may be necessary to persuade future Christians of the essential tragic absurdity of many of their traditional conflicts. It may be a little like the effect of the perspective of Lilliput, or the old games of Monopoly and Trivial Pursuit. Perhaps it will not be surprising that only a cosmic perspective can enable humanity to come to terms with its own limitations. What may be achieved in the conscientization of conscientization is something like a Copernican revolution all over again. But this time it may be a social revolution among the religions. It is as if the untouchables were to become the centre of the sacred. It would be an appropriate response to the thousandth anniversary of the landing of Columbus that the Europeans finally lose their sense of superiority over inhabitants of other regions, and that the old Third World could at last see beyond persecutions to the universalizable benefits in the civilization that went back to the ancient Greeks and beyond. It may indeed be in part the impact of ancient history, in retrieving the common factors in Greek and Indian culture, which helps to consolidate the picture.

One solid result of progress would be a recognition that religious prejudice is almost identical in its operation throughout the various religions. Discrimination against blacks in white-dominated Christianity is almost exactly paralleled by discrimination between castes in India, against members of foreign tribes in Africa and against separate ethnic groups in Asia. Here a wider cosmic perspective may provide a remarkable stimulus to reform on planet earth. It might take the churches another thousand years at least to develop the range of their theological imagination in order to stretch beyond the present limits of their existing cultures. They should therefore be rather careful about being too dogmatic. Openness to new truth should be a constant consideration.

Technological development may well produce changes literally unthinkable today, especially in medicine. This sort of change could affect theology almost as much as the delay of the parousia in the early Church, and create almost as many problems. There have of course been intimations of startling developments in recent times, with the creation of gene maps, body scanners and the development of monoclonal antibodies. But again it may be possible to speed up the process beyond recognition. The widespread availability of such facilities will raise all sorts of new problems for Christian medical ethics. We may wonder what the ancient philosophers would have made of this, with their faculty psychology, natural law ethics and Augustinian anthropologies. In contrast, one of the causes of failure of Christian vision today is the bureaucratic ossification of the churches, which have simply become incapable of action through administrative paralysis. Some of you will have seen the poster which said 'God so loved the world that he didn't send a committee.' In a new world, things might actually get done. People may find it extremely difficult to cope with the new technology at first. To that extent, ancient cultures would have found it literally impossible to comprehend the complexities of modern society. They might also be surprised to find reflection upon the character of the God of Jesus Christ still at the centre of a quest for a better actualization of human potential. Yet that complexity may make it possible for future generations to look with genuine sympathy upon previous societies, locked in their primitive conditions, victims of their own ignorance in so many ways, yet also capable of sustaining brilliance and compassion in what were often difficult circumstances. All civilizations on earth combine plus and minus aspects, high culture, mindless indifference and deep humanity side by side. It would be fascinating to be able to be a fly on the wall 500 years from now, when things will again be radically different in so many ways.

Such speculations, like much of the above, are entirely fanciful, for none of us can actually see into the future. But if they encourage us on occasion at least to slip out of our dogmatic slumbers, and to look more critically at ourselves in the present, in order to create the conditions of the possibility of a more open future, then they will have served some useful purpose.

Common human values

In such circumstances the project of the modern may return to the centre of human concern. Bearing in mind the dangers of foundationalism, it will still be necessary to search for common human values in relation to humanity and God which may be agreed in dialogue across cultural divides. Otherwise there is a considerable danger that we shall return to the sort of dialogue of the deaf which in numerous areas characterized the pre-modern age.

Important developments in this direction have been the subject of two recent sets of Gifford Lectures, John Hick's *An Interpretation of Religion*, and Keith Ward's *Religion and Revelation*.[2] *Religion and Revelation* represents an important modification of the direction in which Professor Hick had pointed, notably in distinctions between exclusivity and pluralism in respect of truth on the one hand and salvation on the other. It is possible to be exclusivist in relation to truth and at the same time pluralist in relation to salvation. A particular faith may believe the ultimately real to have particular characteristics, not seen by all religions. At the same time, it can be held that God acts in a salvific way through different faiths.

Professor Ward's book is innovative and progressive in the directions in which he leads us. He develops in detail a fundamental reappraisal of a Christian theological approach to other religions. If we are to have a peaceful and just future on our planet, then such thinking is absolutely basic, not just to theology but to politics and to the whole process of human understanding. Here is a profoundly critical new approach to constructive dialogue between the great religious traditions, a creative and, to my mind, highly persuasive synthesis between attention to the claims of strict rationality and sensitivity to the claims of revelation. These are not the religious accents most in vogue in our time. Fundamentalism is on the increase, as the religions suffer the withdrawal symptoms of loss of power in a pluralist society. Trying to contribute to enlightened Christian community may seem like trying to fly a twin-engined plane with the port engine permanently in reverse. Yet in the very long-term, obscurantism must collapse beneath the weight of its own inherent absurdity. It may well be to people like Keith Ward that future generations will look with gratitude because they dared to face up to the really hard questions.

Keith Ward writes of God working through the various religious traditions of humankind, and John Hick writes of God working also through such ideologies as Marxism, as a kind of secular religion. I should also like to mention here the importance of the Western liberal humanist tradition as it has developed through the centuries and especially since 1750. Some strands of this tradition have led to a secularism which makes it almost impossible to think of God. But there is a distinction to be recalled, made notably by the late Professor Ronald Gregor Smith, between secularism and secularization. Secularization is at least in some respects a consequence of Christian reflection on the difference between creator and creation. The development of a theology and a spirituality for a secular age, the sort of non-religious interpretation of the Christian gospel, life lived *coram Deo, etsi Deus non daretur,* which much exercised Bonhoeffer and his pupils, especially Gerhard Ebeling, is still perhaps an important strand of the search for a theology of the Christian future. It may be complemented by more overtly religious frameworks, of the sort found in Rahner, and in inter-religious co-operation. Such a concern might play a part in assisting the major world faiths to reach a more mature and self-critical view of their own strengths and weaknesses. The roots of this tradition may be traced back to the Christian humanism of the Renaissance and of Erasmus. Beyond this, it owes much to the manifold development of Greek philosophy, to some extent filtered through Ciceronian *humanitas.* We noted earlier the tendency to write off much in this tradition as a malign Western individualism whose chief monument has been colonial oppression and exploitation. There is a serious negative side. But there is also much that may still be of immense value in the future.

Inter-religious dialogue in practice: Christianity and Judaism

A good example of the necessity and also of the difficulty of inter-religious dialogue is dialogue between Christianity and Judaism, which might seem the easiest of the great dialogues. Here the problem of communication, in the understanding of central concepts, arises at once. I illustrate from a dialogue about the meaning of law and grace in Judaism and in Christianity.[3] I begin from some general considerations.

1. Law has always been central to the Christian tradition, though it has been interpreted in very different ways at different times. The same may be said of grace, which is, however, always related to the loving, self-giving presence of God in Jesus Christ Future interpretation will probably be at least as diverse as past interpretation.
2. In such a consultation there is an obvious temptation to slant the discussion towards what are thought to be the concerns and priorities of the dialogue partner. This may simply result however in what is commonly called 'groupthink'. A consensus is reached which is unrecognizable to anyone who was not a part of the original group. This is a common fate of ecumenical proposals.
3. It should perhaps be recalled at the outset that modern discussion of basic theological concepts is deeply coloured in all traditions by past discussion, and that the formation of these concepts, in the past and even in the present, is often deeply moulded by controversy and polemic. The task before us is to find constructive dialogue in the midst of difference.
4. History has left a legacy not only of intellectual divergence but of pain, suffering and unreconciled wrongs. Persecution seems to produce a circle of alienation which tends to repeat itself. In the Christian tradition we have to be ashamed that precisely in stressing grace we have been anything but gracious, and in interpreting law we have often been anything but just, in specific and repeated cases.
5. Part of the problem lies, I believe, in the failure to recognize that different traditions may mean rather different things when they use the same words. The more effective strategy is to seek to understand and respect the other as other, as in important

respects different, and then to move on to fruitful engagement with the areas of convergence and divergence.

Law is a concept central to the history of the Christian tradition, as it is to the Jewish tradition. In both it has been interpreted in different ways at different times, and this process will doubtless continue. There were of course innumerable codes of civil and religious law, much interwoven, throughout the ancient world and notably in the Near East. The source of law for Christianity is the Old Testament, and the variety of interpretations of law which it displays. Old Testament law both reflects the complex culture in which it arises and has its own distinctive tone. The situation is then developed in the treatment of law in the New Testament. There is the variety of concepts in the various New Testament writers, and the interwoven issue of Jesus' use of the law. The New Testament story suggests that Jesus was deeply interested, as every Jew was, in the correct interpretation of law, and that he had his own interpretation, to the New Testament writers a unique interpretation. The meta-question of how in fact Jesus interpreted the law is, like many other things in Jesus' life and teaching, irrecoverable for us in detail, though we may reckon to have probabilities in certain directions. There seems to have been a radical dialectic or ambiguity in Jesus' attitude to the law, which made it both binding and not binding. The law was summed up in the commandment to love God and neighbour. This was clearly not a new interpretation, but to the Christian community it gained a new significance in the light of the resurrection of Jesus as the Messiah, the Christ. Within this spectrum of New Testament material we have the distinctive writing of St Paul. For Paul there is a striking contrast between law and gospel, which reflects his distinctive background and personality.

Tied up with the interpretation of the law is the interpretation of all the other great concepts of the Bible, God, creation, salvation, grace, the human condition, eschatological hope. For Christians, the law has always raised also centrally the question of the destiny of the Jews, for themselves, in relation to Jesus, in relation to Christian community. This dimension has had awesome, and in the end unspeakably tragic, consequences for Judaism. The charge of deicide against Judaism was a lie. But the charge of genocide against Christianity, admittedly in grossly perverted form, was and is a sad reality. And none of us can bear too much reality.

The history of the Church has seen numerous attempts to define the relation of the law and the gospel, and to define the interpretation of the law. Luther's dialectical distinction of law and gospel is perhaps the most famous, influencing both later theology, e.g. that of Gerhard Ebeling in this century and Catholic opponents of the Reformation. The distinction between law and gospel is usually identical in essence to the distinction between law and grace. I shall come to speak of grace in a short time. It is important to note that the treatment of law was influenced by the juxtaposed treatment of grace. The Reformed followed the Lutherans in developing a threefold understanding of law. The first use, the civil use, is to deter people from civic offences by the threat of punishment. The second, the theological use, is to make people be conscious of their sins and repent. The third use is to guide the faithful in paths of moral obedience to God's law. While the biblical law is superseded by the gospel as a means of salvation, it can still be used in all its detail as a divinely inspired set of rules of moral conduct: all ethical issues can be solved through application of the biblical law.

The Enlightenment brought a further radical revision of the law, in which its value was increasingly to be relativized in various ways. This had good aspects, in that the harshness of the law as interpreted for example in the disciplinary procedures of Christianity was modified. To take one example, thousands of women, we must not forget, had been murdered as witches through the application of what was thought to be the law. But the progress of Enlightenment might also bring on a new tyranny, of the sort graphically portrayed by Foucault, in which a new coercion was born. And those who stuck resolutely to the old ways, like the Orthodox Jewish communities, would find themselves the target of a sub-Christian religious fundamentalist ideology, which substituted ethnic dogma for the love of God, and created hell on earth. It is important to recognize that other groups as well as Jews were equally victims; but Jewish people were by far the largest group.

This brings me to reflect on the relation between religious and civil law. Civil law has been shaped in important ways by religious law, and this has contributed to the understanding of justice. Civil law has been used to coerce religious law, as in my last example, and vice versa. Civil law is absolutely vital to society, and to suppress it in the name of anything, including the Christian gospel, is always dangerous. In a somewhat similar way reaction to religious law, in the form of aspects of antinomianism, has sometimes produced almost identical constraints to those which it has attempted to remove. I shall have more to say about the Christian understanding of law in the light of what I have to say about grace. In substance then, Christians understand the law as a highly significant part of God's story, as they read this in their own way, through the Old and the New Testament and in the history of the Church.

Grace. The first thing that is often said on this subject in Christian theology is that grace is not a thing. This may well be said in other theologies, for talk of grace is by no means an exclusively Christian form of speech. Grace is not a thing. It is not a substance, a lubricating liquid which enables the wheels of divine action to turn more smoothly. It is a way of speaking about the nature of divine action, the presence of God and the effect which God's presence has on our lives.

Christology is of course central to Christian thinking about grace. It is sometimes tempting to minimize this dimension in the interest of inter-faith dialogue, but that is not ultimately helpful. Of course there have been and will be endless debates within Christianity about the nature of the finality, decisiveness and centrality of Christ. What we believe about the character of Jesus in his ministry will affect our conception of grace. What we think about the significance of his death and resurrection will also affect materially what we say about grace. Grace is always interlinked with the divine generosity. An ungenerous treatment of grace is a contradiction in terms. Here we have much to learn from our attitudes to Jews down the centuries, and not least in our own time.

Law, grace and the future of dialogue

In thinking of law and grace it is important to remember the present. It is also important to remember the past. Much of the work of dialogue is inevitably taken up with the difficult and often painful task of the reconciliation of memories. But it is also important to consider the future. I should now like to turn to this area. In the future we shall no doubt look at the past, and indeed the present, rather differently than we do today. Jewish scholarship, along with Christian scholarship, greatly influenced what we see as the European Enlightenment. Though Bible and Torah remain important, there is a shift in much modern theology from the religion of a book to the religion of a personal God as centre. This is clear from Schleiermacher to Harnack, and also in, for example, the South Baden school of the philosophy of the Jewish scholars Cohen and Natorp, which influenced much twentieth-century thought. Reflection on God and history deepened in our time to tragic reflection on God and suffering in the work of Emil Fackenheim and Jürgen Moltmann. (Though it is passing strange that not only Heidegger but even Barth has little if any reflection on the Holocaust in his colossal theology of grace.)

Reflection on God in history includes consideration of God as Spirit. The relation of the divine Spirit to the human spirit, and the centrality here of the central figures of the great world religions, Abraham, Christ, Mohammed, the Buddha, is likely to be a source of continuing dialogue and debate – I think of the recent intensive discussions between American Christian and Japanese Buddhist theologians. Against such ventures into pluralism and cross-fertilization we must set the rise, again equally through the great world religions, of fundamentalism, an extremely powerful modern phenomenon with strikingly parallel manifestation in all the religions. How to tread a judicious path between the Scylla of total relativism and the Charybdis of fundamentalism remains a difficult path for a vast number of the religious throughout the world. And finally we have the new waves of disasters which are threatening to devastate the Third World, especially Africa and Asia, of AIDS, of hunger and of internecine war as a result of spiralling economic decline among the poorest of the poor.

All the major world religions face similar dilemmas in the future. Hence they have common concerns. In the face of all these actual crises, isolationism among the religions is a disaster, and a disaster not only of academic interest. For religion remains at the heart of much of the human enterprise, bringing tensions, constructive and destructive. It is important, if we are to encourage human flourishing and mutuality, to try to ensure that these tensions are constructive. If discussion of law and grace is to help in this process, then it must be in a context which moves consciousness in the direction of peace and concord, and repents of the sort of peace which is no real peace. This is not a reactionary warning against 'false irenicism'. It is rather a reflection that the history of Jewish

Christian dialogue has often had the character of 'too little, too late', and it should not be so.

I return to law and grace. From a Christian perspective there is an intrinsic connection between God's love and God's justice, between the nature of God as gracious, generous love and the gracious, generous love which his children are encouraged to show to God and humanity. In such a framework God's law is a guideline or rule to the conduct of God's people. In so far as it contains absolutes, these are the absolutes of unconditional love. To this centre all other considerations are secondary. But these secondary considerations have their importance in pointing in the direction of the centre. Then interpretation of the law remains a continuing and ongoing task in the community of the people of God in all its branches, and in dialogue between them. God's grace is God's gracious, loving presence. As such it is centred for Christians in the kenotic love of God, which is expressed in the life, death and resurrection of Jesus Christ. But Christians understand this love as a continuation and complement to the engagement of God's love, suffering and bringing effective new creation out of suffering, throughout the history of Israel, continuing in the life of the Jewish people and beyond this in all humanity. Grace is always inclusive rather than exclusive, because it is unlimited, unconditioned and entirely unmerited. Grace affirms, accepts, respects and loves, often in a context of rejection and of pain. Grace is generosity in action.

The dialogue of world religions remains a classic problem for the future. Clearly it will not do to say simply that all are worshipping the same God. They might indeed be doing just that, but many of them have continuing different understandings and concepts of God, which are clearly incompatible with each other. One question is how far they could engage in combined worship and social action, despite their conceptual differences. I suggested earlier that the debate may resolve itself into the old inner-Christian pattern of the actualization of reconciled diversity. It could be agreed to do everything together that could be done together. It may be agreed that nothing decided by the parliament of religions would take away the right of individual religious communities to decide their own affairs.

Christian love must commend itself on the basis of its own intrinsic value to the rest of humanity. It emphasizes the equality before God of all human beings, religious or non-religious. For too long the inter-religious dialogue has simply replaced one kind of imperialism by another. Part of the reason for the very slow development of growth in tolerance may of course be because the maturity of the human race is still far in the future. Perhaps there is something in the old-fashioned dictum that whatever humanity can do, it cannot save itself. It is incorrigibly unable to see the wood for the trees. It may need the dimension of cosmic exploration to bring home to humanity the fragility of its own centre on earth.

It is worth recalling here that a situation of global pluralism will not necessarily lead to a pluralist approach to alternative religious traditions of the sort advocated in this book, and an awareness of the complexity of modern cosmology will not always encourage a radical approach to Christian doctrine. We have already considered the textual fundamentalist options, in which sacred texts become a bulwark against the uncertainties created by accelerated change. But there are other conservative options, the consequences of which it will be instructive to take into account.

A good example of a contemporary conservative approach to the place of Christianity among the world's religions can be seen in Carl Braaten's *No Other Gospel*. He perceives in the work of John Hick, David Tracy and other scholars a basic threat to the heart of the gospel. 'This book aims to make clear what we as the contemporary heirs of the Reformation believe about the uniqueness and universality of the gospel of Jesus Christ.' In brief, Braaten hopes to move beyond the dichotomy between the theocentric universalism of Hick and the christocentric exclusivism of Barth to a new understanding of the centrality of Christ among the world religions, with the aid of concepts of Trinity and eschatology. This enables him to take up a Lutheran tradition on the relative validity of human religion from Soderblom to Pannenberg, and to embrace at least part of the programme of Troeltsch. For Braaten, Christ is God's final revelation, but not the only revelation. Theocentric pluralism has flourished in America because it lacks a Reformation. The Trinity is the Church's model of unity and mission. Within this world, order and praxis are governed by a theology of orders of creation. Other religions than Christianity have a certain value as pointers to God, but the gospel remains inviolate.

Braaten's book is instructive in several ways. It points to the real difficulty in maintaining the centrality of Christ in a Christian theology of other religions. It also shows the difficulty in allowing any real validity to the insights of other religions within the Christological framework. I use this as a caution against a simple utopianism. Braaten's constructive comments on the great world religions can only be extremely sparse. Braaten shows an awareness of the problems of Christian imperialism in the past, but his approach is much better at affirmation of the tradition than at actual communication with other traditions, secular or religious. A mutuality of relationship with the other as other appears always to be out of reach.

Christology in Dialogue

This brings me to the paradox of the role of Christology in interfaith dialogue. How is Christian theology to contribute to a future enrichment of the *humanum*? God humanizes us by coming into humanity. This is the classical sense of incarnation. How will Christology contribute to the Christian future? Sometimes it seems that a new Christian future must involve a radical move away from the classical centre of the gospel in Christology, because traditional Christology has often been used to coerce others, in all kinds of ways. This is forcibly argued for example by John Hick in *The Metaphor of God Incarnate*, and it is worth pausing to reconsider the strong case which he makes for his perspective. There may be difficulties with some of Professor Hick's solutions, but at least he has been willing to enter a dialogue in identification and solidarity with the dialogue partners, and to that extent has often been more incarnational than some of his critics.

Hick's proposal on initial inspection appears to be in the mainstream of post-Enlightenment Protestant liberal theology, from Schleiermacher to Ritschl, a perspective which more traditional theology, Catholic and Protestant, has successfully resisted up to the present. It is a development of *The Myth of God Incarnate*, edited by John Hick in 1977. But while *The Myth* was radical and polemical in its approach, *The Metaphor* is consciously eirenic in tone, aiming to build bridges, and to incorporate the concerns of those who had reservations about *The Myth*.

Hick summarizes six senses of 'incarnation' from Sarah Coakley's 1988 discussion, in *Christ Without Absolutes* (104-7), accepting the first two out of the six:

1. God is involved in human life. This is common to most religions.
2. In the life of Jesus God was involved in a particular and specially powerful and effective way.
3. There is belief in Jesus personally pre-existing his earthly life in some divine or quasi-divine form (usually the *logos*).
4. There is a total interaction of the divine and human in Christ, in such a way that Jesus is fully God and fully man.
5. Jesus has been and will be the only divine incarnation in this sense.
6. Incarnational Christology is equated with Chalcedon, and includes assent to the substance-language of *physis, hypostasis* and *ousia*.

Hick wishes to use the language of incarnation, but as metaphorical rather than literal. 'We see in Jesus a human being extraordinarily open to God's influence and thus living to an extraordinary extent as God's agent on earth, "incarnating" the divine purpose for human life' (26). The argument is spelled out further throughout the book. Jesus lives a life of selfless humanity in concern for others, and of transparent openness to the divine presence. He is crucified. He did not himself claim to be God incarnate. Christians then felt that the presence of Jesus was with them in their experience of God.

Chapter 4 deals with 'the church's affirmation of Jesus' deity'. (Interestingly, the Articles Declaratory of the Church of Scotland seem to mention neither incarnation nor Virgin Birth, though they do speak of confessing our Lord Jesus Christ, the eternal Son.) What are we to make of the Chalcedonian formula, with Jesus as of one substance with the Father and of one substance with us, two natures in one person (47)? Tom Morris (49) suggests two ranges of consciousness, a divine and a human range. Hick objects that on Morris's theory of two minds, those who talked with Jesus were talking to a man whom God the Son was invisibly monitoring and preventing from going astray. He then turns to theories of kenosis, of divine self-emptying. He chooses as an example Frank Weston's *The One Christ*, a pioneer of British discussion, but hardly as sophisticated in his use of kenosis as Barth, Rahner and Jüngel. He concludes of kenosis, 'It is a humanly devised hypothesis: and we cannot save a defective hypothesis by dubbing it a divine mystery' (71). Further examples of kenosis are then considered, e.g. Sykes, for whom, according to Hick, kenosis is a vivid metaphor for the self-giving quality of the divine love as revealed in Jesus, and for the self-giving love to which we are called as disciples (78).

Exclusive claims to Christ have led to exclusion and persecution of those who do not conform to the dogmatic norm: Christian anti-Semitism, colonial exploitation,Western patriarchalism, Western superiority complex in relation to other faiths. A better idea for Hick is plural incarnations in all the great religious figures (98). Chapter 10 turns specifically to the language issue: divine incarnation as metaphor. 'The metaphorical stands in contrast to the literal use of language.' For Hick, Chalcedon assumes that Jesus was literally God and man. That cannot be. This literal language could also be described as metaphysical, since it refers to the divine mind (103). But, 'a human body inhabited by the mind of God would not count as a genuine human being' (103). The metaphor, on the other hand, meaningfully indicates 'that Jesus was a human being exceptionally open to and responsive to the divine presence' (105). (This is fine, but perhaps it does not take account of the classical claim that in Jesus's life the nature of God is revealed, and that incarnation makes a decisive difference to the life of God, as well as of the man Jesus.) Such an idea of metaphor can be developed into myth, or reinterpreted as paradox, as by D.M. Baillie.

How does this reinterpretation of incarnation affect the Christian view of atonement? The traditional view of the Fall is totally unbelievable for educated Christians (116). Salvation may be seen as human transformation, and as part of a world-wide process of human liberation. The achievement of this liberation must involve a reassessment of the relation between Christian truth and other truths. (There is a rather odd discussion of the position of Christian inclusivism, between exclusivism and pluralism, here,148.) Christian self-understanding must move in the direction of a new global consciousness, an opening to universality, in which Jesus is not regarded as the exclusive Son of God, but as our guide to an ultimate transcendent reality (163).

This is all highly attractive. Yet I am not entirely convinced that we necessarily best serve the increased humanization of humanity by reducing stress on the claim that the creator of the universe himself engaged with human life in a way which remains unique, in the quality of the love which it demonstrated and continues to elicit in human life. The centre of Christianity is Jesus Christ, as he comes to us through word and sacrament. Christologies take up the various images which the Christian community has used in attempting to speak of Christ, and put them together to create larger patterns and perspectives. Incarnation and atonement are two of the most common categories. Though rightly subjected to critical scrutiny, especially when used in theories which appear to reduce the mystery to the tightly defined constructs of a particular time and place in the history of Christian thought, incarnation and atonement may still be helpful in the future.

In 500 years from now the ways in which we speak of God will reflect the tradition seen through the culture of an age very different from ours. How will the incarnation of God be conceived? If humanity is fortunate, it will be able to consider God from a much more naturally ecumenical perspective than we have available today. It will also be possible to think in rather different ways of the nature of humanity, not least because of the developments which we may reasonably anticipate in the life sciences and in the nature of society. The insights of groups which have up to now had only a marginal influence on Christian theology, such as feminism and Third World perspectives, may have come to a wider fruition, changing the entire landscape. But all of this will be possible, then as now, by building on the reality of the presence of God. In every generation there are things that help us to appreciate God's presence, and things that hinder. The Bible, the tradition and experience teach us that God was incarnate in a kenosis of self-giving love. The task is to respond to this love in an appropriately generous way in each generation. The gospel of the cross and resurrection, rather than a particular interpretation of incarnation as such, is at the centre of Christian faith, and it includes a call for the transformation of lives, individual and corporate, after the pattern of the love of God. It is a challenge to look at all areas of society which remain untransformed, and to change them further. This could involve a new Christological assessment of human rights, of prison conditions, of economic and social balance on the planet.

The human condition

How does God humanize us? Who are we? Here I want to turn again to theological reflection on the nature and development of human culture. Edward Farley's *Good and Evil – Interpreting a Human Condition* is a good recent reappraisal of the human condition.

It begins with a consideration of cognitive style, and a defence of reflective ontology against possible objections, especially from postmodernism. In Part 1 Farley then considers three spheres of human reality, the interhuman, the social and individual agents. He considers these in their biological, psychological and historical dimensions. The interhuman has a triadic structure, involving alterity, intersubjectivity and the interpersonal. In the sharing of emotions or dialogue, when we experience what Levinas has called the face of the other, there is created a call to compassion and obligation. The interhuman involves vulnerability, fragility, and the possibility or actuality of suffering. There is a salutary reminder of the negative dimensions of vulnerability, the risk and often the reality of disaster. Chapter 2 examines the social sphere. The sphere of the social includes power and society. It too includes social vulnerability, incompatibility and suffering. Chapter 3 deals with the personal sphere. Personal being is elusive and temporal, and includes determinacy, transcendence and, again, vulnerability. Chapter 4 turns to the biological aspects of human beings. Human beings undergo a process of maturation and reproduction, they possess a biological unconscious, they react to their environment to satisfy genetically rooted needs and tendencies. This raises the matter of the elemental passions of personal being, of agents as embodied passions, of subjectivity, of the interhuman, of reality. The element of unfulfilment gives an eternal horizon to the passions.

Part 2 turns to theological analysis, to a paradigm of good and evil.

1. Human good and evil occur in three spheres which reflect three of the dimensions of the human condition.
2. Human evil as a distinctive response is constituted by a distinctive dynamic.
3. Evil and freedom affect and interpenetrate all three spheres of human reality.
4. The vulnerability of the human condition is the origin of the dynamics of evil in individuals.
5. The content of historical freedom is not strictly correlated with human evil as the mere correction of a distortion, therefore new possibilities of good may arise.
6. Because evil arises in connection with the passion for the eternal, freedom has an intrinsically theonomous character.

7. Evil and redemption are interspherical.
8. Human reality is redeemable, transformable towards the good.
9. The workings of redemption require a primacy of the interhuman as a primary condition of redemption in communities of the face.

Idolatry, and the tragic dimension of existence, is the subject of chapter 6. Here Farley explores the classic theological vision of human evil. We respond to our vulnerability by aggression, thereby diminishing freedom for ourselves and others, and by distractions such as drugs. Our basic passion is a desire to be founded, to be secure. This requires courage and trust. Farley now considers corrupted historicity and the creation of beauty. Our autonomy may be corrupted, and this affects our creativity. Our subjectivity may be corrupted and this affects our vitality. The passion of the interhuman may be corrupted, and this affects our capacity for agapic freedom. Chapter 11 considers 'the corrupted passion for reality and the freedom of wonder'. We seek certainty, and we are also given on occasion to a false scepticism. We come then to 'the corruption and freedom of bodily life'. We confuse satisfaction with a false hedonism. This brings us to the nature of wickedness, involving aggression, control, malice and bigotry. This raises the theme of alienation and communion, and the redemption of the interhuman. Communion takes place through forgiveness, in which alienation is overcome. The third face of human reality is the social. Social evil is institutionalized evil, and requires social redemption. This requires first radical criticism, and then the creation of communities of redemption. In redemptive communities, there is a healing interconnection between the spheres of human reality. 'That which unites the spheres in the cause of human good is the face' (287). We need communities of the face.

Farley develops the tradition of Schleiermacher, translating the theme 'that about ourselves which is utterly dependent is our freedom' into 'that about ourselves which is utterly *vulnerable* is our freedom' (130f). We are reminded that vulnerability has tragic as well as creative potential. The human condition is not to be seen with undue optimism but is constantly engaged with passion and tragedy. Historical freedom is not a release from vulnerability but a way of existing as vulnerable and tragic. But human reality is also redeemable, transformable towards the good. Beyond the individual and the social comes the possibility of the interhuman. Lowe suggests that the interhuman is truly affirmed precisely in encounter with the stranger. Here we have a profound and comprehensive treatment of the reality of sin and evil. Together with such works as Marjorie Suchocki's *The Fall to Violence*, it offers solid evidence that a liberal theology is not incompatible with taking account of sin and evil in the most serious possible way.[4]

Critical liberal theology

We come back to the question which to be faced by all theologies, the nature of the interface between faith, praxis and reflection. Faith, we suggested, is faith in God, who is characterized by the self-giving love of Jesus Christ. What this means is the appropriation of the character of Christ, as individuals and community seek to do this within their own culture. It means to be influenced decisively in our humanity, not to be dehumanized. Positive examples of such a transformative pattern may be seen in such studies as Theissen's *The Shadow of the Galilean*, or in the work of Edward Schillebeeckx. A powerful negative example of what conformity to Christ should not be is set out in Eugen Drewermann's *Kleriker*. To engage in discipleship, intellectual and practical, is to be encouraged to develop our human talent in full and autonomous humanity as children of God. It is not to undergo submission and suppression of our own humanity in the creation of a religious stereotype, which may become a barrier to human communication and action at every level. Such stereotypes may be seen in a certain sort of clericalization, which is unfortunately endemic in the churches in various forms. It is also present, however, in a kind of mirror-image laicization, which may become more clerical than the clerics. This kind of subversion of theological anthropology has been impressively chronicled by Drewermann. It is also implicit in Barth's early critique of *das violette Jahrhundert*, the century of the Church, as a kind of supercession of the Gospel.

In thinking of faith and praxis we are concerned inevitably with the use of power. Where there are large and complex social structures, as in church denominations, there has to be the exercise of power, in order that executive decisions may be taken and implemented. The power of God, in Christian tradition, is the power of self-giving love, and is made perfect in weakness. The Church has always understood itself as the servant Church, the Church of the servants of the servants of God. Yet this servant imagery has not proved incompatible with exercising absolute power in an exploitative and dehumanizing way. Indeed the language and imagery of service has often served as a cloak for manipulation of human beings in the most devastating way, while immunizing the institutions against genuine critical reflection on their practice. This blindness has regularly affected religious communities of various denominational colouring. It has been endemic in church politics. A critique of the exercise of power must somehow be built into the Christianity of the future.

Power is not confined to structures and institutions. There may also be a tyranny of ideas, when certain doctrines become mandatory for the expression of Christian faith, in such a way that to deviate from them incurs penalties, of a more or less severe nature. It is one thing for ideas to commend themselves on the basis of their own intrinsic merit. It is another for them to be forced on the obedience of people who may be reluctant to endorse them, in whole or in part. The test of a democracy, it is often said, is the way it treats its minorities. This is a particular problem for the church establishments, whether liberal or conservative in general orientation. It will long have been clear that my sympathies are in general with liberal rather than conservative Christian positions. Yet it does seem to me that the great Achilles' heel of much liberal Christianity has been that it has been just as authoritarian and exclusive in its power groupings and its practice as the conservative alternatives which it has rightly identified as authoritarian and criticized. In this way it has lost credibility and failed to benefit from the positive things which may be learned from its conservative dialogue partners. A new liberal Christianity, which I regard as crucial for the future of the faith, must be a truly self-critical liberalism if it is to succeed.

A self-critical liberal theology must be both consistent and flexible. It must be consistent in its emphasis on a humane, non-authoritarian interpretation of the gospel, as it sees this mirrored in witness to the God of Jesus Christ in the Bible and in the tradition of Christian life and thought through the centuries. It must be consistent in its rejection of all that is contrary to its understanding of the character of self-giving love. It must be flexible in its ability to learn new truths about the gospel from different forms of theology and life, notably from those which may not share a liberal vision, while maintaining its fundamental understanding of the gospel. It must seek to maintain a sensitivity which is genuinely Catholic and self-critical, and which will rise above a mere political correctness, identifying only with those who represent the enthusiasms of the moment. Above all it must offer positive constructive programmes. This is perhaps the hardest part of a liberal theological programme to realize in practice.

If these observations are more or less correct, then it seems likely that a renewal of the gospel in society will require substantial structural changes in the major Christian denominations. Instead of a group of rigidly organized bureaucracies, feeding upon each mutual critique for strength and distinctiveness, there will have to be a reappropriation of humility which is not a romantic immunization against actual humility. It is not clear how this may come about, and it may well take a very long time. On the other hand, sometimes there are unexpected and accelerated changes in over-rigid structures, as in the recent collapse of Marxist regimes in Europe. It may be that outdated ecclesiastical structures will also collapse under the pressure of their own absurdities, perhaps with a domino effect throughout the confronting denominations, in something like a multilateral confessional disarmament. Even a partial easing of defensiveness might be fruitful for dialogue with other faiths, as well as for a joint engagement with such major problems as food, health and welfare on our planet.

Future paradigms of the church

STRUCTURES

Theology will have to take stock, too, of the understanding of the Church. Whatever the structures, the churches will probably not flourish in an open future till they come to see that the essence of the Church is not to be served but to serve, not in a ceremonial but in a real way. To that extent, we may agree that ministry is of the essence of the Church, ministry as service. Self-giving, mutual regard and respect must come not at the end but at the beginning. The Church can do this only by being more believing, not less believing. God is the source of self-giving. God is God, yesterday, today and tomorrow. The Christian gospel is as much the way, the truth and the life as it has ever been.

We may then say that the church is infallible. But this infallibility is the infallibility of the service of self-giving love. Such a universal potential infallibility of the Church suggests a greater sense of responsibility, and brings the possibility of the actualization of service.

In the context of self-giving love we may see a new character in baptism and Eucharist. Every Council looks backwards and forwards in its own way. But recent developments in the sociology of church practice have shown how many church structures were so constructed as to make it virtually impossible to make radical changes. The classic example is the Church of Anyland. No matter how well chosen its committees, no matter how trusted its leaders, no matter how radical or how traditional, it has been impervious to significant change for 1,000 years. When ordinary membership has fallen, committee membership has always increased. Forests are sacrificed to document the inconsequential for the sake of the ineffectual. When the pews are hushed, the assemblies and synods vibrate with business. How could so many excellent people achieve so little for so long? Analysis is not enough. Beyond the paralysis of analysis we have always been prisoners of our past, even of our sophisticated perceptions of the past. What really matters is our programme for the future.

WORSHIP

As far as services of worship are concerned, these may not change as fast in the long-term future as other aspects of community. For here continuity has proved its value, and modernization has not always been a success. Liturgy may still be focused on particular traditions. But much will be learned from other denominations, in the colour and intensity of the Eucharist itself. There may be periods of silence. Prayers may be beautifully balanced, and drawn from many different areas of the Church. Freedom from exclusive historical commitments may in fact release a whole treasure house of new but ancient devotional literature for use and adaptation throughout the Church. We may stop playing off medieval against patristic orders of service and the like. There may be a spontaneity and an imaginative dimension to the service which will be refreshing and profound.

Most age ranges may be represented. One result of the mixing of traditional cultures and races in recent years should be to extend a certain understanding of unfamiliar attitudes. The result may be that the old no longer patronize the young, or vice versa. People will drop in from work. Some will go back to their offices, others to work from home, after a shared lunch. In a sense this is probably how it has always been. But the pattern may be as natural in 2500 as it perhaps was in 250.

ETHICS AND SOCIETY

The Church's relation to society. This is an instance where more theology, not less, may be needed. Sometimes Christians are inclined to react to intellectualist pietism by understating all foundational and dogmatic theology, but that may not always help. Many of the basic philosophical problems of the past will remain. To what extent should life in society be regulated? To what extent must we protect the vulnerable by legislation which includes positive discrimination? Liberal intentions are not always enough. The French revolutionaries, we may often think, had the right ideas – liberty, equality, fraternity. And, in proportion to their modest numbers, they murdered more people than most in a short time, butchered and drowned indiscriminately, created autocratic horror. Right-wing politicians, even quite respectable ones, by cosmic standards, like the Thatcherites of the 1980s, cut back centralized legislation but left the most vulnerable sections of society completely at the mercy of market forces, and diverted much of the weight of the law to the harassment of ethnic and social minorities. It might be tempting on bad days to agree that the world would be a much better place without organized religion. But there isn't much positive evidence for the intrinsic infallibility of the unchurched either.

Theology is full of paradoxes. Christian ethics often provides the most difficulties of all. This is even the case in the theology of peace and war. It has long been agreed that wars are never just and always against the mind of Christ. On the one hand, it becomes clear that a naive pacifism may come close to destabilizing and destroying the world. And on the other hand, here might be a determination that the conditions for armed conflict should never be allowed to arise again. The global destruction of so-called defence industries would be a major contribution to stability, and the establishment of an effective World Peace Corps would ensure the effective policing of which previous generations have dreamed.

For personal ethics, the experience of war and lack of trust on a global scale underlines as never before the importance of such primary values as trust, support, imaginative concern for others, positive discrimination for the vulnerable, and by comparison the disastrous effects of exploitation on a social or individual basis. What this means for a Christian understanding of personal relationships is a renewed critique of traditional chauvinist values, whether male or female. Advances in the social sciences and in medicine may in time largely take away much of the negative aggression and misunderstanding which has destroyed so many human relationships at the end of the twentieth century. This may leave people free to develop positive energies with a new enthusiasm, while leaving them the imagination to see rather the complexities, indeed the wonder, of human relationships in ways that have been hidden from most of their ancestors. Nuclear families may flourish again, though without the destructive elements which have often oppressed people and threatened the single and the widowed in the past. Difficulties there will be in the future, but few will perhaps want to exchange them for the all too frequent institutional violence, public and domestic, of the 'good old days'.

The best thing that may come out of the traumas of the recent past will be a greater realism about people than in the past, when idealism has alternated with increasing violence. There are still problems with so-called mixed marriages in a more pluralist society. But there will also be benefits from the clash of different cultural backgrounds, and the difficulties have absolutely nothing to do with the colour of people's skin. Superstition and ignorance of the sort that are still rampant today may become almost unthinkable in the future. Racism may be simply unacceptable, and people may marvel at the insensitivity of even the more educated of the early moderns. Much will depend on the final achievement of the economic balance between North and South. Only the developments of medical technology may prevent the disappearance of humanity. Perfect love casts out fear: that is as central to the Christian gospel today as it has been from the beginning. Toleration we owe first to the old-fashioned liberals, who may not have been profound systematic theologians but who at least recognized discrimination and prejudice for what it is, and fought it resolutely. Second, we may owe it to new Evangelicals who are learning from shattering disillusion to distinguish concern for Evangelical truth from fundamentalism and legalism, and may be a growing force in the new Church.

When we come to Christian ethics, we ask about authority in decision-making. Authority for Christians is the authority of God. How is God's will made known to us? Traditionally we have turned to the Bible, which is described in such terms as 'the supreme rule of doctrine and life', to the experience of the Christian community through the ages, to the conscience of the individual before God. How does God use the Bible to make known his purpose for humanity? I have suggested (*God in Christian Perspective*, 55) that 'Basic themes in the Bible function to illuminate Christian life and thought in different ways at different times. This is part of the action of God, Father, Son and Holy Spirit, in human life.' We need the Bible that speaks of the unconditional love of God, of grace alone, of the acceptance of the unacceptable, of Jesus who is there for the poor, the vulnerable, the outcast. We have to recognize, however, that the Bible has often been misused in the Christian community. We don't need the Bible which is there to foster religious bigotry, to attack the other, to encourage self-righteousness, and the cant and hypocrisy for which the churches have sometimes been a byword. We need the Bible to inspire the virtues of religion, not to consolidate its vices. In a situation, say, of apartheid you can say 'the just shall live by faith' three times a day before meals and still not bring the cutting edge of the gospel to bear on peoples' lives. You have to put the text in context. Pious, self-righteous platitudes are not enough, even when they are full of biblical language. The Word of God is a reality in actual lives.

I have spoken of liberation theology, which must have its consequences for our own society. I should like to relate this to the debates about marriage and human sexuality, which are the subject of continuing discussion at present and are likely to remain so. The great majority of Christian denominations have traditionally held that sexual relationships are allowed only within traditional marriage, and that all other sexual acts are sinful. There have of course been huge variations in the practices of Christians, and the tradition itself has been anything but uniform. In general, however, the tradition has been strict. Divorce has been condemned, except for adultery, and the remarriage of divorced persons in church has been forbidden. Until comparatively recently, artificial contraception was regarded as wicked by most Christians.

The last fifty years have brought reappraisal in many of these areas. We need to affirm the hidden presence of the loving God to all humanity. We need to respect the other in his or her otherness. We should certainly rejoice in the happiness which traditional marriage brings to many people. But those for whom traditional marriage has been a rewarding experience should not imagine that God's transformation of lives through the gospel will simply make everyone else like the supporters of the tradition. We have to repent for our oppression of many people, notably gay people, single parents and women, in the days when we were able to exercise social control. Now we are sometimes suffering from the symptoms of withdrawal of power, and we don't like it. But the gospel is good news, of affirmation, of rejoicing, not of being judgemental. Sometimes in history people have thought that the Church consists only of the pure, e.g. the Donatist Church in the fourth century. There are existing Christian communities with a similar ethos, e.g. the Free Presbyterian Church in Scotland. But this is not the tradition of the mainstream national churches.

There is a strong element of polarization in the churches today. There does seem to be the beginnings of a resurgence of fundamentalism, in the American style, and it's not without financial resources. Sadly, you only need to look across to Ireland to see the chronic effects of religious intolerance and bigotry. We have to learn to respect the other as other, and not think that God wants them to be just like us.[5]

On the other hand, argument is always a healthy thing, when it is not purely destructive. Jesus didn't say, 'Blessed are they who always close ranks and never rock the boat.' We can disagree and still respect each other. But internal discussion, pulling up the drawbridge, is not enough. The Church must be seen to be able to speak up for those who cannot speak up for themselves in our society-vulnerable people in the community. Christians believe that the grace of God is there for all humanity, at home and abroad. I suspect that the Church will always be judged at every level on its record of caring effectively for those who are in deepest need of God's love. That's the tradition of the Gospel. When it is seen to care, the Church will flourish.

We want to affirm the specific, Christian vision of lifelong, faithful marriage. But as a recent report in which I had some part says, 'we should not wish to exclude from the Christian community

those who responsibly and conscientiously make other life choices'.[6]
I think that the churches are gradually coming round to see deeper connections between love and justice, stemming from the nature
of God, and to look critically at their own practice. In commending
the traditional Christian vision we don't have to make negative
judgements on other loving relationships – unless of course they
involve exploiting vulnerable people. We need to think about people living together in committed relationships, often perhaps as a
prelude to marriage. (True integrity and real commitment are not
always as tidy as traditional moralists have sometimes assumed.)
A recent report suggests 'love, trust and faithfulness as the most
significant criteria by which all relationhips are to be assessed'.

What about same sex-relationships? Aren't these always sinful?
We should not forget the thousands of homosexuals who were
murdered along with the Jews in the concentration camps. God
always suffers in solidarity with those who are made to suffer. The
Church's task today is to reach out to offer the love of God in Jesus
Christ to people, especially younger people, where they are. Many
young people are concerned about equality and freedom, and
they should find these above all in Christian community. When
the issue of discrimination on grounds of sexual orientation came
to the Commons, the late John Smith, a devout Christian, said
simply, 'I think it is a matter of equality and freedom.'

The gospel does not call us to exercise social control, manipulate
people's lives or anything such. People argue about the moral
equivalence of different sorts of human relationships. We might
reflect that true goodness is created by God's grace, not by our
self-righteousness.

Post-confessional theology

I return at the end of this chapter to the present, to reflect again
on the subject of my own particular interests, the foundations of
systematic theology. This is a question familiar to all theologians,
and answered in many different ways. The Bible, the tradition,
the ongoing theological enterprise, the life and worship of the
Christian community – all can be said to be the basis on which
theology rests today, and will rest tomorrow. In a narrower sense,
the foundation is often held to be the Trinity, or revelation, or
the Word, or the Eucharist, as manifestations of the incarnation of

God in Jesus Christ. In the various churches, such concepts as the apostolic tradition, the decrees of the early Councils, justification by faith, the notion of covenant, all play important roles. It is the contention of this study that a greater emphasis on the love of God as normative for the specification of foundational theology would shed light on many of our current theological problems and offer considerable improvements to what is at present on offer to contemporary theologians, for the theology of the future.[7]

Where does the phenomenon of Christian life, lived in different ways in different parts of the world, come from ? Christians believe that it comes from God. It is a result in this world of the outpouring of the over-generous love of God. What we call faith, personal awareness of the meaningfulness for us of the Christian story, is the condition of living with this dawning and deepening recognition. Faith is recognition of the reality of God's love as a force in our lives. It includes experience and reflection on this experience. Christians reflect that God's love is the source both of our existence and of our awareness of the grounds of our existence. What this means is that Word and Spirit, subjective experience and objective reality, are related elements of the effective action of the divine love in the world. This means that the choices which modern theologians have felt compelled to make between the way of Schleiermacher and the way of Barth are fundamentally misconceived. Both were dealing with particular elements of the whole dynamic of the divine love in contingent history. Both saw different aspects clearly. Both were right, and both were incomplete in their diagnosis.

What we often call the world of empirical reality is not, for Christians, self-contained. It is dependent on God, who is the ground of its being. While God's being is unique and inconceivable to us, Christians understand the character, quality and purpose of God's being to be shown as self-giving love. At a fundamental level, God's love has created the physical order, and has intended that it should develop, to express with increasing richness the character of its creator, in such a way that humanity should develop its own authentic and autonomous community of love, regard and mutual respect. This is the shape of the gospel. The substance of the gospel includes the affirmation that despite the evil and suffering in the universe, which appear constantly to frustrate God's loving purpose, God has himself created a dimension of reconciliation, which makes possible that to which God invites. To become aware of God's love as a factor in our world, and increasingly as the decisive factor, as the ground of existence and of meaning, is to come to faith. As we see that all that is of fundamental value in human life is based on God's love, we know what it means to speak of justification by faith alone. Aware of God's love, however intensely, hesitantly or intermittently, we may live in the freedom of the children of God. This life is the life of the Christian community, called to service in the world. The tension between law and gospel is part of the wider tension between love and non-love, between caring and exploitation. The criterion of difference is the same as the criterion of balance between law and gospel, the love of God expressed in the life and activity, the death and the resurrection of Jesus.[8]

At this stage we should look at what may be thought to be a basic flaw in my argument. *Nondum considerasti quanti ponderis sit peccatum.* We do not in fact always perceive the world as sustained by the love of God. Even within the churches there have been tragic and cruel conflicts. Christians are notoriously unredeemed in the way in which they behave towards each other. Even when they believe in God as a loving God, Luther held, they are authentically Christian only when they are aware of being justified by faith alone. For justification emphasizes an important characteristic of faith, namely that it is entirely unmerited, solely of grace. We may agree with this proposition, and go on to consider its wider significance. In a previous age these confessional focal points which we have considered, such as justification, served to discriminate between true believers those who adhered to the 'right' confession, and others whose beliefs were considered inadequate. Today we have to do better. We have to learn to share in and participate in the particular insights of the various denominational theologies, while avoiding the narrowness of historical discrimination which is not relevant to the Christian future. We may continue to enjoy the distinctiveness of the various kinds of denominational witness, but we must not use them as tribal excuses for local self-righteousness. What might the public character of theology in the future look like? I return to this theme in the next chapter.

6

FAITH, THEOLOGY AND

COMMUNITY

Public signs of faith –
towards a theology of generosity

Christian faith understands itself to have a unique responsibility, a responsibility to live according to the gospel and to communicate this at all times, past, present and future. It understands human beings to be created by God, to enjoy fellowship with God and with each other. How this relationship will be expressed will vary in different cultures. But it is intended to be according to the pattern of self-giving, responsive love shown in the events concerning Jesus. (I am grateful to David Griffin for the phrase 'creative and responsive love'. Self-giving is not self-imposing, but respects always the otherness of the other.)

This pattern has often been reflected in the political and social documents of cultures deeply influenced by Christianity. A good example is the American Declaration of Independence. Yet, as is often noticed, this declaration did not prevent the continuance of slavery for almost a hundred years thereafter, together with racism and a neglect of the most vulnerable members of society up to the present. Clearly, declarations need to be backed up by legislation, to protect the vulnerable. Christian faith is not only concerned with the vulnerable, but it is particularly concerned for them. If the vulnerable happen to be, say, Muslims, and the oppressors are formally Christian, then the Christian duty to the vulnerable is even more imperative. This concern for the vulnerable, for those who are the victims of physical or mental violence, of institutional violence or exploitation by individuals, is of the essence of Christianity, though it is not of course confined to Christians. Bonhoeffer said memorably that only he who speaks up for the Jews has a right to sing hymns in church. This applies to all vulnerable minorities, without exception. But individuals and societies are not only to be protected from exploitation. They are also to be encouraged to live life to the full, to rejoice and be glad in God's world. They can only do this if efforts are being made to increase the opportunities open to all people.

I turn to divinity. Basic to Christian faith is the belief that God is there, as a loving presence. Humanity finds its fulfilment in the worship and service of God, and through this in service of our neighbours. Even more crucial, Christians believe that God is present to humanity, inviting, encouraging and enabling participation in relationship with God. It is not easy to understand this central belief in a world where so many people live and die in desperation and isolation. Indeed it would be highly insensitive and unrealistic to be unmoved by this mountain of human suffering and apparently unanswered pleas for help. Yet Christians believe themselves to be aware, on occasion at least, of God's presence, and they seek to encourage others to find God's presence as a reality in their lives.

Humanity has developed numerous concepts of God over millennia, and will very probably develop more in time. Christians believe that God, creator of our physical universe, has made himself known to us in a way that is decisive for our understanding. In the life, death and resurrection of Jesus Christ this love is shown within the sphere of human practice. We believe that other religions and world views also have contributions to make to our understanding of God, within the mystery of providence, and that we have a duty to listen to such views. We believe too that there will be an eschatological fulfilment for humanity, in which the love of God in Jesus Christ will be more fully understood. We believe that humanity finds fulfilment as co-humanity in the worship and service of God.

Faith in transition to faith

It is important that we should attempt, from time to time, to stand back a little from our usual perspectives and consider the future of our faith. When we do this we may be surprised by the colossal gap between the actual and the possible. In history people have often reacted to such reflection in despair, in anger and in puritanical zeal for reform. These are legitimate reactions. But we shall not make progress merely by substituting one set of dogmas for another. As always, we need cool and differentiated thinking. There are areas in which radical, painful and immediate changes may be necessary, in which institutions which perpetuate institutional violence may need to be abolished. I mentioned the abolition of slavery, an institution supported by the churches for nearly two millennia, or the emotive struggle for women's rights in the churches, still by no means won. It seems to me that the hard-edged confessional triumphalism which spreads rigidity through all the Christian confessions, and is today on the increase, requires to be dismantled, as decisively as Soviet communism has been dismantled. There may be other areas in which it will be necessary to work slowly and patiently within the institutions. There is always a need for fine judgement to discern on which issues progress may be made most effectively. The gospel invites to patience, gentleness, kindness, self-giving. But it does not invite the marginalized to practise self-effacement. It does not counsel acceptance of exploitation of the vulnerable. It is concerned with the fullness of life for all people. That may entail shaking many more of our received perspectives than we care to imagine.

I have suggested that the Christian world of the future may be in many respects very different from today's world. Experience of sterile conflicts and intolerant ideologies may lead to a genuinely open society in which the fortress mentalities of the past may simply vanish. There may be a transformation of sociological structures in the Church which have ossified tradition, inhibited change and effectively crushed dissent. The collapse, for example, of Roman Catholic rigidity may lead to a collapse of Protestant defensiveness, with corresponding effects on Orthodoxy. In relation to other world faiths, and to secular value systems, there may also be a developing openness, in the absence of a need to 'hold the line' in the face of the claims of other Christian bodies. Such an openness would remain a Christian openness, which respects particularity.

In any future, as it were post-defensive theology, there would inevitably be radical shifts in perspective.[1] This might involve a reasoned eclecticism, in that approaches like the experiential-expressive theology of Rahner, to use George Lindbeck's categories, would be applicable in conjunction with the ontological theology of the sort currently practised by Plantinga, together with the cultural-linguistic perspective of someone like Lindbeck. Theologians in our time who have been able to exemplify this sort of freedom of imagination would include Schillebeeckx and Tracy, perhaps because they have had to make a conscious effort to break out of narrow ideological constraints. In a more open society the possibilities for creative thinking about God might be exponentially increased. Since future theologians will also have access to developments in information technology unimaginable to us, with perhaps instant recall of and comparison with all previous thinking, there may be scope for swift development and evaluation of concepts which hitherto have taken centuries to mature.

We cannnot, of course, write the theology of the future now. If we could, it would cease to be future and it would be present. But we can try to anticipate the sort of moves which might lead us in a future direction. God is a presence expressed for faith through numerous clusters of imaginative patterns. Different studies come up with different sections through the conceptual spectrum, different numbers of central paradigms, different perspectives. It seems probable that most Christians will continue to understand the divine presence as the presence of God as Spirit, illuminating the reality of God as the God of human life through Jesus Christ, and still the cosmic creator and reconciler. In other words, some kind of Trinitarian framework is likely to continue as the most enduring model for expressing our Christian experience of a living God, who manifests personal being and action. This Trinity will not be an exclusive Trinity, for it will be open to dialogue with non-Trinitarian concepts in other religions. But a Christian concept of God will retain this internal quality of essential relationship.

A public invitation

How then will Christianity be communicated as a public invitation? It will continue, as it has done, to commend a vision of ultimate reality as the core belief of a caring community within the wider human community. Those who continue to believe that God the reconciler is the creator of the physical cosmos, and I see no reason for that belief to disappear, will not imagine that 500 years make a significant difference to the mode of God's presence and action in the world. But the response to God's active presence could well be quite transformed. If there are grounds for pessimism about some of the future prospects for communities based on faith, there are also grounds for optimism. Christianity in a post-defensive age could be a basis for human renewal, of the forging of trust and support between individuals and communities on a new level of magnitude.

In such a community, Jesus, understood more fully as a figure whose supreme goodness, expressed in total vulnerability and pastoral sensitivity, may become visible again, when layers of obfuscation created by ecclesial ideology are removed by the pressures of a genuine Catholic ecclesial theology. One could imagine that this may involve in part completely new symbolism, in part hermeneutical retrieval of apostolic notions such as the Prince of Peace.

It may also be that a new understanding of God as Spirit, as the centre of human and cosmic well-being, may again become conceivable, after the various plausibility criteria which militate against such a conception in a fragmented and often self-destructive Church and society begin to dissolve. Anyone who looks at present trends in religious bodies is likely to see grounds for disquiet. But a person who believes that God's love is effective to all eternity will also have serious grounds for hope.

It may be at least in part because we are so damaged by the immediate pressures of our ecclesial and social institutional violence, as individuals and as groups and denominations, that we are unable to have the confidence which would produce a tangible reality of life in the Spirit of God. We have learned that the abuse of children often creates instability, and that social deprivation contributes to crime levels. It is at least conceivable that a new ecclesial atmosphere, and a new level of inter-faith dialogue in a transformed society, could produce a quality of social life which we can today hardly conceive of. If so, then the future may well be much more interesting than the present. It is important to leave open as many options for growth as possible. The gospel is there not to close down, but to open up, the truth of God for all humanity. God is creator and sustainer of the physical cosmos and of humanity within this cosmos. God is reconciler of this cosmos, and of humanity, to himself, transforming structures through participation in them. God is Spirit, creating new possibilities within the cosmos, not least within the life of humanity.

I am interested to see that Moltmann increasingly stresses the Spirit in his developing systematic theology, most recently in *The Spirit of Life – A Universal Affirmation*. The volume is characterized on the dust-jacket as 'an invitation to openness, to the experience of the life-giving Spirit and the affirmation of life in the threats posed to it'. It evolves out of the logic of the doctrine of the Trinity which is the basis of the entire systematics, and also from experience, from practical experience in the struggle for peace and against war, violence and poverty. Clearly, a study which combines both the poles of human experience and Trinity as sources is worth attending to. He discusses the spirituality of Jesus. The Spirit suffers in Jesus' suffering, and brings Jesus up out of death. The Spirit creates expectations in the community, through signs of hope and lamentation. This is an immensely powerful section which is largely a meditation guided by the central biblical themes. Moltmann speaks of 'the streaming personhood of the divine spirit'. This brings us to a vital definition: 'The personhood of God the Holy Spirit is the loving, self-communicating, out-fanning and out-pouring presence of the eternal divine life of the triune God' (289). This is a Trinitarian personhood. Concepts of Trinity are explored, monarchical, historical, eucharistic and doxological. The triune God is worshipped and glorified for his own sake. The *Filioque* is superfluous. Trinitarian doxology is paralleled by the social analogy of the triune God, creating communities of Christian love and friendship. *Veni Creator Spiritus.*

The understanding of God as the Spirit of love within the universe is a central theme of Christian life and thought. It has sometimes given rise to anxiety, if Spirit was understood in separation from the physical world, for that appeared to undermine incarnation. It has to be understood too in relation to God's sustaining creativity, for it is a transformation precisely within the structures which God has originally created. As the transforming Spirit of love God is ceaselessly active within the cosmos at all levels, at the human level inviting and encouraging imaginative response. This response takes different forms, not least in theology and the churches, where it is shaped from within very different social and intellectual cultures.

From its source in the being of God, the Spirit of self-giving, responsive love is a hidden presence throughout the structures of creation. It is understood through faith, when the character of the Spirit's action is perceived as the pattern of the reconciling kenosis of Jesus Christ. The Spirit actualizes the possibility of service, and is at the same time a judgement on inauthentic spirituality, even when carried on in the name of Christ. The Spirit of God is in time, before time and after time. As such it is not bound to the structures and thought patterns of any particular period of human history. It is not shackled to the pre-modern, the modern or the postmodern. Thinking about the Spirit can make available the thought forms of different cultures and periods for fresh development, because it is always a challenge to received norms and conventions. Faith believes that the Spirit is always there before us, inviting and enabling, making possible trust. The Spirit engenders Christlikeness, sometimes explicit, sometimes implicit, sometimes with the churches, sometimes against them. Between the excesses of 'enthusiasm' and the dead hand of ecclesiastical bureaucracy for its own sake, the Spirit encourages us towards a path of universal reconciliation and renewal in the created order. Because the Spirit engenders Christlikeness it is both exclusive and inclusive. It is exclusive in that it fosters only that which is consonant with the character of Christ, with whom it is in constant communion. It is inclusive in that it operates throughout the physical cosmos, a presence to all human striving for ultimate meaning.

Awareness of Spirit in an open, inclusive concept of God which includes a Trinitarian dimension should make it possible to deepen our understanding of creation as God's reconciled creation. David Tracy has spoken of the options of pre-modern, anti-modern, modern and postmodern concepts of God. As I see it, a future theology should be able to benefit from the insights of all of these cultural patterns in our thinking, employing the advantageous and discarding the disadvantageous elements. I should be inclined to describe this as a critical modern approach to theology, but I am willing to call it postmodern provided that the critical dimension is not weakened.

In speaking of Spirit I want to emphasize the active presence of God equally in Word and sacrament. I can see no great benefit in playing off one line of spiritual growth against the other, theologies of experience and expression of Word against theologies of community, of sacramental presence. This is the kind of cultural limitation which I would expect to diminish in a church in which the great traditions refresh each other. Both Word and Sacrament equally encourage us to respond to the participation of the divine reality in our world as the subject of our faith.[2]

We may note too that a future perspective will also involve an inevitable reassessment of the past, of the memory of the Church, and this will itself be a stimulus to a new vision for the future. Facts are facts. What is done is done. Yet the interpretation which we put on the past often has tremendous consequences for the future, and indeed becomes the stimulus for future action. In the future our faith in God will take new directions, our action in community will take new forms, and one of the roots of this impetus will undoubtedly be a continuing fresh assessment of the history of the Christian tradition. Just as we look at church history very differently from the ways in which Christians looked at these traditions 500 years ago, so our successors will no doubt consider the past, and our own century, from very different angles than those familiar to us. In particular, the ways in which perspectives have been shaped by the interests of the predominant religious groups and parties will become clearer, and the concerns of the less successful groups will come to more adequate expression. The future will always bring surprises, and none of us owns the future.

Relating to basic needs

In the longer term the Christian vision will commend itself to humanity, Christians believe, not because it is able to force itself upon people's attention, but because it will speak to their deepest needs. It will be appropriated in different ways at different times, by Christians, by believers in other faiths or none, in different combinations. At its centre lies an understanding of God as the ultimate reality, a reality completely and decisively characterized by self-giving, responsive love. We return to the Christology of the future. Christians believe that God has participated in a unique and mysterious way in his own creation by engaging in the life of a single human being, Jesus of Nazareth. God is self-differentiated in relationship, neither male nor female, constantly encouraging the created order towards a final fulfilment in love, justice and peace. Part of this fulfilment is the existence of communities of relationship between God and humanity, and between human beings, bearing the quality of Christlikeness. It is as a pointer to the basis of reality in kenotic love that Jesus Christ will be trusted in the Christian future.

To develop this community further we need the theology and liturgy of the more traditional elements of Christianity without its exclusive and coercive elements. We need the theology and practice of the more liberal elements without the evacuation of intellectual rigour and emotional profundity which this has sometimes entailed. We need to turn to the rest of humanity with openness, generosity and hope, in order to create a future in which these qualities are at the centre of social reality as God's reality.

Jesus comes through the New Testament as a figure of supreme goodness, expressed in vulnerability to others, in pastoral sensitivity and in witness to the truth of creative love in action. He is the mystery of the incarnation of God, the substantially enacted parable of the nature of God as kenotic love in creation and reconciliation. He is the source of the spirit of self-giving love which creates Christlikeness in the new creation. A fully human being, Jesus of Nazareth, he lives in a world of terror and counter-terror and opposes evil and inhumanity in its characteristic forms of oppression and intimidation. As Word and Sacrament for the world, his presence is a judgement on all that is unloving, and an encouragement to the human rights of the children of God. One way of exploring a Christology for the future may be to conceive it as a Christology of human rights. There has been in recent years an enormous interest in and debate about rights and human rights. Rights bring privileges and responsibilities. Perceptions of human rights vary from one culture to another, and agreement on their status may require careful discussion, with a self-critical awareness of the dangers of unconscious cultural imperialism. Despite the difficulties, agreement on respect for human rights, for human dignity and freedom, is clearly an essential future task for the inhabitants of our planet. To this task, Christians believe, the gospel offers a vital contribution. For the goal of creation is reconciliation and the peace of God, the effective delivery of salvation after the pattern of the events concerning Jesus.

In constructing a Christology for the future, it is important to maximize the advantages of the christological traditions of the Church towards the realization of a positive response to God's invitation to enter the peace of his Kingdom, and to minimize the disadvantages. In the words of St Paul, love is kind, patient, humble, long-suffering. In genuine dialogue it should be possible to respect both one's own tradition and that of others equally. It is necessary neither to reduce one's own position in order to produce an artificial harmonization which will then immediately threaten to fall apart, nor to underestimate the strengths of the views of dialogue partners.

Christians believe that the creator and sustainer of the physical universe has been involved in the life of the man Jesus in a way which includes but goes beyond his involvement in all human life. The life, death and resurrection of Jesus make a difference to the life of God. God takes the particularity of one human life into his own experience as God, and this opens up a new direction of reconciliation in the cosmos. We believe that all humanity is affected by this divine action, and that God will be recognized in an eschatological dimension as he is seen in the character of Jesus Christ.

But Christians also recognize and respect the perspectives of believers in the other major religions. They accept that for Buddhists the Buddha has a unique place in the understanding of God, and Muhammad for Muslims. They may recognize and respect the belief that God has also acted in a unique and special way through the founders of these religions. They are unable to say how this is so. But a Christian understanding of mutuality and respect will enable them to take a positive and generous view of the beliefs of others.

At the same time, we should feel encouraged to act in an open and affirmative way towards people who may have no religion, and who embrace humanist perspectives of various sorts. These people, too, are children of God and part of his loving purpose. The gospel has no preferential option for the religious over against the non-religious. All are loved equally by God. But those who are called to Christian faith are called to be conscious instruments of God's love in the world.

In an ideal world, there might be no better alternative to maintaining the traditional expressions of Christology. Incarnation in the classical sense more truly represents what Christians believe than non-incarnational theory, it may be held. Yet there is no doubt that in times of a traditional Christian majority, classical Christologies have often become a problem and even a threat to all kinds of minority communities of those who did not conform, from Incas in America to Quakers in England, Hindus in India and Muslims in Britain. It may be said that a turn to a more generous position in the face of decline and loss of power on the part of Christianity is scarcely convincing. Even a belated attention to the centrality of kenosis in Christology and in discipleship is preferable to no change at all. We have seen, however, that there is a strong tendency, both in the smaller church groups and in the mainline churches, to retreat to a fortress mentality in response to the challenge to change.

The spirit of hope

Hope of divine love. It is of course necessary to be realistic about the difficulties which may face the human community in the future, and to work patiently through the problem areas. But it is also vital to human flourishing not to get bogged down in the problems. Christian faith contains a dimension of promise, of hope of God's love in the future as well as in the past and the present. I want to concentrate on the future of what I experience as good things in the Christian tradition. Others will have different preferences, but I expect that there will be some areas of common agreement. Those who hold to the Christian faith do not always stand out in society from other citizens. They may be good citizens, hard workers, caring persons, socially engaged in efforts for the welfare of the community. These activities do not necessarily distinguish them from other citizens, though the element of concern for others is basic to Christian commitment. But they are distinguished by believing in the God of Jesus Christ. They usually come to believe, and they express this belief most distinctively, in participating in worship, in the services of the church.

In worship, when this is properly conducted, they experience refreshment and renewal. They express their devotion to God, and they experience the peace of God. This may of course make them uneasy with aspects of themselves or of the society in which they live. If the worship is ill thought through, they may be frustrated. But at its best, worship is for most Christians an occasion of spiritual communion, of the sense of the presence of the Spirit of God, incarnated in Word and Sacrament in Jesus Christ. How this spiritual awareness of communion with God is appropriated will depend on the denomination, the particular service or the practice of the community. Some liturgies centre on Word, some on Sacrament, some on both. Liturgical renewal is important. Ancient services which bore people to death are clearly pointless. But the experiments of recent decades have shown that Liturgical renewal cannot succeed simply by substituting modern words for ancient words. Unless the result is aesthetically satisfying to the congregation, whether in an Evangelical Protestant or in a Catholic context, it simply will not do. What is needed, here as everywhere, is an intelligent adaptation of different styles of service for different contexts.

There are times and occasions when only the ancient services of the Church will cut any ice, with people of any age. There are times when a thoroughly modern liturgy will be vividly effective. God comes to bless people with his presence through Word and Sacrament. God's continuing presence in the sanctuary, in good times and bad, must belong to the centre of our Christian hope. Christian service has been central to the gospel in which the Sermon on the Mount and the Kingdom of God have always been integral parts. No single denomination or style of spirituality has had a monopoly on service. Quakers and Carmelites have been equally faithful: this too must be part of the centre of hope for the future. The whole notion of disinterested love, of regard for others as others, with a priority for the poor, the sick, the disabled, outcast and the disadvantaged, will always be at the centre of Christian faith. Worship and service arise from and in turn encourage a belief in God. The centre of the Christian hope is that God will continue to be present in human lives as a basic experience, pouring out, inviting and eliciting love for God and humanity. Christians believe that this is the power at the heart of the universe, and they expect that it will be an ever more present force in human development in the long-term future.

Constructing the future

How can we utilize the resources of the present to move towards a more constructive future? Once we have taken on board the liberation theologies, then there ought to be a dividend of creative understanding, affecting all our perspectives. What, if anything, does liberation theology teach us about the Christian doctrine of God? Not a lot, it may appear. For it tells us nothing of what it is for God to be or to act, it may seem. Yet it may help us in other ways. Liberation theologies, theologies with a human rights dimension, may help us in our thinking about the anthropological element of talk of God. Man is made in the divine image. God is person. (God's presence is in some ways like human personhood, in other ways not. God cares for us in a personal way, we learn from the Old Testament and from Christian experience of the personal presence of God's gracious invitation. God cares, God identifies, God communicates, as a person does. Not simply as a male person does, but as a female person does also. God communicates as one who is identified with the poor , though he is concerned also for the rich and powerful as persons.) Whereas in history God has been identified personally with the rich, the powerful in human society, God may now be seen as also identified personally with the persons of the marginalized. God is not only sovereign, kingly, majestic, but his majesty is displayed in human self-humbling.

This is particularly significant when we come to see the christological dimension of God. For God to be is to act in love, after the pattern of the character of Christ. Liberation theologies may help us to look at our Christologies with fresh eyes, and so our doctrines of God. Jesus is not only the royal man, the king, the high priest. God's priorities turn the world upside down. God himself is the one for whom to love is to be incarnate, to identify with the poor and the marginalized, to be poor and marginalized and outcast. There can be a false romanticism here, when God is identified with every current politically correct trend. Yet there is evidence in the Bible that God engages with the weak and powerless in this world. He is crucified as a criminal, and that is decisive. He does not, how-ever, take on himself the bad side of humanity which can affect weak and powerful alike, exploiting others, being rapacious or self-pitying. Being poor does not create salvation, any more than being rich brings salvation. Only being God makes possible rec-onciliation. What is decisive is that in this particular, contingent person God is there as salvation for all humanity, regardless of colour, race or creed. As we come to a more humane view of humanity through deeper reflection on the gospel, so we may come to find through this reflection a deeper view of the source of our humanity, which is God. As in Christian worship we pray to be guided to a better understanding, so we may see theology again as Anselm saw it, as prayer and the answer to prayer.

What in a nutshell are the priorities of a more humane theology for the future?

- We are called to live out the consequences of faith in the present, not in the past.
- What of the role of the Church as an institution in relation to the rest of society, and not least to government?
- A Church that never feels awkward, embarrassed, unpopular and even vulnerable should perhaps ask itself whether it can possibly be carrying out its proper mandate.
- We live in a society with huge social problems. Crime and punishment. Ours is a Christian and a democratic society. Here is an area where human rights are of decisive significance.
- We live in a society in which the power of business is formidable. Business ethics is another of our concerns. I shall not speak of religion and the rise of capitalism, Calvinism and Max Weber, and all that. There are clearly problems with the relation of market philosophies to justice as fairness.
- We live in a society with tremendous economic contrasts. Poverty, at home and abroad, is and remains a continual affront to human dignity and human rights.
- We live in a society with all kinds of ethnic tensions. It is right to be proud of local tradition. But national churches have to be especially sensitive about the dangers of nationalism, however discreetly expressed, particularly in relation to our nearest neighbours.
- In an international context the matter of human rights is clearly also central. It is not surprising that concern for human rights has been attacked, from Marxist, Islamic, postmodern and numerous other perspectives. And of course Western liberals have often been selective in their views. But for the Church the basic central principles of compassion and human commitment are not negotiable. Particularly where rights are violated by those who should know better, the Church must not be afraid to speak up. We can hardly advocate these principles abroad if we don't practise them at home, not least in the Church.
- The centre is the hidden love of God in Jesus Christ, effective through solidarity, infinitely vulnerable but also infinitely enduring and sustaining. It is this inexhaustible love of God which makes possible hope and peace in hopeless situations. It comes from above. But at the same time, God's love is committed in trust to those who take up the way of discipleship, in fear and trembling, in error and in hesitation. Nothing can separate us

from the love of God in Jesus Christ. For this reason no obstacle need ever prevent us from attempting to respond in the way of love, however impractical this may seem. Bruised reeds and still small voices may be the Christian order of the day, in a century which has already seen tens of millions ruthlessly murdered. But we may perhaps reflect quietly that God's love is the force which moves the stars, and the universe in its development towards its goal in God.

It is because God has given himself away to others and yet produced effective love out of darkness that there is good news. At future Councils there will be opportunities to translate good news into direct action. Will we actually give absolute priority to genuine mutuality and equality of regard? We find it easier to take shelter in doctrinal discussion than to become vulnerable to the reality of resurrection. The uniqueness of Christ, in unconditional regard, in perpetual intercession for humanity, is precisely what summons us all to Evangelical generosity.

What do we do with theology when liberation is achieved for all the oppressed? History shows us that it is hard for human nature to avoid finding new forms of exploitation. That is why the risen Christ is still the crucified Christ, and will be till God himself brings about his eschatological peace. Humanly speaking, the task of working towards and maintaining God's goal for us of love, peace and justice will always be before us. Pursuing this further, we need to consider the impact of specific questions in an unmilitant manner. Here are some crucial examples.

RACE

Was Jesus black? We don't know his skin colour. But it was probably the pale brown colour characteristic of the Middle East. It was highly unlikely to be white, and in that sense more black than white, but perhaps more yellow than black.

I think white theologians have to be sensitive about sitting in judgement about how black theologians view Jesus. They will probably decide that in some circumstances it is right to think of Jesus as black, and in others it is not. It is easy for black theologians to be portrayed as an inflexible and extreme stereotype which is then easy to rubbish. This is a common form of racial discrimination. There is no reason why people of one colour should be less reflective and intelligent than people of another colour. Jesus was Jewish. It is interesting that black theologians have themselves debated the significance of Jesus' colour. The point is not Jesus' colour as such but solidarity with all the oppressed.[3]

It may be important to see Jesus as black in some circumstances. In other circumstances, it may be right to see Jesus as white. Jesus was male, but that does not mean that men should be privileged over women. Jesus came from the Middle East, but that does not mean that Arabs should be privileged over Africans. Ultimately, in Christ there is neither Jew nor Greek, male nor female, black nor white. But it is quite natural for people to identify Jesus with their own local culture, because he belongs to them. But he also belongs to all of us. Jesus is one with God the Father and the Spirit, and God is not colour-determined. In paintings, Jesus has been depicted as of many ethnic groups, Chinese, Japanese, etc. Always he is the man suffering for and with others on the cross. Jesus is for all, inclusively rather than exclusively. If there were verses in the Bible which suggested that Jesus was exclusively black or white, then we would need to challenge them in the name of the heart of the gospel, which is about God's love and God's justice, justice equally for all humanity

Christians and Muslims disagree on the relationship of Jesus to God the creator. But they agree on the fact that we are all created to love God and our fellow human beings. We need to work together to maximize the consequences of our agreements and minimize the consequences of our disagreements. Where Christians have persecuted Muslims in the past, and vice versa, I have no doubt that God has always been on the side of the persecuted, as a suffering, identifying presence, bringing new creation out of destruction.

GENDER

I have touched on the question of what can we learn from feminist theology. Without subscribing to militant feminism, we may note that one big change in the future may be the impact of a much higher proportion of women in the decision-making processes of Church and state.

My soul doth magnify the Lord, and my spirit hath rejoiced in God my saviour. The adoration of Mary in history is a long and complex story, a tale of human devotion, human fallibility, human imagination in most of its moods. We have had the romantic Mary, the queen of heaven, the inaccessible Virgin, full of humanity and purity. We have had Mary the down-to-earth mother at the kitchen sink, the Oxfam Mary. We have had Mariologies designed by men for men, to put woman on a pedestal where she belongs, adored but disbarred from exerting any undue influence on Church and state.

As Rosemary Radford Ruether has said: 'We have to look back over a broad sweep of the history of culture in which a male ruling class conquered nature and the female.' I am conscious that we men still think we can act as gatekeepers, graciously allowing women a little more freedom today.

It is with a sense of critical realism that many contemporary Christians have turned to a new appreciation of Mary, and to a new expression of a Christian understanding of the role of women in our world. We all know that women do something like 90 per cent of the manual work in the world and earn about 15 per cent of the income. In the face of this sort of world there has been a reappraisal of the Magnificat, in which Mary may be understood as identified with the voice of the poor, of the oppressed, the marginalized and the sidelined in this world.[4]

He remembering his mercy hath holpen his servant Israel. Perhaps for too long God has been for us the managing director, the male macho figure who controls and fixes everything with mechanical precision. God is neither a male macho figure nor a female macho figure. God is a God of mercy. But God is not a wimp either. Absolute powerlessness corrupts as much as absolute power does. He hath filled the hungry with good things, and the rich he hath sent empty away. God is there for the poor, and he does not tolerate the rich and uncaring. God is not indifferent to suffering and the relief of suffering. God suffers as Mary suffered when her child died. God cares, with the care that Mary has. The song of Mary is the song of God, as the passion of Mary is the passion of God. To be God is to exhibit all the human virtues male and female, and more, and to exhibit these in forms beyond our capacity to understand. In the womb of Mary God is made small for us, said Martin Luther. So God participates in the whole cycle of human birth and development, in the whole, world feminine as well as masculine. Mary's child is a boy. But God participates uniquely in the entire human experience, in the female conscious- ness and sensibility as much as in the male. The God whom Mary worships is a God for all humanity, who is there for us all, for all sorts and conditions of women and men.

PRAYER

A future theology will still be a theology of prayer. We can't afford to let the dimension of prayer be hijacked by fundamentalism. Be still, and know that I am God. The Spirit of Christlikeness is active in the entire cosmos, and in particular in the commitment of women and men in Christian community to service. The Spirit is present in our community, in Word and Sacrament and in charitable effort.

This is the God into whose presence we come in prayer. We can expect there to be prayer in the future as in the past. All forms of prayer can be well used or misused, can be infinitely rewarding or downright tasteless. Sometimes we are completely unsuccessful in prayer, for no reason that we can think of. Then we may begin to wonder. But is there a God? A bleak and lonely question. Suppose it's not true. Many Christian people have felt the experience of the blank wall, Lord I believe: help thou mine unbelief. And they have believed that God is there as a caring presence encompassing all men and women in his love, whether they are aware of his presence or not. Sometimes we can feel drawn by God into his presence and sent back refreshed into the communities of which we are a part.

It is not strange that God's love for us should reinforce our love both for God and for our fellow human beings. The divine love is love to the loveless shown. In this way all Christian life takes place in the context of prayer. Yet this prayer may be all the more effective for being quietly in the background of Christian life. For it is not so much an end in itself as a means towards the effective communication of the divine love through human faculties, of perception, of imagination, of action. Our prayer is our prayer. But people have often perceived prayer as participation in God's active love. If you had not been seeking me, you would not have found me. God is there before us, encouraging, inviting.

Prayer is related to the service of the poor. If there is an underclass, Jesus is in it, upholding, affirming, celebrating all that is good among adverse circumstances. Jesus comes through the Gospels to us as a very human figure. He certainly doesn't come across as a sort of grey man. He was prepared to be joyful, to celebrate. He took risks. He affirmed people in their individuality and their interdependence. He knew what it was to be defeated. Out of the dire consequences of his devotion, God brought new creation.

One of the striking things about the humanity of Jesus was that he prayed a lot to God his father. In our society there appears often to be a great gulf fixed between us, the respectable who pray, and them, the marginalized and disadvantaged in our culture, whom we hear and don't hear, whom we see and don't see. If we think that in the late twentieth century we know all that there is to know about the nature of discipleship, I suspect that in truth there is still much to learn. That's one reason why we all need each other's support in the human community, in a spectrum looking 500 years back and looking 500 years forward. And sometimes, not only for the sake of others but for our own sake, we need to stand still, just sometimes stand still, and be open to the presence of God.

Perhaps much of the time we don't. But the gospel points us to the character of Christ which is the character of God. God is the one who exists by giving himself in the service of humanity. The mind of Christ is the mind which visits the sick, the hungry, the poor, the prisoners, those who are marginalized and oppressed. The fruits of the Spirit are long-suffering, patience, kindness, gentleness.[5]

True Christian spirituality should relate to creation and reconciliation of all humanity. Gospel priorities – not to damage but to encourage people. Things may possibly get much worse. But we may expect further light in future, even on the evidence of the present. It is then possible that the Church will embalm itself in a fundamentalist fortress mentality. Some young people will be attracted to this. The idea of beacons of light in a dark world is always attractive, and sometimes valuable. But sometimes beacons can scorch and burn as well as cast light, and we have to be very careful. Salvation has nothing to do with cultivating a smug, complacent sense of self-satisfaction.

Basically, the Church will always show signs of real spiritual life, almost despite our worst intentions, because it is the Church of God. If the Church were only a human invention, then very often it has indeed been a pretty unfortunate invention. Looking at its history, often of repression and persecution, we can see that the Church must repent. There is no room for satisfaction about church history. Many good things have happened in the lives of millions of people through the love and care shown by Christians through the ages. But there is a dark side, known only too well to people of other faiths, to minorities of all sorts, to those who have dared to stand up and criticize the prevailing orthodoxy.

What is the Christian gospel about? We are called to affirm the hidden presence of the loving God to all humanity. We can certainly rejoice in the happiness which traditional family values bring to many people. But none of us should imagine that God's transformation of lives will simply make everyone else like us. Not everything goes. But the gospel of God is good news, affirmation, rejoicing, not being judgemental, sheer grace, always.

Steps forward

We cannot anticipate the future, in political, social and environmental developments. We can expect that much will change, and also that much will remain similar to current arrangements. That has been the pattern in human history up to the present, and it would be strange if part of this pattern did not continue. We cannot anticipate the completely unknown. But we can attempt in the present to maximize the benefits and minimize the evils in the areas with which we are familiar, and which we can expect to remain a feature of the future.

A theology of generosity, grounded in the generous love of God, should lead us, in my view, to a much more open approach between Christian denominations and between the world religions. Despite the dangers of 'enthusiasm', it is clear that the scale of priorities among the churches in their relations with each other need to change. It may be that federal unions are not the answer. But still there could be much more united activity in confederal association.

Similar considerations apply in inter-faith dialogue, which is for practical purposes still in its infancy. Here the work of pioneers has been severely criticized for being too ambitious, too inaccurate, too sweeping. Yet without the challenge of the work of such scholars as John Hick the impetus to dialogue would be even less than it is today. It is through dialogue that standard stereotypes can be assessed critically and differences realistically discussed. All the great world religions have probably at some times been guilty of excesses, of exploitation through alliance with totalitarian political regimes, of using moral codes to exercise power over individuals in an unscrupulous manner. They have also brought great benefits to humanity, promoting love, peace and justice in individual and social contexts. It is urgently desirable that they should face together their shortcomings rather than attribute these to each other, and work together for the good of humanity, as God intends. It is through this process that we may expect truth to prevail over untruth.

In specific areas, for example in the realm of ethics, social and personal, the need to give realistic priority to generosity, to oppose all forms of exploitation in all cases and within that framework to respect difference, to respect minority views, remains a continuing task. For Christians this is related to the pattern of Jesus Christ, who is the self-expression of God. For non-Christians this pattern may be assimilated and appropriated in different ways. We can safely leave God's love to make its own impact on the subjects of its creation and reconciliation.

In global politics, the divide between North and South becomes ever greater, as opportunities are lost for transforming the quality of life of a major portion of the inhabitants of the planet, most of whom still are born, live and die in obscurity, their needs unacknowledged by the literate and privileged minority of their fellow human beings.

Within this framework the task of the theologians may not necessarily be very different from what it is in the present. It will be necessary to engage in dialogue with conservative religious frameworks in various forms, and with various kinds of religious fundamentalism. It will also be necessary to engage in dialogue with humanist perspectives of a secular sort, as more people cease to find religious frameworks persuasive. There will probaby continue to be mediating positions of a more liberal kind. These may be under increasing pressure from both sides. But they may be of vital importance in facilitating engagement in the common search for the human good. Much will depend on the capacity of all these groups to see the welfare of humanity as a whole as complementary to the special interests of the culture with which they themselves have particular associations, to their ability to blend genuine universality with genuine subsidiarity.

However conceptually unsatisfactory for us, there is, it seems, a paradox at the heart of our understanding of God. God is infinitely beyond our full comprehension, not a being but the ground of being, beyond the concepts of the religions. God is also, Christians continue to believe, fully and definitively expressed for us in Jesus Christ, through life, death and resurrection, in vulnerability and self-abandonment This is the contribution which Christians bring to the dialogues of the future, in trust and humility, not knowing whether these will lead us but trusting in the God of Jesus Christ to use them as instruments of his love.

Despite many changes, there have also been amazing similarities between human cultures over long periods. It may be true that we find it difficult to imagine societies which until fairly recently were happy to burn thousands of women as witches, regarded illness as a visitation of Satan and did not have the benefits of modern technology which we take for granted. Yet historians cheerfully imagine that they are able to make pretty accurate reconstructions of Greek and Roman history and politics. Generations in Europe right up to the present were brought up steeped in the Classics, and often developed an abiding affection for the literature of an age long past. It is possible to develop and draw strength from traditions derived from previous cultures if these traditions commend themselves by virtue of their intrinsic values. We can still read and recognize the human emotions of the poetry of Homer or the Old Testament, though we realize that some of the nuances may be lost on us in an untutored reading. Much has changed, but much has remained, if not the same, at least remarkably similar. You might have expected otherwise, given the accelerated change of at least the last century, when more people have lived on earth than in all previous centuries and technology has affected human society in endless important ways. It may be that many of the same human values will as be central to the development of the future as they have been of the past – trust, affection, friendship, loyalty, peace and justice, fairness.

Certainly these values continue to make science fiction intelligible to us. For it is hard for us at least to conceive of human community in any worthwhile shape without these. We regard unjust totalitarian states as abhorrent precisely because they distort these values. It may be, then, that society in a thousand years from now will have great similarities to the present, as well as significant differences. If that is the case, then it may well be important that the Christian tradition, which, with others, recommends the most altruistic of these values, continues to make a seminal contribution to such a future society, despite the differences. This accords with the promise of the gospel that it is always central to human concerns past present and future, as the light that shines in darkness, as the ground of the fruits of new creation. How to express the generosity of the love of God in the long-term future will be a central challenge to humanity in that future.

PART II

GENEROSITY

7

GENEROSITY IN THE
CHRISTIAN FUTURE

A theological tradition of generosity

In this section I want to develop further the basis of a theology of generosity, and theology which seeks to develop further openness to cultural development and change, while retaining the centrality of the God of Jesus Christ for the human future, as the catalyst of human rights, dignity and development. The programme I propose may be described as both liberal and pluralist. It is liberal, in that I regard a development of a liberal tradition as likely to come closest to the truth concerning matters of doctrine. It is pluralist, because I regard the contributions of other theological traditions as important discussion partners in the communal search for truth. An important precursor of such development must remain, as I have already indicated, Schleiermacher. But a successful programme for the Christian future must have the flexibility to draw on a much broader range of tradition and innovation than the direct heirs of Schleiermacher. And indeed, despite the high profile of theologies at opposite ends of the Christian spectrum, there has been a dynamic tradition of Christian thought which is Evangelical and Catholic and open. It is by no means impossible to find a number of illuminating precedents in the twentieth century.

I begin from the thinking of John Baillie, who combined in a remarkable way an Evangelical Christian tradition with openness to a liberal culture. Baillie is a theologian of grace, grace not constantly dividing the sheep from the goats as so often in the Augustinian tradition, but grace extending graciousness outside the magic circle. In this way he may be regarded as a theologian of generosity *par excellence*. Notably in his last book, *The Sense of the Presence of God*, he suggested ways of thinking of the divine mysterious presence as pervasive in all human endeavour and yet dependent at every level on God's grace through Jesus Christ. Grace is both the medium of Christian worship and the medium of Christian action, and theology is directly related both to prayer and to social engagement. John Baillie's analysis of soldiers' experience in the 1914–18 war led him to reflect on the gospel as reflected in, with and under the common human values of loyalty, trust and sacrifice for others. Reinhold Niebuhr's battle with the Ford Corporation led him to affirm the infinite worth of the individual, at the same time as to call for social structures in which common humanity was to be enhanced rather than diminished.[1]

In his concern to relate metaphysical to social theology Baillie was influenced by the work of his friend and former colleague Reinhold Niebuhr, for whom also fundamental power structures of society were the sphere in which the gospel was to come to expression, notably in his magnificent Gifford Lectures, *The Nature and Destiny of Man*. Both Baillie and Niebuhr were concerned for the centrality of the divinity of Christ, but they saw the consequences of Christ in social as much as in individual terms.

In this they were paralleled in some ways in Anglican thought by Geoffrey Lampe and Donald Mackinnon, who differed on approaches to Christology but shared a commitment to social justice and to ecumenical openness. Lampe and Mackinnon both stressed the need for social justice and the transforming power of the gospel, of Christlikeness, in society. Mackinnon says characteristically in an essay on 'Christology and Protest', in essays for Trevor Huddleston, 'From Christ there issues a continually repeated question, and his Church is his authentic servant only so far as it allows that interrogation to continue. It is always easier to escape its remorseless probing, or to blur the riddling quality of its disturbing challenge by conformity to the standards of the age. Here we have no continuing city' (Honore, *Trevor Huddleston. Essays*, 176). Generosity, as Huddleston knew, does not always make for a quiet life.

In continental Europe we can think, on the Catholic side, of Rahner, Schillebeeckx and Küng, and on the Protestant side, of both Bonhoeffer and Barth. In all these theologians there is a serious attempt to relate the gospel to society in such a way as to maximize its impact on social life throughout the world.

It is no accident that Barth continued to have enormous respect for Schleiermacher, for even in his critique he was concerned with the breadth of the scope of the gospel, not with its narrowing. Though his theology has often been used in the service of defensive and authoritarian theology, a use which, it must be admitted, corresponded to a significant characteristic of Barth himself and perhaps even of the Calvinist tradition in general, Barth was much concerned that we should not seek to be as God, but to find a transformative human justice under the Word. Barth remains, as Aquinas remained for Rahner, an important resource for a transformative theology of the future.

Above all Bonhoeffer in his short life typified, in his own brilliant way, the tensions between the exclusive demands of the gospel for faith and the unconditional demands of the same gospel for service to all humanity. Indeed Bonhoeffer may join Augustine and other classic Christian figures in providing inspiration and stimulus to generations with very little in common beyond a common desire to lead a Christian life in the real world of their own particular time.

Bonhoeffer saw that generosity always meant going the extra mile, loving those who were under threat from the powers that be.[2] We have suggested earlier that this may mean on some occasions a turn towards the classical traditions of theology and on other occasions a turn from them. Developments of the christological concentration of the early Bonhoeffer may be crucial to the relation of the gospel to humanity. And this leads to the concern for solidarity with 'this world', and the identification of the suffering God of all humanity, of the later Bonhoeffer. Bonhoeffer's haunting phrase to the effect that 'only he who speaks up for the Jews has the right to sing hymns in church', must be a constant reminder, not simply of a romantic history of resistance in the past, but of a pressing need for solidarity with the vulnerable, and that always includes in the first instance the poor, in the present.

Mention of the poor is extremely important, and brings me to the name of Jon Sobrino. It was in my view the Achilles' heel of most modern liberal theology that it made little difference to the facts of enormous social injustice in the nineteenth century and left it to a doctrinaire socialism in the form of Marxism to articulate the need for basic social justice. In the work of Sobrino and his colleagues, largely in Latin America, a theological response to poverty has been impressively worked out.

Generosity involves both an acknowledgement of the presence of significant others and an individual imaginative response to that presence. All effective theology includes both an individual and a corporate element, and a balance between the two. All effective Christian theology articulates the dimension of Word, addressed to the conscience of the individual believer, and the sacrament of sacrament, addressed to the community of the faithful, as servants in God's world.

Rahner, Schillebeeckx and Küng were all in their varied ways agents of transformation in Catholic thought, making possible Vatican II, as a challenge to a more open Catholicism in the very long-term future. Rahner's kenotic Christology demonstrates the power of imaginative reflection on the sequence of life, death and resurrection to open us up to the heart of the gospel. Schillebeeckx has related this theological framework more directly to the historical and sociological labour of New Testament exegesis. It may be that this practice is always dated by later research, as for example Schillebeeckx' stress on the centrality of eschatology in Jesus' message is superseded by further sociological and historical study. Yet it remains of crucial importance to seek to earth christological theory in cultural praxis. Küng has engaged in both metaphysical and historical study, and has also taken the great risk of relating his conclusions openly and controversially to the power structures of the Church. This is a high-risk course, full of problems, yet future generations may be grateful for the debates begun here. 'God's power "tells us who we are" only in the risk and reciprocity of God's life with us in Christ, as God displays his identity in terms of human freedom and human vulnerability.' (Rowan Williams in Honore, (ed.), *Trevor Huddleston. Essays*, 150).

Generosity, human rights and Christology

How does one do theology in the present, with generosity at the centre of our concern? We have already considered a particularly imaginative approach to the problem of a postmodern theology in Peter Hodgson's *Winds of the Spirit*. It seems to me that Hodgson has at least shown an awareness of the main issues which Christology has to tackle in the near future. Christology has to be constantly aware of the issue of liminality, of an option for the marginalized. But at the same time it has to sustain and encourage those who do not find themselves at the margin, who are somewhere at the centre, and who in fact often function as the energy of the Church in making possible the effort at the margins. We shall not serve the gospel by discouraging those whose simple obedience provides the stability and indeed the funding essential to outreach.

For me Hodgson's christological reflections chime in with some of my own reflections about the relationship between generosity, human rights and Christology. One might think in the first instance that there were not many connections, beyond the obvious commitment of Jesus to love and justice. However, as with many such issues, nothing is entirely obvious. We recall as soon as we start to think about it that the commitment to Jesus of European Christendom for nearly two millennia was compatible with slavery, capital punishment for the most trivial of offences, and all kinds of savagery. To show forth God's praise, not only with our lips, but in our lives, has never been easy, as indeed the example of Cranmer vividly demonstrates. It may be that despite our long tradition we are only beginning to see the real connections of Jesus with love and justice, and there is no guarantee that such awareness will persist in the future. There has been endless debate about rights in general and human rights in particular in recent decades. The whole question of whether there should be an emphasis on rights or on duties, for example, has had significant political as well as philosophical dimensions. The debate about postmodernism has thrown up the problem of cultural pluralism and the relativity of ethical stances: to what extent do the values of the Western Christian tradition apply to different contexts, e.g. to a critique of the literal application of Islamic law?

When we think of human rights we think of the minimal conditions for human flourishing, material and intellectual, which, it may be thought, should be guaranteed by any form of civilized society.[3] Below these standards treatment of people becomes inhumane, dehumanizing. This clearly cuts across many patterns of human conduct in history, involving the deprivation and often the destruction of groups of people and of individuals. Sometimes such negative treatment has been legitimated by reference to secular ideologies, sometimes by religious ideologies, including Christian ideologies. In effect the result is the same.

Christology, it might be thought, leads us automatically to take a liberal view of the matter. History tells us that that is not the case. Devout Christians have deprived each other of basic human rights in wars for centuries, without being aware of a problem. The doctrine of the just war was a major element in this process, and it was not hard to persuade oneself that any given war was just, and that destruction of human life was an inevitable necessity of war, in which, too, excesses inevitably happened. Despite elaborate codes of chivalry for the upper classes, medieval battles between Christians were usually brutal and merciless. Salvation through Christ had little impact on the inflicting of mindless cruelties. In the present, too, e.g. in the Gulf War or in the conflict in Chechnya, strategists remind us that effective action may require techniques which inflict unmentionable suffering on enemy forces. There are no pleasant ways of killing thousands of people in a short time.

It is often thought that modern liberal theology reduces the claims of traditional Christology. I would contend the opposite. On the contrary, the tradition often reduced the impact of Christology to matters of personal spiritual salvation, to issues concerning life after death and to rescue from individual sin often defined in terms of sexuality, and then precisely in a very narrow understanding of sexuality. It could be argued that a concern for God's love in incarnation as radically transforming in every sphere of society makes an infinitely larger claim on human attention than such traditional limitation. It is not simply that Jesus is an example of concern for love related to justice, especially for the marginalized and the poor. It is rather the case that self-giving love is, in Christian understanding, the core of the nature of being, and the sustaining source of all that is. If anything is the basis of natural law, that is it. Hence coercion of human beings along lines opposed to self-giving love, freedom, vulnerability, goes against the grain of the universe and is not conducive to human flourishing. It would seem, then, to be the case that human rights and Christology may be mutually illuminating concepts. By thinking of human rights we think of the shape of the human in God's self-giving purpose. By thinking of Christology we think of the basis and dynamic of all that is, creating authenticity and capacity for self-giving in mutuality in others. Human rights, where the sharp end of persecution is found, are a kind of litmus test of generosity. They include, for example, the treatment of those who seek asylum from persecution in other countries.

I want to bring in here two further guides to Christology as witnesses in my case. The first is Ingolf Dalferth, who has recently set out a magisterial reconstruction of traditional classical Christology, in which he stresses the centrality of the resurrection of Christ for the Christian understanding of God and humanity, and understands the logical grammar of Christology as leading from the resurrection to the cross. It is reality of faith in the presence of the Spirit of the risen Christ which leads us to see the cross as the focus of the power of kenotic love. This is, as it were, the ontology of an effective kenotic presence of God, the objective pole of divine action in the world. Focus on generosity is not an alternative but a stimulus to analysis of the depth structure of Christology.

British theologians often begin their theology from a German discussion. Here we have the reverse situation. Dalferth begins from the debate about the Myth of God Incarnate, offering an analysis which hinges on the distinction between christological titles as identity statements and titles as predicates. The centre of Christology is not the incarnation but the resurrection, the presence of Jesus Christ in the world. This theme is developed in a second chapter, on the relationship between cross and resurrection: the Word from the cross. The testimony to resurrection becomes the basic logical structure for talk of the Christian God. For Dalferth there is a correct grammar of Christological construction: from the resurrection to the cross, from the cross to the life of Jesus Christ.

Clearing the ground now makes possible the construction of a systematic grammar of Christology. There follow sections on the personal identity of Jesus Christ, the salvific significance of Jesus Christ for us, the divine ground of the being of Jesus Christ for us, and a chapter on christological thought structures, looking at the two-nature Christology, *communicatio idiomatum* and the meaning of person in Christology.

The last two chapters spell out the wider consequences of Christology. First, Dalferth considers the theological relevance of the cross for language about God. To think of God is to think of Christ, and to develop a Trinitarian grammar of God. Second, to think of Jesus as dying for us means a reassessment of the whole conceptuality of sacrifice, leading to Christian life after the end of sacrifice through Christ.

To read the above might well be to gain the impression that here we have all over again the old old story, with nothing fresh to surprise us. That would be a pity, for Dalferth has much to contribute of an original nature. The most obviously fascinating thread is the careful attention to logical distinctions, in which he brings contemporary analytical philosophy to bear on traditional discussions, sharpening the issues and producing clarity out of ambiguity. The distinction made, for example, between statements of identity and statements of predication in the first section is characteristic. But Dalferth's achievement goes much deeper than an exercise in logical housekeeping. He demonstrates a fine grasp of the underlying theological issues, respecting the mysteries, and the irreconcilable elements, aware of the pointlessness of a seamless system which explains everything and nothing. For example, the discussion of resurrection is a wide-ranging project which explores every aspect of the historical and theological issues, the language and the events which they seek to articulate.

The formal exposition of Christology is equally lucid, relating Christology eventually to Trinity. Trinity is 'the regulative basic framework of the whole Christian life' (213). He can speak of the doctrine of the Trinity as 'the combinatorial grammar of the fields of the imagery of Father, Son and Spirit' (215). Trinity stresses 'the fundamental and indispensable difference between God and all our pictures, models, images and concepts of God' (217). Turning to the concept of redemption, he traces the development of the concept of sacrifice, and then develops an understanding of the Christian life on the basis of the end of sacrifice in Jesus Christ. Thus Christian life becomes a life of faith.

Dalferth's use of the central concepts of logic and grammar is effective on at least two levels. In the first instance it serves to dissect and lay bare the many strands of argument in christological construction. In the second place it offers an imaginative construct for developing a fresh perspective on traditional problems.

Does this Christology supply all our contemporary needs? It may be that the days are simply over when we could look to Germany for a solution to all our theological problems. Perhaps that was always an unfair expectation. Now radical pluralism throws up dilemmas which are perhaps not susceptible of solution from the resources of any single branch of the Christian tradition. For example, Dalferth's strength in using logical devices and imagery may also raise problems for us. Is the Trinity really best understood in the framework of combinatorial mathematics? I sense a danger that the contingency of incarnation may be dissolved here into the concinnity of abstraction. The problems of historical evidence and probability are resolved with bravery and confidence. The sociological and political dimensions of incarnation, the hermeneutic of suspicion which to some extent at least characterizes the winter of our postmodern discontent, appear to melt away in the bright matrix of logical clarity. There is perhaps an inherent tendency in the language of mathematics and mathematical physics to understate the sheer messiness, the unresolved tensions and the jagged edges of much to which the Christian gospel invites us to attend. The Apollonian God fails to redeem our Dionysian reality, and we are left in our sins, corporate and multinational as well as psychological and introspective. The emancipatory dimensions of Christology, from institutional oppression of race, gender and economics, the world of marginality, scarcely appear in this narrative. Reassuringly, the world is not turned upside down.

But our final word must be one of solid gratitude. This is the classical model of German theology at its deeply impressive best. It is a highly intelligent, sustained and immensely careful restatement of a traditional Christology. It is always elegant and always suggestive, never dull. As such it deserves to become a major point of reference for the contemporary systematic theologian.

When we come to the practical effects and implications of such a kenotic presence we are brought into the realm of experience of the divine presence, and the transforming effect of such experience in a social context. Here I find illumination on a kenotic generosity in a rather different quarter, in the theology, today somewhat muted but in my view potentially immensely creative, of Edward Schillebeeckx.

Let me recall the basic thrust of Schillebeeckx's christological programme. In the early New Testament material, notably as represented in Matthew and Luke (the Q community), there is experience of Jesus as present now and yet to come. Resurrection is important, centred not on the person of Jesus but on the experience of his presence in community. Repetition of the saving experience leads to transformation of human life, and to a challenge, not about formulas but about our social structures. Jesus is the Mosaic-messianic 'eschatological prophet'. This 'maranatha' Christology is the centre, a centre of experience by humanity of God and the world, then and now. Christology is to be done by reflection on experience of life in modern society, and the impact of the Christian tradition on this reflection. We may not simply 'apply' biblical models to the modern world in the hope of illumination. We look to Jesus' own experience, the experience of his followers and the experience of God in community ever since. Christology is concentrated creation, Christology can only be understood as a specific way of making belief in creation more precise. In this way we begin to understand more deeply the human significance of Jesus and his relationship to us as individuals and in society.

I have commented elsewhere that it is not yet entirely clear, perhaps, on this account, what difference it makes to God the creator that he is involved in incarnation in human life. I am not sure that Schillebeeckx has spelled out this dimension fully in his work. Yet it does seem to me that Schillebeeckx's account is in genuine complementarity, as the subjective pole of an account of reconciliation, with the objective accounts given of the self-giving love of God, for whom to be is to create being in others, of Rahner, and even more particularly of Dalferth, who stresses the intimate connection between effective new creation and the cross. The experience of the presence of God, the Spirit of Christlikeness, as Geoffrey Lampe called it, is always an invitation to solidarity with the shape of the cross in the infrastructure of our social order. God is present as the reality of reconciliation at the heart of the creation. As Schillebeeckx puts it, 'Here the cross is the symbol of resistance to death against the alienation of our human history of suffering, the consequence of God who is concerned with man: the resurrection of Jesus makes it clear to us that suffering may not and will not have the last word' (*Christ*, 836). As the New Testament reminds us quite simply, when we visit those in prison, feed the hungry, support those who are persecuted for the sake of justice, we are turning to God where he already is. Hence a Christology which attends to the specificity of human rights issues may hope to be a guide to a pattern of contemporary discipleship, and so of contemporary understanding of the Christ. The shape of Christology and the particularity of rights may be seen as basic to the deep structure of the generosity of God.[4]

Retrieving a tradition of rights

It is customary today to regard consideration for human rights as essentially a product of the Enlightenment (Berlin, Lauterpacht, Pagels, etc.). This follows a comment by Condorcet that 'the notion human rights was absent from the legal conceptions of the

Romans and Greeks: this seems to hold equally of the Jewish, Chinese and all other ancient civilizations that have since come to light. The domination of this ideal has been the exception rather than the rule, even in the recent history of the West' (quoted by Pagels in *On Human Dignity, the Internationalization of Human Rights*). Much more important is obedience to the laws of God in religious codes, or the idea that society confers upon its members whatever rights, privileges and exemptions it enjoys. The latter notion means that human rights are seen as an internal affair of sovereign states, not to be criticized from outside.

There are indeed traces of concern for the rights of individuals as such in history, and, according to Elaine Pagels, these need to be consciously appropriated and reaffirmed. 'We need to recognize that our task is not simply to rediscover and reaffirm ancient cultural traditions, but to select elements of them in order to construct an intercultural rationale to support the principles of dignity, equality and justice' (7).

There have been hundreds of studies in the law and the philosophy of human rights in the last fifty years, not to say thousands on the nature of rights, and much debate about the possibilities of cross-cultural agreement on basic common affirmations. The rhetoric of rights is as subject to abuse as any rhetoric. There are often intractable conflicts of rights. The assertion of individual rights can detract from social values. But the abuse does not take away the proper use. Meanwhile, as for example, Amnesty's reports on torture show, the violation of human rights continues as before in many parts of the world.

The churches have contributed for some time to this discussion, for example *A Lutheran Reader on Human Rights*, eds J.Lissner and A.Slovik. There are lists of specific rights, following the United Nations' Declarations. For example:

1. the right to live
2. the right to enjoy and maintain a cultural identity
3. the right to participate in decision-making
4. the right to dissent
5. the right to personal dignity and
6. the right to choose freely a religion or belief.

Much of the theological discussion speaks of the creation of man in the image of God. I begin with a quote form Alexander Hamilton, back in 1787: 'The sacred rights of Mankind are not to be rummaged for among old parchments or musty records. They are written, as with a sunbeam, in the whole volume of human nature by the hand of Divinity itself, and can never be erased or obscured' (quoted in Joyce, *The New Politics of Human Rights* (7)).

It might be thought that there is no obvious connection between rights and generosity. Claims to rights often encapsulate individual self-centredness, and may if granted diminish the rights of others. All kinds of dubious dogmatism can be advanced under the rhetoric of rights. How do we distinguish between appropriate and inappropriate claims to rights? Here I should want to bring Christology, and Christ as the new image of God and the basic form of humanity, more explicitly into the discussion. If we take the phrase of the Creed, 'suffered under Pontius Pilate', to be central to our faith, then here God has characterized his nature definitively for us, as both committed to identification with oppressed humanity, and as bringing a universal new creation out of that particularity. We are invited both to a priority for the oppressed and to a concern for the wider dimension of human society in all its potential for development. We are called to be a pressure group for the oppressed, but not to become trapped in a culture of marginality.

Christ and vulnerability

We are also called to respond to the resurrection of the crucified one, to see Christ crucified as *Christus Consummator*, as the transformation of the wider layers of culture. In that way the cross may be a catalyst for opposition to oppression, and a wider society may be mobilized on behalf of the specifically oppressed. God himself, the pressure of self-giving love, invites us to respond to his active presence in the widest possible perspective. I would be inclined to see the incarnation as a standing provocation in history to attend to human rights, as God seeks to humanize us further. Jesus' concern for those in prison, for the sick, the outcast, the unaccepted and especially for the poor is a direct reminder of this divine pressure. It may sometimes be a call to direct action. But it is also, and most importantly, a call to work through the structural processes of civil society for a tangible reflection of the priorities of the gospel throughout that society. This may not mean a return to outmoded notions of Christendom. But it may mean a structural critique of a society based on old-fashioned vices like personal greed and dressed up to look like modern virtues like success.

In these chapters I have laid stress on the centrality of Jesus Christ as the realization of God's being as self-giving love in the created order. I have commended the vulnerability of self-giving love as a basis for the development of human values and human rights, suggesting that for Christians there is an intrinsic connection between Christ and human rights. I have deplored the rise of religious fundamentalisms, which are a kind of reverse image of vulnerability, a bid for exclusivity. But is my own position not a kind of fundamentalism, of the sort that I have deplored in others? My response is that it certainly could be, but that it is in fact not at all a form of fundamentalism. However, the question deserves a careful answer. Let me begin from some useful distinctions, which Reinhold Bernhardt makes in his recent book, *Christianity without Absolutes*, between fundamentalists and Evangelicals. Both groups regard as central the authority of the Bible, the atoning sacrifice of Jesus Christ and personal faith in Christ as a condition of salvation. In addition, fundamentalists believe in the verbal inspiration and infallibility of the Bible, reject modern critical biblical scholarship and tend to regard all who do not share their viewpoint as not true Christians.

I am not suggesting an infallible religious text, a rejection of critical enquiry, or a rejection of those who do not share my particular perspective on God. I could still be a conceptual fundamentalist, an Enlightenment rational fundamentalist, of the sort well criticized by Gellner. I would have to refer in turn to my appeal to Bernstein's 'engaged fallibilist pluralism', taking our own fallibility seriously, being committed but being willing to listen to others without attempting to deny the otherness of the other. There is a world of difference between having commitments, including basic beliefs, based on reflection and open to discussion, and a literal adherence to the ahistorical truth of an infallible text. Christians do not expect to find that reasons for opposing the priority of self-giving love will ever prove stronger than reasons for affirming it, in the interest of ultimate human flourishing.

Critical awareness and a measure of humility is itself a protection. We need to be aware of the vulnerability, ambiguities, cultural heritage of our own positions and the danger of absolutizing them. We must seek to enlarge the horizons, not limit them. We must encourage freedom for the other to be himself/herself as other. But not at the expense of the freedom of others to be themselves.

Here is my justification for offering the pattern of self-giving love, which Christians understand as the reality of God in the events concerning Jesus, as a contribution to dialogue about the human future. Self-giving love recognizes, respects and encourages the other, and invites the expansion of generosity. It is firmly opposed to all exploitation and coercion of the other, or of third parties, because that is damaging to the humanity of the exploited. The only valid ground for force would be to prevent the probability of greater coercion.

Such a perspective will not accept, in a false guilt complex, that it is only another form of fundamentalism. That in itself would be a tribute to coercion, a contribution to the progress of a culture of violence. To say that coercing people is just as rational as respecting and supporting them is to learn nothing from human experience. It is true that a Christian understanding of love has sometimes been exploitative in the past, and for that we must repent. But the abuse does not take away the proper use. All cats are not grey in the night. Fortunately, too, there are indications of an understanding of kenotic love in many religious and humanist traditions, which may serve as bridges towards communicative action. It is not necessary to be a Christian in order to share in this project, but for Christians it has its own dynamic.

This raises the practical question of how to engage in dialogue with perspectives which do not themselves welcome dialogue. Sometimes liberal Christians may find themselves in the curious position of being able to relate to other religions yet quite unable to relate to fundamentalism in their own religion. Yet other religions may include significant communities with a much more fundamentalist approach to sacred texts and the enforcement of moral values than is common in Christianity. I think it is necessary to try patiently to keep open lines of communication between the different cultures – liberal, Catholic, Evangelical, fundamentalist – in Christianity. It may be that this can be done in part by entering into dialogue, however difficult, concerning the application of Christianity to basic human social issues, and their implications for basic human values. Such dialogues would have value as examples within the Christian tradition, and might encourage similar dialogues in other traditions, and eventually between traditions.

There is a considerable amount of material relevant to Christianity and human rights in Christine Gudorf's *Victimization, Examining Christian Complicity*. Gudorf begins by noting the frequent failure of victimizers to recognize what atrocities they perpetrate, and the extent to which victims may become resigned to, and even perpetuate, the very victimization which oppresses them. The study is divided into five short but closely argued sections. First, Scripture and victimization. God liberates the Hebrew slaves in Egypt and Jesus supports the outcast. On the other hand, children are to obey parents, wives to obey husbands, all are to be subject to the powers that be, regardless of the circumstances. Paul opposes unnatural sexual relations, but what is natural for some may be unnatural for others. Hatred and discrimination follow. Violence must be purged from our concepts of God and our own actions. We are not to be sacrificial victims but to offer our lives for the elimination of the causes of violence. Some parts of Scripture are counter-revelatory (16), possibly encouraging victimization, child abuse, domination. We need courage to see the Bible as ambiguous in parts, a record of 'a people who often misinterpreted God's will, and sometimes cloaked our own half-conscious needs or desires in the divine mantle' (27).

The second section covers the preferential option for the poor in Christianity, and the counter-tradition of a temporal retribution for sinners – their poverty is their own fault. The poor are those in material poverty, and in conditions such as sickness or discrimination which result in material poverty. Preference does not mean giving privileges but redressing deprivation, considering the consequences of sin not just for the sinner but for the victims of sin.

We come to the romanticization of victims. This is élitist. What we need is political education. It is the poor who struggle against poverty who are closest to God. Neither poverty nor those who suffer from it are necessarily good. Women, children and the poor are romanticized as good and innocent – what God desires. But the poor are often made 'non-persons'. There are problems with a death/resurrection paradigm. Suffering may lead to joy but more often to despair and death. We are called to pursue life, not to be preoccupied with death.

Section four is devoted to prudence and victim-blaming. 'One of the most consistent types of victim-blaming relies on accusing victims of lacking prudence' (75). 'We know from the cross that not all victims are blame-worthy'(76). But in North and South America blacks and whites have been blamed for being victims, often for acting without enough likelihood of success. Yet there is an evangelical obligation to resist injustice. 'The gospel is risky business. Prudence should be used to minimize the risk of pursuing the fullness of the kingdom, without decreasing in any way efforts to realize it' (89).

The last section deals with sexual victimization and sexual abuse. 'The structures of our churches affect the Christian complicity in abuse' (91). People are too often victims simply of sexual ignorance and its consequences. The attempt to emphasize sexual complementarity not only fuels the victimization of homosexuals but also victimizes single people in our society, who are understood as incomplete. 'The men who hold the majority of power in our churches feel threatened by homosexuality' (99). In considering repression, Gudorf reminds us that 'Every human action, to a greater or lesser degree, is sexual, because it is performed by sexual persons. Thus in some areas of our lives it becomes difficult to draw the line between what is sexual and what isn't' (103). She suggests that 'the overly romantic image of spouses as a self-sufficient unit put utterly unrealistic pressure on marriages, for no one person can satisfy all the intimacy needs, much less all the other needs, of any individual'. As for unmarried couples, 'they intuitively understand that shared intimate physical contact bonds persons together in care and trust, and that there are different degrees of trust and care, one building on the other' (106).

'In conclusion, we do not have to be Freudians to recognize that sexuality colors every aspect of our world, every structure and decision that we make individually and collectively. Sexuality is not a distraction from the work of liberating victims, but an integral part of that work, which needs to be taken seriously by the Christian' (112). There is no doubt that here is a well-argued, tough and realistic case for a serious reappraisal of the role of the Church in the creation and liberation of victims, in social and, connected with this, equally in personal relationships.

This plea from Gudorf may remind us of Sobrino's suggestion that the main task of Christianity today is not so much to tackle intellectual atheism but to tackle the reality of the inhuman, of man's inhumanity to man. In such a perspective traditional battles between Evangelical and liberal and Catholic become less important. The problem is how to build bridges to harness joint Christian action on issues of justice and peace and also to provide mutual illumination on theological issues which divide. This suggests that a theology of generosity must attempt to see constructive tensions in the reconciled diversities of Christianity rather than to labour the traditional divides.

God, dignity and ethics

I have spoken of Christology in relation to human rights. At this point I should like to clarify some of the concepts employed in such discussion before returning to the christological dimension. There is a good recent survey of these areas in Kieran Cronin's *Rights and Christian*. Cronin begins from a discussion of the roles of definition and imagination in metaethics, and refers to controversies emanating from Hohfeld's distinctions of different sorts of rights. He takes due account of various levels of scepticism concerning rights, and develops his own constructive understanding of a covenant model of rights.

For Cronin the ultimate foundation of rights is the notion that humanity's dignity comes from being created in the image of God. The image gives a specifically religious justifying reason for acting morally, and is preferable to such notions as God's rights and our rights against God. Sometimes, in fact, religious justifying reasons offer little practical guidance in particular areas of moral controversy. The image-of-God concept suggests that humanity is the high point of creation, that human beings have a capacity to enter into dialogue with God, and that man may work, or decline to work, as an instrument of God's action in the world. God empowers us with power in weakness, to work in community.

This, in my view, is a useful study because it engages effectively with non-theological discussion of rights. The image-of-God concept is useful both in dialogue with secular philosophers and in inter-religious dialogue. In addition, however, Christianity speaks of the image of God in Jesus Christ, as a transformative power in the cosmos. As we have noted, this often leads to exclusive rather than inclusive concepts, but it should not do so, for in Christian understanding the gospel is there for the service of all humanity, and is always an invitation rather than a command.

Christian theology needs to be a theology of correlation, and it also needs to be Christian. An effective theology of correlation is no easy task. Paul Tillich will, I believe, be seen to have been an important figure in the quest for correlation, though he was perhaps less successful in articulating the distinctively Christian elements in concepts capable of stretching the theological imagination. The balance of relationship between fundamental theology and praxis, at this time notable in social justice, together with the dimension of worship, appears to me to remain central to the theologian's task.

The correlation of theology and praxis in relation to social justice was pioneered in a remarkable way, as we have seen, by Reinhold Niebuhr, in his battle with Fordism and his classic exposé of the social dimensions of alienation in an industrial society. What he had to say is still, in my view, theologically correct. Yet American industry was soon to be almost overtaken by similar industrial cultures on the Pacific Rim, and Niebuhr's perspective appears to have been overtaken by events. The contemporary state of America, much influenced by right-wing Republican values, appears at least in some areas to have little recollection of the values of one of its greatest theologians. Yet not all is entirely lost, for much current interdisciplinary reflection on business ethics and industrial practice goes back to the tradition pioneered by Niebuhr.

In developing the shape of a theology of generosity I return to the correlation between theology and human rights, and to three useful texts, the excellent symposium *Understanding Human Rights*, ed. A.D.Falconer, *Human Rights in Another Key* by Johan Galtung, and *Human Rights in Perspective*, ed. A.Eide and B.Hagtvet. In the Falconer volume there is a useful survey by Jürgen Moltmann on 'Christian Faith and Human Rights'. Following the Universal Declaration of Human Rights of 1948, Moltmann agrees that the dignity of man is not itself a human right but a source and ground for all human rights. He makes the important point that 'The task of Christian theology does not lie in presenting once again what thousands of experts, jurists, parliamentarians and diplomats in the United Nations have already completed. However, Christian theology cannot also dispense itself from the discussion of and the fight for the realization of human rights' (193). The theological discussion stresses man as made in the image of God, and reconciled by Christ the Word of God. There is a third starting point, our own life experience, where we have encountered man's inhumanity to man.

The gospel promises liberation from slavery, and points to fulfilment in God's future. There is a parallel and particularly valuable reflection on 'Human Rights and Islam', by Rashid Ahmad Jullandhri. Muslim thinkers consider freedom as the most essential value in human life, while slavery is an evil opposed to human dignity. No one has the right to impose his faith on others. There is, as the Koran says, no compulsion in religion. As far as political rights are concerned, non-Muslims should be equal to Muslims.

'In the end I wish to say that responsibility for the denial of human rights in a Muslim country lies with the ruling class and not with Islam. It is hoped that Muslim peoples will be able to put their ideals into practice, because application is the measure of all ideals.' The same could of course be said of the abuse of power in all religions.

Falconer himself recalls David Jenkins' talk of *The Contradiction of Christianity*, of coercion within the Church, and suggests that theology is a theology of the wayfarers, in which God appears as a scandal to challenge many of our certainties and call us to a deeper commitment.

Moltmann develops further the relation of Christianity to human rights in a further essay, 'Christian Faith and Human Rights', in a collection *On Human Dignity*. He stresses that 'The image of God is human beings in all their relationships in life' (23), and quotes the Scots Confession of 1560, article 14, which states that as a consequence of divine freedom, human beings are called 'to save the lives of innocents, to repress tyrannie, to defend the oppressed'. The image of God is human beings together with others. Human rights in a hostile world are made real through the ministry of reconciliation, in which 'love accepts the person and forgives the sin' (31). Christians can be expected to act in this way.

In the struggle for human rights and human dignity they will represent the unassailable dignity of human beings and thus also the indivisible unity of their human rights and duties. For the sake of God they will stand up with all the means at their disposal, acting as well as suffering, for the dignity of human beings and their rights as the image of God (35).

171

In the introduction to the essays Douglas Meeks reflects on human dignity. Dignity is the worth of being human, the norm by which all forms of human acting and deciding are to be judged. Human rights spring from human dignity 'Human dignity, however, requires human rights for its embodiment, protection and full flowering. Human rights are the concrete, indefeasible claim of human dignity' (xi). The complexity of concepts of humanity is of course enormous, and the key elements have long been much disputed, as a glance at a modern critique, e.g. Peter Scott's *Theology, Ideology and Liberation,* will immediately confirm. In his book on *Human Rights in Another Key* Galtung examines rights in relation to the Western tradition, the legal tradition, human needs, social structures and processes. The collection by Eide and Hagtvet, *Human Rights in Perspective,* looks again at the question of the universal validity of human rights. In stressing rights I am aware that these can be interpreted in a narrow and adversarial manner against the rights of other individuals and groups. Here again the framework of generosity may be a constant reminder of the need to develop in partnership with others rather than over against others in any particular society.

Religion, politics and the secular world

In discussion of the future of faith as a servant of human rights it is important to pay attention to the influence not only of the Church, and of inter-faith dialogue, but of the secular in the world. I want to look here particularly at the legacy of Marxism. Few subjects might seem more dead today than Christianity and Marxism. Communism has collapsed in most of the world, revealing a sham of corruption, oppression and massive denial of human rights, beneath a facade of fine-sounding principles. Russia sometimes seems to be returning to an imperial Christian and Orthodox past. Religious fundamentalism is emerging everywhere, in Islam, in Judaism, in Christianity. Spirituality is back. Few men may seem to have been as ungenerous as Marx, always embattled, creating a legacy of terror.

Yet it is not clear that Christians will want to rejoice in everything that has followed the collapse of Marxism. And in any case, the secularization of Europe, which had some connection at least with socialist viewpoints, is still an important fact of our time, distinguishing the culture of Europe for example from the culture of North America.

Marx studied in Bonn and Berlin, and was greatly influenced from an early period by the great Berlin philosopher Hegel. It was Hegel's God especially that Marx was to find redundant. Later Christian Marxists and others were to suggest that other concepts of God might not have been so unacceptable to Marx. In 1843 he moved to Brussels, was expelled from there to Paris, was thrown out of Paris and spent the rest of his life in London, supported financially by his friend Friedrich Engels. Here he developed his ground breaking economic theories. Goods, he believed, were exchanged at rates decided by the amount of labour that went into them. But the labourers produced goods worth more than their wages, making profit for the capitalists. The masses should therefore take over the means of production to produce a free and just society. Much in society is decided by the mode of industrial production – historical materialism. Revolution could give reality to justice and liberty, by recognizing their basis in materialism. Matter is a unique reality. Society may develop in revolutionary moves which may resolve internal conflicts and tensions. Religion, as a symptom of unjust social conditions, is doomed to disappear.

Marx's basic ideas were to be developed in different and sometimes conflicting ways by his many followers over the next century, in philosophy, politics and social structures. It was to be Marx's misfortune that the socialist experiments of the twentieth century were often to degenerate into a new totalitarianism of the left, notably under Stalin and his successors in the Soviet Union. Their collapse does not prove the moral superiority of capitalism, only the need to go on searching for small steps in the direction of greater realisation of justice and human dignity. Man is alienated, in a capitalist society, from himself, his work, his products and his fellow man. Alienation must be overcome by a process of liberation. As for religion,

> Man makes religion, religion does not make man. . . .The struggle against religion is therefore indirectly a struggle against that world whose spiritual aroma is religion. . . .Religion is the sigh of the oppressed creature, the sentiment of a heartless world, the soul of soulless conditions. It is the opium of the people. . . .The immediate task is to unmask human alienation

in its secular form, now that it has been unmasked in its sacred form. (Introduction to his *Critique of Hegel's Philosophy of Right*)

We turn now to Marxist criticisms of religion. These cover two main areas.

RELIGION AS A PROJECTION OF HUMAN ASPIRATIONS.

Philosophers of the Enlightenment wrote treatises on human nature – David Hume. They reflected on human rights and human dignity – the Marquis of Condorcet. They asked themselves what aims and goals man had (usually man, for feminist conscientization still had, and has, a long way to go). In this they followed the ancient search for moral values – *De finibus*, on moral ends. They were also influenced by traditional theology. What is salvation, which is somewhere at the centre of faith? Salvation is negative, rescue from some great evil which threatens our humanity. It is also positive, God's love moving us towards a goal which God has for us. But salvation has to be appropriate to humanity. It would be surprising if it did not relate to man's aspirations and needs.

For Feuerbach it can be established that religion is a projection of human aspirations. Therefore, it is false. Given the traditional force of religion as a divine sanction affecting every area of human life, it is not surprising that this came to Feuerbach and many others as a liberation. Against Feuerbach, it could of course be argued, for to every argument there appears to be an equal and opposite argument, that a God who created humanity would most naturally include in his creation a religion which projected and reflected human aspirations. Man is made in the image of God, according to Scripture. And a religion which did not reflect human aspirations would be of no practical use whatever. Somewhere between these positions comes the mediating view that religion has both subjective and objective dimensions, the former naturally reflecting human aspirations and the latter reflecting the reality of God, as a challenge and corrective to undue anthropocentrism.

But in any event, the influence of Feuerbach was to soften the traditional sense of the absolute divine sovereignty. Later of course Karl Barth was to suggest that Feuerbach had put his finger on the weakness of nineteenth-century theology, which was to advocate a man-made religion. The answer was to turn back behind the Enlightenment to the pure Word of God of the Reformers, not the word of man but the Word of God. This was deeply impressive, but it could be taken up in turn by other major world religions, and might be thought to be a retreat, leaving all standard human consciousness to the realm of unbelief. Karl Rahner was to retrieve the spirit of man as the instrument of the Spirit of God. But Marx could have known none of this. If God was no more than a symbol of our subservience to oppression, then in the new society God would be redundant.

RECONCILIATION WITH INJUSTICE?

There was, however, a potentially equally grave charge, that religion reconciled people to injustice. Here is where the famous phrase about 'the opium of the people' can be brought to bear. Religion, it could be argued, tends to encourage a form of fatalism. Whatever is, is right. Bless the squire and his relations, and keep us in our proper stations. Did the Bible not advise us that the powers that be are ordained by God? As a matter of historical fact, is it not the case that the churches have lent a vitally important veneer of respectability to innumerable tyrannies? Increasingly at odds with the Prussian and then the French state, Marx had perhaps reason to criticize a religious establishment which seemed to gravitate naturally towards power.

Alistair Kee has summarized Marxism usefully as a doctrine, a way of life, and a historically discernible tradition of thought and action. Peter Scott stresses Marx's importance for the development of a hermeneutic of suspicion – a central Marxist point is that ideas are not innocent. We must ensure that theories are not used to support social oppression. This can of course also become a powerful tool for criticizing Marxist theories themselves. Thought must be self-critical. He argues that 'the self-presentation of the Christian God is the denial of human attempts to be gods, and is thereby the election of human beings into their freedom to be creatures' (260).

We may ask whether the Bible, which we have just reconsidered, is to be regarded as a confirmation or a refutation of Marxist criticisms. It will be clear fairly soon that the answer is not straightforward, for the Bible is not a single seamless narrative with a cohesive theme, but a library of texts of very different character and genre, many of which explicitly contradict one another.

The Bible may be read as a record of the experience and aspiration of numerous social groups. As such it can be seen as nothing but a record of the protection of human aspirations. It can also be seen as reconciling people with injustice, and has been so used by totalitarian regimes throughout history. It has been used to justify all sorts of oppression, from capital punishment to apartheid. But again, it may be argued that the abuse does not take away the proper use.

There are counter-examples. The Bible has been the engine of liberation theology, priority for the poor, even a Marxist reading of Scripture. The text may be interpreted differently in different contexts. Yet Christians would argue that not every interpretation is as good as any other. There are limits, set by the priorities of the gospel within the Bible itself. These too are contested, but are related to Jesus as the Christ, as the revelation of the unconditional love of God, always on the side of those who are oppressed.

We come to the more general question of the relation of Christianity to Marxist ideology, with particular reference to liberation theology. It should be recalled at once that though Marx had little use for religion, modern Marxist philosophers have paid serious attention to theology, notably Ernst Bloch, Theodor Adorno and Max Horkheimer. There was in the 1960s a flourishing Marxist – Christian dialogue, notably around Hromadka in Czechoslovakia, and an internal dialogue in which Christians have sought to learn from Marx, often quite critically, and reinterpret Christian faith in the light of this experience. An excellent example of such critical appreciation is Christopher Rowland's *Radical Christianity*.

Much traditional theology has been concerned with the salvation from sin of the soul of the individual, and the cultivation of the spiritual life. At various times there have been attempts to articulate a social theology, on the basis of the biblical narratives, but the systematic construction of a theology of social responsibility has been a comparatively modern development. There has been discussion of the need to create a responsible society. Recognition of the failure of the churches and of governments to create just and responsible societies has led in turn to calls for a theology of revolution, clearly owing much to Marxist impulses, stressing the revolutionary and apocalyptic elements in the Bible, and the emphasis on the need to look to the future as well as the past and the present.

These accents have been further deepened in a variety of theologies of liberation in the last thirty years or so. Gustavo Gutierrez classically expressed the main concern of liberation theology in this way.

> Universal love comes down from the level of abstraction and becomes concrete and effective by becoming incarnate in the struggle for the liberation of the oppressed. It is a question of loving all people, not in some vague, general way, but rather in the exploited person, in the concrete person who is struggling to live humanly (*A Theology of Liberation*, 276).

How are we to learn from this perspective to express the centre of Christianity in ways which will engage with the roots of alienation? Generosity must relate, and be seen to relate seriously, to structures as well as to individuals, to the roots of alienation in culture as well as its symptoms. In the life of Jesus we see the character of God, in identification with the poor – Christians should never become bored with repeating this – the unloved, those in prison, the marginalized of every sort. The Gospel points us to the character of Christ, which is the character of God. God is the one who exists by giving himself in the service of humanity. The mind of Christ is the mind which visits the sick, the hungry, the poor, the prisoners, those who are marginalized and oppressed. The fruits of the Spirit are long-suffering patience, kindness, gentleness. We are called to affirm the hidden presence of the loving God to all humanity. We can certainly rejoice in the happiness which traditional family values bring to many people. None of us should imagine that God's transformation of lives will simply make everyone else like us.

We have to learn to respect the other as other, and we may need to defend those who are unable to speak up for themselves. The voluminous debates on human rights and human duties, on different levels of needs and rights, on social and individual aspirations, on the cultural relativity of rights and the relation of human rights to civil liberties will doubtless continue. Clearly not every appeal to rights or even human rights will do. No concept is free from the possibility of misuse, as the legacies of Marxism and capitalism have both demonstrated, and those who wish to oppress others are always adept at turning the concepts of freedom to reactionary uses. The Christian gospel is concerned with the understanding of humanity in the light of God, whose being involves the experience of being the victim of torture and execution, and the bringing of light out of darkness.

8

GENEROSITY THROUGH
THE TRADITION

Generosity and the metaphysical frame –
God and Christology

THE QUESTION OF GOD

Here we must turn to a reappraisal of the three main areas of the metaphysical, the historical and the cultural dimensions of a renewed theology of generosity, taking account of recent research in all these dimensions.[1]

Perhaps nowhere is pluralism more evident today than in the wide diversity of approaches to the metaphysical issues involved in talk of God. On the one hand, there is the approach to God-talk of the various forms of fundamentalism which are enjoying a revival in the present – a revival graphically illustrated in Gilles Kepel's *The Revenge of God*. On the other hand, there are the continuing descriptions of a non-realist approach to God in Western thought, notably in the work of Don Cupitt and Gordon Kaufman.

We may find it salutary to listen to Don Cupitt in *After All – Religion without Alienation*. 'Here's a paradox: the cultural resources and the wealth of knowledge about everything that are available to us today are far greater than ever before – and yet most people live in a fog' (1). The rest of the book continues in the same highly readable style, trying to show us ways to cope in the fog, between the Scylla of the old-fashioned authoritarian world view and the Charybdis of pure hedonism. The Enlightenment has changed everything. By the end of the nineteenth century 'metaphysics and systematic theology were dead in the water' (3). (Students ploughing through Barth, Pannenberg and Rahner might sometimes wish that it were so!) We need a reinvention of metaphysics, but not of the old kind. What is needed is a minimal creed, 'a post-postmodernist attempt at reconstruction'.

Chapter 1 considers the emergence of post-Christianity. Now we see how the Christian tradition has arisen. 'Indeed the entire body of Holy tradition, which seems so real and coherent, so grand and timeless, and so thickly-populated with human beings, is a purely contingent human tradition. We made it all up!' (14) Cupitt says that the postmodern, post-Christian age is an age when people can live without ideology. We don't need it any longer.

The position is spelled out further in chapter 2, the 'Death of Tradition'. Philosophical realism is dead, and with it traditional religion in all forms. 'Today the language of fundamentalism is ugly and empty ranting, and the language of liberal religion is soothing but empty waffle' (33). Chapter 3 explains how it is. Since the Enlightenment the old religious systems have become ever more irrational and authoritarian. So we need to escape. 'We cannot any longer look for timeless and objective standards of meaning independent of the flux of current human usage . . . There is nothing off the page, nothing between the lines and nothing behind the scenes' (55). The world is a continuous stream of language-forming events, in which the world of nature has gradually evolved into the world of culture. Because we are ambivalent about life and death, we tell cosmic stories in order to understand ourselves. The mind is the body's own ever-changing symbolic expressions. 'And we are fleshwords.'

There is no 'objective' value. We make values: they are socially established, and they get written into our language games. Moral action involves changing the way certain words are habitually used, and changing public policy. There never was a Golden Age, and there never will be. The book ends with the vision of Jesus. 'Jesus of Nazareth did not envisage a peaceful restored Eden. On the contrary, the Sermon on the Mount throughout envisages the continuation of stress and conflict, persecution and suffering. But he promises joy in affliction: no more, but no less than that' (117).

This is a remarkable short volume, stimulating and thought-provoking. One does not have to follow Cupitt all or even half the way down the path of his particular sort of antirealism to find his comments on the state of Church and theology today perceptive and challenging. There will be those who will find support in his 'Sea of faith' perspective. For myself, I still find grounds, in reason, revelation and experience, for believing in community that our human constructs of God, while entirely human, are at least sometimes responses to the presence of a God who is transcendent to our world, and who comes to us in self-giving love through Jesus Christ, and that this unprogrammed love is central to our future.

Don Cupitt's gentle creed, which mirrors his own style as a sympathetic and popular teacher, is in many ways a much more persuasive pointer to religion than the abrasive certainties of traditional fundamentalism. It reminds us powerfully of a need for humility in our claims to detailed knowledge of God and his will for humanity. (It is interesting to see that the Templeton Foundation, from a very different perspective, has stressed recently the importance of humility in theology.) There is an important link between generosity and humility. Generosity implies concern, but is always ready to listen to the other, not to prejudge every issue. But I think this project binds itself too closely to its own conceptual fundamentalism. For Cupitt, it was Kant who ended metaphysical realism, and then regarded God as a regulative ideal, as a supreme human moral value. We cannot know things in themselves. We are always inside our own vocabularies. We cannot jump out of our limitations and achieve absolute knowledge.

There is no doubt of the lasting value of the Enlightenment development of critical reason. It will take a long time still to work out its legacy fully. Anti-Enlightenment theology is often not much more than an excuse for hallowed superstition. But philosophers cannot jump out of their own cultural skins. Kant too was shaped by his particular culture, and we need not absolutize his perspective into a new dogma. People have been around for millions of years, and no doubt each generation has regarded itself as the expert on God. God may have a few surprises in store for us in the next few million-odd years.

Human life is lived in the tensions between the one and the many, the particular and the general, the personal and the social. Humanity is itself a product of selection and specificity in the gene pool, between different possibilities, different molecular combinations in different environments. To be human is to be bounded, particular, distinctive. A God who meets our deepest desires and aspirations will be unambiguously our God, personal, local, there for us. God in human tradition has always been the God of our tribe, of our nation, of our village, rather than theirs. In the Christian tradition God is the God of Jesus Christ. God is, for most of the tradition of the gospel and the Church most of the time, the sole mediator of the forgiveness of sins, of salvation, of eternal life.

God is an exclusive God. This is not an opinion to be welcomed or regretted. It is a fact. It is also a fact that a militant fundamentalism in various forms is on the increase in most of the major religions, and not least in Christianity.

Yet humanity becomes more human by learning to respect the other, to respect difference. It will be largely agreed that one of the most significant features of Christianity in the last hundred years has been the development of the ecumenical movement, and especially the work of the World Council of Churches. Denominations are slowly learning to be less exclusive. There are often as many steps back as there are steps forwards, but there are fewer anathemas hurled back and forth these days. There is an incipient, hesitant and much-debated inter-faith dialogue. The work of the pioneers in this area is often heavily criticized, but the significant fact is that they are there.

It has to be conceded that much of the humanization of Christianity has been stimulated by sources outside the tradition, and therefore quite logically condemned by Christians who continue to fight vigorously against 'post-Enlightenment individualism'. We have learned from Michael Foucault that the Enlightenment has not all been gain, and from Charles Taylor that the abuse does not take away the proper use. The task as I see it is to learn from the critique of liberal theology and to build on its strengths. Liberal theologies are not always inherently generous, but they have the capacity to become generous, through their basic opennness to constructive, engaged dialogue. I see this as a programme for developing a theology of generosity, as a sequel to the confessional theologies of the past.

RESHAPING CHRISTOLOGY

The past, as Pannenberg has classically reminded us, is an important springboard for the future, both at the level of our own personal motivation and at the level of corporate strategy. I have argued that the generosity of Christ is at the heart of the gospel. This means that the person and work of Christ may be reconsidered from that standpoint, and such reappraisal may be expected to shed new light on our understanding of the centre of the gospel.

An economical way to approach this is in dialogue with a recent constructive Christology, traditional but excellent of its kind, Gerald O'Collins' *Christology*. In doing so we can see the force both of the objective strand of Christology in the Anselmian tradition, stressing the givennness of incarnation and atonement in the realities of the cosmos and of human life, and also the creative/responsive dimension in the Abelardian tradition. From the perspective of this study the Abelardian tradition emerges as the most progressive, provided that the weight of the counter-theme is incorporated, as in a Christology of kenotic, generous love, with profound social implications. It is at once interesting that Abelard receives only minor attention from Gerald O'Collins. O'Collins is a distinguished modern theologian, whose work deserves the greatest respect. Yet it is remarkable how very conservative his latest study turns out to be. Six initial chapters introduce the problems of Christology. These are followed by three chapters on the history of the christological tradition, and then five concluding chapters of systematic reconstruction. We shall look here at the three historical chapters. It should be said that O'Collins performs a major feat in condensing a subtle and detailed history of the tradition into seventy pages. What is fascinating is the nature of his selection of data and the effect which this has on the argument.

The first section takes us from the apostolic fathers to the first council of Constantinople. Four themes are pursued. The historical and cultural context fades into the background, and with it the enormous diversity of the strands of Christology around the Mediterranean world. We then move from Ephesus in 431 to Anselm, with Chalcedon as the centre point. The third chapter brings us from Anselm to the present, again following a classical pattern, and leaving almost no space for Schleiermacher, for example. This leads to a reconsideration, in which, perhaps not surprisingly, Küng and Schillebeeckx do not emerge as very reliable guides to the way forward.

It is true that O'Collins notes that, for example, over two hundred million people have been killed in our century. But this has no decisive impact on the historical reflection. This is rather a contemporary illustration of our fallen condition. It seems to me that there is an urgent need to analyse further the historical grounds of our ecclesial failures. Can we be sure that we have done enough in the name of the gospel to challenge the plausibility criteria of a world often alienated from itself?

If we ask ourselves why the sort of radical interpretation of Christology and human rights expounded by Moltmann and Sobrino did not come to the fore in the Middles Ages, part of the answer must surely be that medieval society was in important respects a closed and totalitarian society, in which freedom of expression for social critique was almost non-existent. Romantic enthusiasm for the Middle Ages and for the Pre-Reformation Church should not blind us to what we owe to the modern democratic process. In this respect the states of the Protestant Reformation were not much better than the Catholic. Those who were merely branded and had an ear cut off for subversive religious criticism could count themselves among the fortunate. Even in the nineteenth century, dissent from the status quo, as the cases for example of John McLeod Campbell and William Robertson Smith demonstrated, often had painful social consequences. Recent freedoms are easily taken for granted. Debates about Christology do not automatically foster communities of generosity.

This does not make the christological tradition irrelevant. On the contrary, the social dimensions of Christology need to be supplemented by the spiritual dimensions, not least in the areas of prayer, liturgy and literature. The richness of the tradition is essential to encourage and sustain devotion. A good example of the connection between social theology and spirituality is Charles Elliott's *Praying the Kingdom*. Indeed to be emancipated from discrimination is not only to be given rights but to be given responsibilities, to be empowered to share in the fullness of the devotional life of the Christian community.

Christology is central. But its central significance is tied up with the paradox that the person of Jesus Christ is at the heart of the Christian understanding of God as creator and sustainer as well as reconciler of the cosmos. The particularity of the man Jesus is itself a clue to transcending particularity in mutuality of relationship. This is indicated in the relationship-centred life of Jesus, in the cosmic significance of his crucifixion and resurrection, and in the relationality which Christians see in the essence of God as relational, Father and Son. It is developed further in the keynote of mystery signalled in the language of the Spirit, of God as indwelling in new creation through the Spirit of Christlikeness. An effective theology of generosity must bring together the emancipatory authority of Jesus as the Christ with the shape of the concept of a God for whom to be is truly to be self-giving, and in doing so give fresh meaning to the understanding of life in the Spirit. None of this is new to the tradition of the gospel. But it does need to be spelled out in language to fire the imagination in each new generation.

Having been somewhat critical of O'Collins' account of the tradition I find it interesting, and encouraging, that the final chapter is devoted to a theme which I also regard as fruitful for future exploration, 'The Possibilities of Presence'. He sums up his reflection in this way. 'Love is the content of salvation through Christ; his various presences form the mode' (318). He adds that 'Respect for the multiform variety of his presences allows us to acknowledge Christ as everywhere present but in an infinite variety of ways' (322). The book ends with a justification of some sort of confessional approach, claiming a kind of knowledge of Jesus, even if limited, quoting Augustine: *Nemo nisi per amicitiam cognoscitur.* I would agree that none of us can claim to be a true friend of Jesus, that our following is always partial. But if we can believe that Jesus is always a true friend to us, then a theology of generosity becomes possible, through our participation in the generosity of God.

I return to the God who is the God of the oppressed, the one whose name is for Christians forever bound to the symbols of cross and resurrection. How are we to reconceive God as a God of overflowing generosity in the Christian future? A useful guide to the magnitude of what is involved may be found in Gordon Kaufman's *In Face of Mystery.* I confess to a certain disappointment on my first reading of this text, a feeling that the urgency and excitement had been taken out of faith. But I have come to think that the issues with which Kaufman struggles are indeed central to the future of a theology of generosity, though Kaufman would not himself claim to have dealt exhaustively with all the issues.

Kaufman's thesis is that 'Our concepts of God and of Christ must be reconceived with attention to our modern understandings of ourselves and of the universe, and to our new consciousness of the destructiveness we humans have worked in the world as well as on our fellow humans' (xi). Indeed 'only as we appreciate more fully the actual interconnectedness of all humans with one another will we discern clearly the extent of the injustice and oppression which our religious (and other) institutions, symbols and hierarchical structures have been creating and sustaining for so long' (xii).

What is required is 'an empowerment for radical inclusiveness rather than exclusiveness, and empowerment that encourages gratitude and respect for the humanity of every human person and community, not only for those who happen to agree with us' (xiii). Notions both of God and of humanity include the mysterious and the unknown. We seek to articulate the sense of mystery in pictures and symbols, notably symbols for God. I do not intend to go through Kaufman's argument in detail, since his proposals are in many ways broadly similar to those of Hodgson, whom we considered at length earlier. But I do consider it highly significant that both are concerned with a radical reappraisal of the basic dogmatic tradition, especially with reference to the emancipatory dimensions of the gospel.[2]

At the centre of Christian faith metaphysical and moral issues are intextricably intertwined, even though they can be separated out for purposes of analysis. This is because faith understands God to have been incarnate in a human being, in that part of the cosmos which has come to self-consciousness. Basic to incarnation, however further interpreted, is self-giving, creative and responsive love. In God's most significant engagement with the cosmos, the selfish gene becomes the selfless gene, as it were. The relation between individual and community is balanced in such a way as to preserve both the uniqueness of the individual self and the essential relationality of human being, both to other human beings and to the cosmic process in creation of which it is a part. Precisely because of God's particular concern for humanity, theology relates foundational theology to ethical issues at many levels.

A theology of generosity interlinks the dimensions of fundamental theology, social and symbolic theology, and looks to each of these dimensions to enrich the other. God is a generous God. Concepts of meanness, narrowness and unreliability are inappropriate. It may be said that in the Bible God is often a jealous God, mindful for his self-interest. To this I would respond that large tracts of the Bible may in God's providence be counter-revelatory, the Word of God telling us precisely how not to respond to God.

One could take this much further. Large parts of the tradition may also be counter-revelatory. Large parts of what we regard as contemporary experience, whether personal or cultural, may also be counter-revelatory. This does not mean that God is not at work in them. God may use them precisely to remind us of what we ought not to be doing in Christian discipleship.

If everything in traditional Christian norms and sources is falsifiable, then are there grounds for belief at all? In my view what counts is the final balance of the individual and the community. Faith retains the character of trust against the odds, at least till the odds become entirely overwhelming, and faith believes that that point will not be reached.

Talk about God is justified by the exploration of language about God, by considerations of evidence for the existence of God, and perhaps most immediately by conviction of the presence of God in the context of Christian worship. For this reason the maintenance of a rich tradition of worship is essential to the health of Christian community. Here in the gospel of Word and sacrament is the entrance to the world of faith. If the entrance proves to be unattractive and poorly presented, then the invitation of the gospel is made less accessible. If the image of the Church is such as to discourage people from worship, then the results are dire. For this reason it is important that different patterns of worship should be available to meet the aspirations of people approaching worship from different cultures and backgrounds. A theology of generosity is a theology of prayer, preaching, sacrament, response in thanksgiving and praise. Worship can be counter-revelatory in all its forms, revealing how things ought not to be. But it can also be the entrance to faith.

The humane, the inhuman and God. Liberation theology has spoken eloquently of the relation of Christ to humanity. It has perhaps been less well developed in terms of the relationship between Christ, humanity and God. The relation of reconciliation to creation, and to the understanding of God as the ultimate source and ground of reality, is always basic to the life of faith. This dimension appears to me to be lost in non-realist approaches to theology, even though there are lessons in metaphysical humility to be learned. I want then to reconsider the transcendental dimension of a theology of generosity which is a theology of human rights. It seems to me that where the connection is neglected, both sides of the equation come back in ways which are often profoundly unsatisfactory. For example, in America today, there is, at least in some quarters, much stress on the transcendence of God and little awareness of the radical social conseqences of this sovereign presence, *etsi Niebuhr non daretur*!

The metaphysical frame

Modern theology owes its sense of the radical transcendence of God as much to Karl Barth as to any other single thinker. In the case of Barth himself, stress on transcendence did not preclude concern for justice and for the engagement of the gospel with specific social and ethical issues. But Barth was inclined often to believe that the transcendent God could be best understood by Christians only in one way, namely his own. It has been pointed out, however, notably recently by Ian Markham in his *Plurality and Christian Ethics*, that stress on transcendence may encourage a humility about the efficacy of one's own concepts, and hence prepare the ground for an acceptance of pluralism and a genuine capacity for dialogue. Here there is a need to move beyond the traditional idea that there is only one authentic Christian metaphysical framework. Gordon Kaufman has proposed a new and comprehensive transcendental framework for talk of God in his recent *In Face of Mystery*. It seems to me that its perspective might need to be supplemented by that of Barth and Rahner, let us say, to bring out the richness of Christian experience of the sacramental presence of God in Jesus Christ. But I do think that he has important insights into the nature of the theological enterprise. He stresses, rightly, that in important respects traditional concepts of religious truth were fundamentally authoritarian (65). Religious truth tended often to be understood on the model of property, owned by one party and thus not directly available to others. He recommends that theology should become more of a conversation. If different metaphysical frameworks may be properly regarded as conversation partners, even when this involves argument, constructive tension and contradiction, then a much richer spectrum of opinion becomes available to the critical theologian than has often hitherto been the case. The danger of a reductionism which finds value only in one style of theology, whether of the right or of the left, is less likely. It still remains a critical responsibility for the individual theologian to make the decisions about the framework which he considers most relevant to the urgent problems of the day.

God is other, alterity. Karl Barth was right to emphasize the otherness of God, and the importance of letting God be God and man be man, of seeking human justice for human beings and leaving God's justice to God. It is when man seeks to be as God, and to act in God's place, that he becomes demonic. But equally, Karl Rahner was right to emphasize that for God to be is to give himself for others, to allow the other to come into being as authentic being, to relate in perfect self-giving. It is in this reciprocity of relationship, internal and external, that God is and acts. An anthropological approach to theology, which explores the creative response of the human spirit to the divine spirit, may provide a paradigm for listening to the other, when it is seen that the other is also a child of the transcendent and sovereign God. A critical realist approach to theology, in which the transcendence of the cosmic creator is expressed, would be the way in which I should approach the metaphysics of generosity. It is in the light of the immensity of the cosmic love of God that humility concerning our local certainties can be sustained and bridges built. On the one hand, we need to build bridges to dialogue quickly, in order to prevent continuing waste of our human energy and resources. On the other hand, we have to remember that significant change in our culture is inevitably a slow process, and that attempts to speed it up can create resistance to change which further slows down development. The move to abolish slavery in the world was infinitely worthwhile. But it took almost two thousand years, and has still not been completely successful.[3]

The historical matrix

We have just considered the profound importance of the tradition of Christian humanism, in its enrichment of the human imagination. But it may be objected that the historical Jesus, the primary datum of the character of Christ, was probably a Palestinian peasant, embedded in a peasant culture and quite probably not sufficiently articulate to appreciate the nuances of the rich cultural and religious heritage of the religious tradition with which he was to come into conflict. It is right to take this dimension seriously, and we shall reconsider the historical particularity. Jesus' locus in an oppressed and impoverished society is rightly seen as an affirmation of God's priority for the marginalized. But at the same time, the Spirit of the resurrection is not confined to a particular period in time – though it is never in contradiction with the basic structuring elements of the New Testament gospel. This means that the impact of the Gospel on all human culture, from Boethius to Britten, may be seen as data for the theologian's reflection.

I return to the continuing search for the historical particularity of Jesus. In his *Jesus in Contemporary Scholarship*, Marcus Borg begins from Jesus scholarship in the 1980s. Here the old consensus that Jesus was an eschatological prophet who proclaimed the imminent end of the world has disappeared. Jesus is now understood as a teacher, a teacher of subversive wisdom. Studies of the social world of Jesus have become central, concentrating not on his words but on a cross cultural typology to see him in context. 'As a charismatic who was also a subversive sage, prophet and renewal movement founder, Jesus sought a transformation in the historical shape and direction of his social world . . . "Following after" Jesus means to take seriously what he took seriously: life in the spirit, and life in history' (14).

An examination of recent portraits of Jesus emphasizes a strong socio-political dimension in his ministry (Borg, Horsley, Fiorenza). Jesus was a peasant whose primary audience was peasants (Crossan). 'It is clear that he engaged in radical social criticism of the élites of his day' (Borg,105). The ideology of the élites was a purity system. Jesus replaced the politics of purity with a politics of compassion. Borg compares his conclusions with the textual work of 'The Jesus Seminar'. 'The glimpse provided by the red and pink passages highlights Jesus as a wisdom teacher who used parables and aphorisms' (172). Borg sums up his view of Jesus as follows: 'Historical scholarship can help to keep alive the liberating memory of Jesus as one who provocatively and courageously protested against systems of domestication and domination, who pointed beyond himself to the sacred mystery in which we live and move and have our being, and who brought into existence an alternative community with an alternative and egalitarian vision of human life in history' (196).

A very similar assessment is provided by Richard Horsley in his *Sociology and the Jesus Movement*. This is in large part a criticism of the work of Gerd Theissen, also a pioneer of the use of sociology in New Testament studies, and a defence of the work of earlier Americans, Shailer Mathews and Shirley Case Jackson. Theissen is criticized for using the categories of modern social structures, and a particular approach (structural functionalism) to interpret ancient culture. Horsley concludes that 'The Jesus movement both envisioned and, to a degree, realized an independent and revitalized local social order. The Jesus movement proclaimed God's overcoming of the old unjust and unfree order and insisted on the possibility of free, just, even creative personal and social life' (154).

It is clear that an incarnational theology must place the life of Jesus in history at the centre of theology.[4] It must also take into account the force of the death and resurrection of Jesus, and the impact of the presence of God in the Christian community ever since. Here is the continuing value of a theological aesthetic, of the sort developed by Hans Urs von Balthasar. The tradition of community response, and the fact of present experience, may of course be counter-revelatory as well as revelatory. Ebeling saw church history as the history of the interpretation of the Word of God. There is a sense in which this may be the case, though human response to the gospel is rather wider than church history. But the various dimensions of human response to the gospel, from worship and liturgy to social action, are an important source of theological reflection.

From this survey of humanity and human rights in relation to Christology we conclude that though the technical aspects of human rights legislation are appropriately left to the experts, the Christian understanding of humanity has a distinctive contribution, based on the humanity of Jesus as the humanity of God. Christian faith suggests a scale of values and priorities, and is in turn responsive to and challenged by continuing work on human rights, which may be seen as God's way of inviting us to draw more profound conclusions concerning the meaning of salvation, and to act on these. It is important too to recall that Christian faith suggests positive images of humanity in individual and social perspective, and encourages the formation of what Edward Farley describes as redemptive communities.

Why should it have been the case that the Christian humanism of such thinkers as Baillie, Niebuhr and Lampe apparently failed to make a lasting impact on the societies which they sought to influence? At one level it may be thought that the absence of a measurable legacy is not necessarily a sign that there has been no effect. Their work fed into an ongoing process which is always in a state of continuous change. Yet it could be argued that change has often been in directions which they would have neither welcomed nor recognized. Here we must take note of that dialectical relationship between the modern and the postmodern which has been present in much of this study. The modern is to be welcomed, the Enlightenment is to be affirmed. There can be no return to a medievalism whose advantages were decisively overshadowed by its limitations.

Christian theology needs to be a theology of correlation, and it also needs to be Christian. An effective theology of correlation is no easy task. Paul Tillich will, I believe, be seen to have been an important figure in the quest for correlation, though he was perhaps less successful in articulating the distinctively Christian elements in concepts capable of stretching the theological imagination. The balance of relationship between fundamental theology and praxis, at this time notable in social justice, together with the dimension of worship, appears to me to remain central to the theologian's task.[5]

The ethical dimension

All human life is lived *coram Deo*, before God who is creator and reconciler. God is understood to be in his essential nature love, love characterized in the self-giving, creative and responsive love of Jesus Christ, creating the Spirit of Christlikeness in new creation. The divine love is a love 'whose breadth, whose height, whose depth unfathomed no man knows'. But it remains part of the invitation to discipleship to wrestle with the nature and implications of the divine love in the world in which we find ourselves.

There is an instructive contemporary attempt to reassess the Christian understanding of love in Vincent Brummer's *The Model of Love*. Part I of the volume is a judicious – and for the theological student highly useful – discussion of the role of models and metaphors in religious language. Brummer then develops the thesis that most views of love take it to be an attitude rather than a relationship. Part II deals with romantic love, as exclusive attention (Ortega y Gasset), ecstatic union (nuptial mysticism) and passionate suffering (courtly love). Part III is devoted to neighbourly love, whether as need-love (Plato, Augustine) or as gift love (Nygren). Brummer enquires whether these attitudes have a role to play in the love relationship, and in the final section develops his own understanding of a relational concept of love which can serve as a key model in theology.

In part I Brummer brings out the need for a hermeneutical dialogue with the biblical tradition. 'The hermeneutical dialogue between the interpreter's horizon and the text is a creative process which brings forth something new, and leaves neither the text nor the interpreter's horizon unaffected' (32). Brummer wishes to counter the prejudice that there are only two sorts of reality, substances and attributes, and to develop the force of relational reality. Love should be interpreted as an interpersonal relationship rather than as an attitudinal or emotional attribute of persons.

The section on romantic love focuses on exclusive attention, exemplified in the writings of Ortega y Gasset, and on ecstatic union, through the eyes of St Bernard. Passionate suffering in courtly love is explored through the world of medieval courtly love. Need-love as neighbourly love is then viewed through the work of Plato and Augustine. The last of these sections is on gift-love, and is largely devoted to the much-discussed distinction made by Nygren between *agape* and *eros*, with some attention to Nietzsche and Scheler. Outka's *agape* is perhaps a surprising omission from contemporary treatments.

There is a somewhat old-fashioned air to these chapters, in which we pass through the pictures of a sort of *Rijksmuseum* of love, in a fascinating world rather remote from contemporary reality. We may wonder whether there is not much to be learned from love as portrayed in the art of the twentieth century, in cinema and television, in the alternative cultures of twentieth-century fiction, often angry, passionate, violent and tragic. On the other hand, it is always salutary to be reminded of the vast significance of cultural change in the perception of love's priorities and demands, and of the transience of what past generations have regarded as the perennial essence of love. It would be instructive to know what Brummer would feel about the cultural relativity of his own preferred model, and the way in which he might see it developing in the future.

The last section begins with an analysis of feelings, attitudes and relationships. This is developed in distinctions between personal and impersonal relationships, fellowships and agreements, and then discussion of the relation of human love to human sexuality. As love deepens, sexuality is no longer the motivation of love but its expression. A chapter on the breaking and restoring of relationships leads into a discussion of atonement and the love of God.

A concluding chapter returns to the five attitudes discussed in the opening sections. Love can be characterized as a form of mutual identification. I identify with you by treating your interests as my own, including acceptance of each other's mutual individuality. As persons we need to love and to be loved. God bestows love on us as freely as a gift. The spontaneous nature of the divine love might, we suggest, be underlined here by invoking the imagery of generosity in which love is a responsive but still proactive commitment. Generosity suggests the gracious and even lavish nature of the love which God creates and encourages, encouraging initiative and going beyond the bounds of justice.

Once again the analysis of love through literary texts creates something of an impression of 'through a glass darkly'. Apart from the single instance of the incarnation, we may miss the immediacy of love manifested through deeds done in history, the passion and devotion of real people in particular circumstances. This may go some way to explaining why the book concentrates on the personal dimensions of love, rather than the social dimensions, and the connection between love and justice, not least in Jesus' own life. It may of course be argued that somewhat as *Schindler's List*, with all its plastic Hollywood limitations, has brought the reality of Holocaust to millions who knew nothing about it, so the exploration of texts acts as a mirror to illuminate life. If so, then Brummer succeeds in challenging us to reconsider what we mean by love, and how we express it in our lives, as lives lived before God who is love.

The cultural construction of generosity

As I have just suggested, an interpretation of the gospel which is to meet our human needs must address itself to the culture in which we live. But today many of us live in a plurality of overlapping cultures. We have to remember the plea of Geertz and others that we must respect the particularity of specific cultures, not seeking to reinterpret them by criteria drawn from alien cultures. But at the same time it is of seminal importance for the human future, we have argued throughout this book, to build bridges, make connections, encourage conversation and mutuality. The Christian gospel claims to speak to all humanity, by pointing to God as the source of true life, and to God in Christ as in solidarity with all who are denied true life by their fellow human beings, whose human dignity is in any way diminished.

How is theology to succeed in embracing cultural pluralism, in being specifically generous in its engagement with unfamiliar cultures and religions, and at the same time in maintaining the distinctive character of the Christian gospel? This is a central issue for a theology of generosity centred on the generosity of Jesus Christ. Gareth Jones has made an imaginative attempt to do something like this in his recent *Critical Theology*. The purpose is to analyse and deconstruct, but then to move towards constructive and imaginative reconsideration of Christian theology. This book is properly ambitious in its determination to take stock of all the essential dimensions of theology. Why critical theology? Critical theology creates conceptual frameworks for argument, takes due account of the modern (rather than the postmodern) and takes seriously God's eschatological revelation in Jesus Christ. The themes of modern theology may be reconsidered within frameworks of mystery, event and rhetoric. These can be contextualized in the development of twentieth-century theology. Jones begins from the encounter between Harnack and Barth, on first principles in theology. He sums up his own findings thus:

> What is the task of critical theology? It is to communicate the message of the gospel in terms of mystery, event and rhetoric, the last-mentioned of which is itself understood as a form of sacramental narrative, something which mediates the relationship between faith and society as they engage with each other in the lives of individuals and communities. . . . The hermeneutic 'circle' thus relates the theologian not only to the Bible, as one source of authority, but also to the Church in its broadest possible sense, and the world in which it lives. (31)

This is spelled out in seven propositions about critical theology. This leads Jones to Bonhoeffer, and 'naming the crisis in the world'. How does Bonhoeffer name the mystery, and why does

194

he name it Jesus Christ? Here is an attempt, beyond Barth and Harnack, to bring God and world together. Bonhoeffer speaks of the mystery of Christ in the social structures of the world, though his Christology is not as open to every dimension of creation as it might be. We move on to Moltmann and Rahner and the presence of eternity. Like Bonhoeffer, Moltmann brings together Christ and society in the particularity of the cross. Rahner speaks of God's participation in death, in a Christology based on grace. For Rahner theology relates faith to society, but gives priority to faith. Theory must relate to practice, but cannot collapse into praxis. This affirmation is now tested in relation to the work of Jon Sobrino. For Sobrino 'there is a clearly noticeable resemblance between the situation here in Latin America and that in which Jesus lived' (87). Christ challenges prevailing oppression with an alternative culture. Jesus' power is that of the Kingdom of God. This makes his rhetoric exclusivist, unable to speak effectively to different sectors of societies.

How is rhetoric (social context) to be related to event (Christology) and to mystery (religious background)? Jones calls in evidence David Tracy, in a chapter entitled 'Tracy, Halting the Postmodernist Slide.' For Tracy theory must lead to praxis. But it lacks, for Jones, a sacramental narrative, a grounding in the experience of a particular community.

We now have the basis for a positive reappraisal of the seminal themes of mystery, event and rhetoric. Mystery involves 'the spiritual primacy of immanence', the need for engagement with issues of change and development, completeness, incompleteness and potential. Mystery is appropriated through the three names of Spirit, Kingdom and Trinity. The centre of mystery is Christology, and Christology must respect the dimension of mystery. This leads to 'Event: Christ and the Predicament of Scale'. Claims for Christ are made in faith. Our knowledge is incomplete. The story of Jesus is to be told around the focal points of Spirit, power and Kingdom. Christology also has a basic kenotic character. The final main theme is rhetoric, and the necessity of a sacramental narrative, relating the gospel prophetically to social context. In conclusion, critical theology points forward, to the primacy of the possible as a challenge to the actual, based on the continuing mystery of God in Christ.

Here is an argument that it is both necessary and possible to be open to genuine inter-faith dialogue, to maintain the decisiveness for human flourishing of Jesus Christ and to communicate the Christian faith within the complexities of modern society. This approach has numerous perceptive individual insights and passages of sustained theological power. It reflects a serious engagement with the central themes of Christian theology, and is in itself a creditable witness to the primacy of the possible, an impressive platform for a programme of radical and constructive theological exploration for the future. If we may believe that a theology of generosity in the nature of the case can take a number of forms, then here is a good example of the genre. It leads me back to face the issue of the ancient dialogue between the gospel and humanism in our Western culture.

The culture of humanitas.

For European citizens the way into the culture of *humanitas* is of course the legacy of Greece and Rome. This remarkable civilization had strengths which later generations had to disparage in order to impose different values on society, and which in some respects have only recently come to light. It also had weaknesses, notably in its élitism and exploitation and enslavement of other peoples. Succeeding societies created a Christian humanism, fusing the values of Athens and Jerusalem in the miracle of the Renaissance, with its wonderful art, music and literature. This was capped again by the Enlightenment, now fusing Classical and Renaissance values with the spirit of the Reformation and the new movement of Romanticism. From Plato to Goethe, Bach and Mozart there is an amazing flowering of the humane spirit. In the systematic murder of a hundred million people the twentieth century seems to have set a giant question mark against all this. The culture and imagination which can humanise, can also dehumanise and brutalise at the turn of a switch. Behaviour can be programmed at will. Yet the abuse does not take away the proper use, for to despair would be a tribute to evil. In Christian terms, the torture and execution of Christ is the gate to resurrection, the light never overcoming the darkness. This can never be a popular or easy message, for the darkness persists, and the light may often be no more than the feeblest lightening. But it remains an encouragement and an affirmation of the good. I do not take the view that Christian humanism is somehow refuted or rendered vacuous by modern barbarism, either in European or in global history. Somehow the disasters of our time are a challenge to rebuild, like the dome of the Frauenkirche in Dresden.[6]

Theology may be fruitfully related to all areas of the human sciences, though uncritical correlation is clearly unwise. Even such apparently unpromising areas as management studies can be related, as we saw in the case of Charles Handy. Theology will always exercise its own critique of underlying ideologies, here as elsewhere. Christian communities require to be managed properly. The gospel sets up its own range of priorities, with unconditional, creative responsive love at the centre.

One further important contribution of theology to the human future will be its continuing input to world literature. Much world literature has been influenced by Christian faith, theology and life, and this legacy will continue and develop. It would be hard to think of modern writers like Solzhenitsyn, Eliot or Auden, Steinbeck or Baldwin without awareness of their deep interaction with the Christian tradition. Literature is much more than morality plays. But here are narratives of generosity and ungenerosity, not least in the development of the modern novel. Faith is and will be reflected in art in general. Faith is articulated in music and drama, in architecture and painting. Again, the names even in recent times are numerous. We think immediately of Britten and Tippett, Le Corbusier, Arthur Miller, even Picasso.[7]

Presence in Word and sacrament

Central to Christian theology is the realization of the sense of the presence of God. When God is perceived to be absent, the opposite of God tends to fill the vacuum. When God as the source and goal of human rights and human dignity is forgotten, darkness may not be far away. (There has of course been darkness in the midst of a sense of presence, for example in the ritual burning of heretics by the Church. But the presence of God is not identical with the presence of religious belief and observance.) This presence is a presence with a memory. David Tracy has well said that

For the memory of the Christian is, above all, the memory of the passion and resurrection of Jesus Christ. It is that dangerous memory (Metz) which is most dangerous for all those who presume to make his memory their own. And that memory releases the theological knowledge that there is no innocent tradition, no innocent classic, no innocent reading. That memory releases the moral insistence that the memory of the suffering of the oppressed – oppressed often by the Church which now claims them as its own – is the great Christian countermemory to all tales of triumph: both the social-evolutionary complacent narrative of modernity and the all too pure reading of 'tradition' by the neoconservatives.[8]

Postmodern thought has sometimes followed Marxist philosophy in criticism of presence. Not the static present but the dynamic future is important. Yet without presence the past and the future have no grounding. For Christian theology, the basic presence is the presence of God, the ultimate source and reality of the universe.

We have seen that the major world religions went through a stage of basic reliance on a corpus of sacred texts. These texts have remained authoritative. But as understanding of the nature of the texts and their interpretation has changed, so understanding of the authority of the texts has developed. There are Christians who are able to combine for example a sophisticated hermeneutical interpretation of Scripture with an acceptance of the givenness of the scriptural canon by revelation, and the ultimate inerrancy and infallibility of the text. But more often, reappraisal of interpretation leads to reappraisal of authority. In my view such reappraisal is necessary and vital for the intellectual growth of the Christian community.

Similar considerations apply to the concept of a corpus of sacred tradition, which may include the canonical Scriptures. As theories of doctrinal development become more sophisticated, traditional loyalties can be affirmed, yet combined with comprehensive reappraisal and reconstruction. Throughout this process, appeal to reason and experience brings the entire range of modern knowledge to bear on the articulation of the gospel in the present. At the centre of this process is the critical assessment of the complex interaction between Christianity and culture in various parts of the world in past, present and future.

A striking example of this process of reassessment is to be found in the reappraisal of the Bible, for example in the recent production of the Roman Catholic Pontifical Biblical Commission of 1993, *The Interpretation of the Bible in the Church*.[9] This document is divided into four parts. Part I, Methods and Approaches for Interpretation, considers first the historico-critical method, which it describes as 'the indispensable method for the scientific study of the meaning of ancient texts' (13). It then goes on to New Methods of Literary Analysis, including rhetorical, narrative and semiotic analysis. The next section covers Approaches based on Tradition, the canonical approach, the approach through recourse to Jewish traditions of interpretation, the approach from the influence of the history of the text. All these are evaluated positively. (*Wirkungsgeschichte*). The next section is devoted to approaches that use the human sciences. These are a sociological approach, an approach through cultural anthropology, and psychological and psychoanalytical approaches. Here doubts creep in, especially on the last. The next section of Part I is devoted to contextual approaches, liberation and feminist. The last section covers fundamentalist interpretation, which is firmly condemned.

Part II deals with hermeneutical questions, philosophical hermeneutics and the meaning of the inspired Scripture, and deals with the literal sense, the spiritual sense and the fuller sense or *sensus plenior*. Part III covers characteristics of Catholic interpretation, interpretation in the biblical tradition, in the tradition of the Church, the task of the exegete, and relationship with other theological disciplines, notably systematic and moral theology. The fourth part is devoted to the interpretation of the Bible in the life of the Church, and covers actualization, the appropriation of the text today, inculturation, and the use of the Bible in liturgy, in meditation (*lectio divina*), in pastoral ministry and in ecumenism. The report concludes that biblical exegesis fulfils, in the Church and in the world, an indispensable task, that the diachronic research of historico-critical method is essential, complemented with synchronic approaches. Beyond this, Catholic exegesis should maintain its identity as a theological discipline, the principal aim of which is the deepening of faith (96).

In a collection of essays in response (ed. L. Houlden,1995) the critics point out that here is a work by nineteen male priests and one layman. It has problems with feminism, and there are definite limits to the critical process. Robert Carroll says that 'It is in fact an attempt to come to terms with contemporary reading methods in Biblical studies while maintaining the integrity of the *magisterium* in support of a rather traditionalistic interpretation of the Bible in accordance with the dictates of Christian dogmatics' (143). Cardinal Ratzinger, who wrote the preface, would probably agree, though he is careful to avoid giving the document official status. 'The Pontifical Biblical Commission is not an organ of the teaching office, but rather a commission of scholars' (4).

If we ask ourselves in the light of these chapters how the interpretation of the Bible is to be reconceived, we may perhaps expect an answer along these lines: The Bible has always been at the centre of Christian faith, and will no doubt always be there. Without the Bible there would be no faith, no gospel, no Church. Without the Bible we should know nothing of the character of God as self-giving, creative, responsive love, shown in the events concerning Jesus Christ.

The Bible is one, but it is also many. Right from the beginnings, there have been innumerable different interpretations. 'Both read the Bible day and night, But thou read'st black, where I read white.' We may think Blake's couplet unduly sceptical, but it does reflect the fact that Christian communities and individuals have read the Bible differently, and that these differences have sometimes created conflict. We need the Bible, it may be said, which guides us to the unconditional love of God, to his justice and mercy and grace, his concern for the poor and the outcast. We do not need the Bible which supports racism and anti-Semitism, encourages vengeance, genocide and capital punishment, slavery and the subordination of women. Yet a sanitized Bible which cuts out the areas we don't like would also have grave disadvantages. Christians have at least sometimes thought that it is in God's providence that we have the Bible as a whole, containing what is emphatically the Word of God and what is emphatically not the Word of God.

It should be noted here that even, and particularly, where the Bible is considered to have unique authority, it is always interpreted and used within the life of a community. It has immediate social implications.

The Bible has traditionally been central for the Church's understanding, not only of humanity but of God, and will no doubt continue to be so. How are we to reconceive God in the Christian future? Explorations of the understanding of God in relation to humanity are not neutral in respect of the methods, sources and norms of faith. They invite reappraisal of authority and its legitimation, and with this, of the practical accompaniments of authority, power and influence. The history of the ecumenical movement seems to suggest that we are most unlikely to see a sudden convergence of views on authority within the Christian denominations. The most that can be expected, and this at least has the advantage of not replacing one monochrome view with another, is that there will emerge a reconciled diversity which facilitates greater understanding and co-operation, a stress on the inclusive rather than the exclusive. In time we may hope for a similar outcome of inter-faith dialogue, and of dialogue between religious and non-religious quests for humane values.

How can we interpret the Bible in a creative way today? First, we will want to recognize the text as it is, and the varieties of possible legitimate interpretation. We then move to actualization, both intellectual and practical. Both the recognition of the legitimacy of a range of interpretative frameworks and the imaginative actualization of biblical insights call for generosity, of a kind that is not instinctive but which has to be learned, negotiated, worked at. If we were ever inclined to doubt this, a glance at the bitter conflict which has often surrounded Biblical interpretation should remind us of the need for a much more creative future.

God uses the Bible to invite us to deepen our faith, and our understanding of creation and reconciliation It is often in the context of meditation on the text that such imaginative insight occurs. Augustine in the garden. Luther on the psalms. Bonhoeffer in his prison cell. Psalm 119. (*Meditating on the Word*, 114):

> 'Happy are they
> Who never do any wrong
> but always walk in his ways.'

With God one does not arrive at a fixed position; rather, one walks along a way. One moves ahead or one is not with God. God knows the whole way; we only know the next step and the final goal. Whoever sets his foot on this road finds that his life has become a journey on the road. It leads through green pastures and through the dark valley, but the Lord will always lead on the right pathway (Ps. 23) and he will not let your foot be moved (Ps. 121)

'Through the Bible we may appropriate divine revelation through human experience, appreciate the relation of creation to new creation, work towards a Christian view of authority in community, deepen the dimension of prayer, develop participation in liturgy, communicate the Word in preaching, gain insight from various translations.' (*Bishops on the Bible*, 1994). We may also develop a sense of the unity of Word and sacrament as the presence of the incarnate God within our world. This is not simply a nominal presence, but a generous and healing presence among us.

Faith in the Christian future will be concerned, as it has been in the past, with response to the presence of God. The mystery of the divine presence is mediated to us through Word and sacrament. The Word was made flesh. God's word means that God communicates through language. This language is the means of expressing the connection between divine reality and human reality. As such it brings focus and personal relationship into the action. Language is also subject to misunderstanding, to obscuring and masking reality. Even the most exalted language can turn truth into a lie. The Word of God has a kind of dialectical function between law and gospel, which cannot easily be overcome.

God communicates also through sacrament.[10] Christ is God's sacrament for humanity in the physical cosmos. Here we are enabled to participate in the life of God. Sacrament too is open to misunderstanding and manipulation. The self-giving of God can be appropriated as a vehicle for sanctifying violence and oppression. God's sacrament is the reality of the divine presence in solidarity with the victims of oppression, bringing new creation out of innocence, love and justice out of victimization. Language about God and divine substance refer ultimately to this God of Word and sacrament, characterized by kenosis, living through giving being to the other.

9

GENEROSITY UNDER PRESSURE –
HERESY, RECONCILIATION AND THE
CHRISTIAN FUTURE

Truth and history

Latimer, Ridley and Cranmer were burned to death. A whole burnt offering, eminently fitting. This was done not by godless atheists but by devout Christians. It was not done because the accused were atheists but because they had different Christian beliefs from those who tried them. It was not done by mindless thugs but by doctors of divinity – presumably exclusive categories even then. Of course, everybody knew that it was a perfectly respectable thing to do, prayerfully. If Oxford went in for a measure of holy smoke, Cambridge, it was said, burned the dead as well as the living. This book is concerned with the future, but the future, I have suggested, crucially involves every generation coming to terms with the past.

In his recent powerful and immensely learned volume on the prehistory of the Holocaust, Professor Stephen Katz offers a moving and convincing account of the immense burden laid on Jews by Christians through the ages. He shows how they suffered oppression upon oppression.[1] And he is at pains to document the uniqueness of Jewish suffering, because unlike other victims the Jews were forced to live in cohesive and highy visible communities, to facilitate their own persecution.

And yet, however diminished its scale, it also remains a fact that Christians in this country have a pretty shady past, particularly in relation to their fellow Christians. Charles Davis has suggested that 'Since religion is not part of the structure of modern society, it cannot legitimately use violence or coercion to promote its values. Its social action must find expression in non-violent forms. (*Religion and the Making of Society*, 47). While I agree that religion cannot legitimately use coercion, I am not sure that religious coercion has been removed from the pluralism of modern society in all its sectarian profusion. Certainly, weariness with religious conflict is often seen as a source of secularization. Though it must be said that conflicts are sometimes succeeded by great movements of faith. And it can be argued that both sides in religious conflicts are defending the truth, as they see it.

I turn here to the naive and simple question, what is truth? Are there at least two truths, a secular truth, and a spiritual truth, each of which is better, or worse, than the other, depending on where you stand? This too, you may feel, is a typical academic question, though Salman Rushdie, or the Bosnian Muslims, might not entirely agree.

Memoria, for St Augustine, is part of the threefold cord of the knowledge of God. Not the Platonic *anamnesis*, but the grace of the Word incarnate. The history of Christian doctrine might be read as the history of the memory of the love of God. But that would not be the whole story. The history of doctrine can also be read as the history of the battle for Christian truth. And what has truth to do with history, if in truth history is bunk? Collingwood is long since dead. Of course, as we have said for at least 2,500 years, it depends what you mean by truth. On a huge hill truth stands, said Donne, and it's true. At the top of this hill for Christians there is a cross. I am the way, the truth and the life. 'I am the truth' may be no more meaningful than 'you are a poached egg'. Theology will not necessarily make sense of the world, though it does have a duty to try to help us to cope with the world. None of the symbols is innocent. Even the cross which has brought comfort to many has been a sign of terror and exploitation to others. We have to pick up the pieces, trusting that God is doing the same before us. Generosity and orthodoxy may be compatible, but only as orthodoxy reflects the truth of the unlimited love of God.

Ancient Near Eastern traditions

How are truth and reconciliation to be achieved? What can we learn from the tradition, or the traditions of traditions? In the beginning, God. To understand the roots of our present problems with truth and reconciliation, we must go back far into our traditions. Theology in the Old Testament is much more like our own than some of our teachers might have cared to imagine. There is a lot of adhocery, combined with sometimes fairly desperate attempts to lay down definitive markers for future strategy. As in all corporate company activity, the needs of internal structure within the religious community have to be balanced against those of external relations, from Abraham and Isaac to Waterman and Peters. Areas of excellence have to be targeted, achieved and monitored. In the process the company culture shifts, sometimes drastically. So with The People of Israel, PLC. We may say that attribution of modern sociological categories to ancient cultures is always a misleading activity. In many ways the cultures of the ancient Near East were so different from modern times that comparisons are simply a distraction. The last hundred years of human history have changed many things irrevocably. Yet we must be aware that compared with the span of human activity on the planet, 3,000 years is not such a very large slice, and there are instructive observations to be made on the immediate source of much of our Christian present.

The societies in which what we know as the biblical Israel was formed were largely feudal societies, mirroring their immediate ancient Near Eastern predecessors, in Babylon, Assyria, Sumeria, Ugarit. In this way three of the major world religions, Judaism, Christianity and Islam, share a common background which must be significant for attempts to achieve truth and reconciliation between them. They are of course divided as much as united by a common history and a consequential history of conflict, and deploy sophisticated internal hermeneutics to cope with the results of any possible developments in historical research. Yet the task of critical reason remains to work towards better communication and interrelationship, and to resist the privatizing of truth for the special privileging of one section of the human community.

The complex strands of the Old Testament narratives provide fascinating evidence of the impact of the law, and of religious observance in all its aspects, on the culture and politics of one important section of the ancient world. Tensions are created, diffused and developed into new patterns through the narratives, from the dramas of Kings and Chronicles to the meditations of the Psalms. The mix of following precedent and complete unpredictability in outcomes, even in heavily edited and stylized narratives, underlines the diversity and contingency as well as the continuity in the tradition of Israel.

We have already considered the importance of the law in the Old Testament, in the New Testament and in Islam. As in modern times, it appears that law develops, like other social institutions, in irregular ways, sometimes reflecting a sense of the need for severity of punishment against threats to the stability of community, sometimes reflecting religious pressures, sometimes moderating severe penalties in the name of mercy and human dignity. All of these pressures are reflected in the Hebrew Bible, in which the legal measures of inherited codes are modified, sometimes in a more severe, more often in a more lenient direction. In communities with official religions at their centre, religious and civil law inevitably overlap. It may of course be that the religion will eventually lose significance, so that an officially non-religious state may be more influenced by religious considerations than a state with an official religion (compare the UK and the USA today). But that was not the case in the biblical period.

We have seen the problem with the interpretation of law. God speaks, it may be said, in, with and under human speech. How far is the specificity of religious laws or related civil sanctions a matter of the culture also, and how far is the culturally specific itself a matter of divine providential will? On this it may be impossible to achieve agreement. The most that is possible may be an agreement to disagree, and to resolve to do together everything that can be done together. The problem is compounded for Christianity by the conflict between the law and the gospel at the heart of the New Testament, and the subsequent continuation of that conflict in the Church. This is reflected in interdenominational disagreement and within denominations on justice issues, e.g. on the equality and dignity of women. In Judaism and in Islam there are likewise important historic disagreements on the role of the law.

In the nineteenth century many scholars felt that these conflicts would gradually diminish in importance. That was before the Holocaust. Perhaps equally significant for immediate reflection is that this horror, and the murders of up to 100 million people in our time, can be largely banished from our memory by technocratic reason, and the space filled up by popular entertainment in the media. What was once a rather puritanical and élitist suggestion becomes a basic piece of commercial data. The common response of theology and Church, to retreat further into a private community, is hardly consonant with Christ who died in a public place and whom God raised from the dead for the salvation of all humanity.

Christus veritas

'I am the truth'. I have already discussed the liberative dimensions of Christology at length, and reflected on Jesus in his social setting. The Johannine claim that Christ is the truth was to make an immense impact on the development of the early Church. Christianity was the true philosophy. It was the intellectual claim that Christ was the absolute truth which appeared to be the scandal of the gospel and the key to its development. The ultimate fruits of the claim were to take the form of the doctrines of the incarnation and the Trinity. The deepening of this truth was to be the bedrock of Christian community and of Christian mission. This claim that Christ was the truth in the highest philosophical sense was also to be the focus of martyrdom and persecution, of identification with Christ in his suffering.

The idea that Christ as truth implies a dimension of liberation theology, of emancipatory solidarity with the disadvantaged and the outcast in the world, was certainly never absent from Christian thought. Care for the poor and the vulnerable within the Christian community was a concern from the beginning, as it was in the Jewish tradition. Yet the kind of comprehensive social concern which we find so powerfully articulated in much modern theology, based on reflection on Christ as the truth of the exploited and the dehumanized, appears to have little place in Patristic thought. It is true that there were protests against many state practices, e.g. pleas for pacifism, or against the worship of the old gods. Origen is a good example of intellectual argument combined with readiness for martyrdom. The early Church did not lack courage. One could no doubt find by ransacking the Fathers quotations to support almost any kind of perspective. Why then, we may ask, is there so little trace of any sort of embryonic liberation theology?

We know that the early Church was simply not in a position to be in the business of large-scale social reconstruction. It struggled in groups of usually poor people to exist and to deepen its faith. Part of the price of toleration was the creation of respectability – we are not socially unstable, we are loyal and reliable citizens. Dissent and critique is a luxury not available in such conditions.

Equally important, it can hardly be underestimated how great a difference the coming of modern democracies, however imperfect, has made to the possibilities for articulating social critique. Those who decry modernity in the name of a romantic longing for the past might find this particularly trying. The societies in which venerable traditions, including the Jewish and Christian traditions, were basically shaped were feudal societies, autocratic, totalitarian and oligarchic. Unless you were a member of the privileged élite it was extremely difficult to develop social criticism, and even then it was likely to be highly dangerous. Freedom for social criticism is a vulnerable plant, and unless tended carefully may again become an endangered species.

With the consolidation of the Constantinian settlement Christianity became established and the old religions became the marginalized minorities, for whom there was scant sympathy. Even in establishment, Christians had to observe the rules of the feudal state, or suffer the consequences which were always an option – compare the fate of Boethius.

Christ is the truth, and his truth is in conflict with untruth, with evil.[2] There is in Christianity, as in Islam and Judaism, a strong sense of the conflict between sin and grace, between good and evil. I want to look at this briefly in the great theologians. For Origen this conflict is largely between the material and the spiritual, the things of this world, of the flesh, and the things of the spirit and of the next world. For Augustine there is a profound reflection on sin as the sin of the flesh, corrupting creation and characterizing the gulf between the earthly and the heavenly city. Saved from the sins of the flesh, we may rise to the life immortal. For Thomas there is the flowering of a new understanding of man as creature, and of the natural as a norm, within which the supernatural may be nurtured. What for modern thinkers is a philosophical construct is for Thomas something like an empirical fact, a natural order, within which binding rules and classifications can be made which reflect God's will. For Luther and Calvin God's grace may put this whole order in question, but only to refreeze it in a new dispensation which is in many respects a mirror image of the old. It is perhaps a reflection of the ineffectiveness of this complex Christian taxonomy that its most immediately striking result was the long-drawn-out atrocity of the Thirty Years War in the heart of European civilization, echoed in the lesser conflict of the Civil War in Britain.

Religious organisms have a wonderful capacity for recovery. Yet serious questions had been raised about truth, which were to evoke the Enlightenment and to change the whole framework of understanding the universe. Modernity and the theology which it provoked was itself to come into question in the same way 300 years later in the Holocaust and the deaths of millions in Europe and Asia, and increasingly in Africa, in our own time. Christian triumphalism rejoiced to think that the time had come again for a new Christendom, without any appearance of having learned lessons from the past. Truth for Christian faith is the truth of the generosity of God in action. Any other reading of truth is a contradiction in terms.

Christianity and kenosis

One consequence of establishment was that Christian voices have been listened to, at least in Europe and America, by governments over a long period. We may now be returning in some respects to the period of the early Church in which Christian views have no automatic access to the consideration of those who make decisions. This may be seen as a consequence of bad advice, when for example the churches on both sides were enthusiastically in favour of the First World War. Power abused should be diminished. It is true that the Pope is still instant media news on any topic on which he pronounces. But it is hard to gauge his actual influence, given the degree of dissent which many of his views arouse.

It seems to me that the need for the future will often be not so much to determine where secular discussion can be fitted into a religious framework, but where the priorities of the gospel can be brought to bear on an ongoing secular discussion, namely the negotiation of continuing ordinary life on our planet. This will of course need to be sustained by a strong Christian tradition of worship. I see this as an appropriate task for the theologian in the present, not in discontinuity with the tradition but in development of the tradition in critical and constructive response to the needs of the present. This will, however, need to be inspired by a continuing solid basis in faith, doctrine and worship.

This brings us back to my theme of generosity and truth. The theme of kenosis, of God's self-giving, creative, responsive love in Jesus Christ, runs through the tradition of Christian doctrine. It may not by itself solve all the problems involved in doctrines of incarnation, but it does indicate areas of engagement with social reality. It does not do so automatically. Reflection on kenosis in the seventeenth century led to acrimonious conflict about the nature of that kenosis. Often it has been internalized, to become a source of personal spirituality. But it may also be deployed in the service of truth and generosity. There are instances of this throughout the tradition and I think here of Karl Rahner and Donald Mackinnon in the present. Even in the midst of seventeenth-century conflict, however, we can find a correlation of concern for generosity with concern for Christ as truth. I think here of the life and work of Robert Leighton. Leighton's extant writing is largely meditation on personal piety. But he was at least acutely aware, in the midst of a cultural clash of extremes, of the need for the truth of Christ to create structures of reconciliation. Such attempts are an important witness to Christ as truth, even where they are not successful. It remains an imperative to make them more effective.

There has been much discussion recently about the doctrine of the incarnation. No less a figure than Gadamer has described incarnation as the great contribution that Christianity has made to civilization, which increasingly means a community of cultures. It seems to me that we may soon be able, thanks to scholars like Rahner, to add that dimension of kenosis effectively to the Christian contribution to a future civilization. Human flourishing is indeed made possible through the self-giving, creative responsive love of the creator in reconciliation through Jesus Christ. This affirmation will be heard effectively when the churches themselves are seen to reflect a community of generosity. In the interval it is up to Christian communities to indicate the priorities of kenotic love in their contributions to the public square. This means abandoning the triumphalism which is juxtaposed with insecurity, creating alienation outside and complacency within. Christ as truth is a source of critical judgement as well as affirmation. The Church will not automatically support any group, poor or rich, male or female, white or black. It will recall that there are poor fascists who terrorize other poor people as well as rich fascists, self-indulgent feminists as well as other-regarding, murderous blacks as well as whites. But it will take into acount the multiple deprivation which is itself one of the sources of alienation. It will judge specific instances rather than general impressions, remembering that St Paul, who promoted patriarchy and intolerance in many areas, also reminded us powerfully that love endures all things, suffers all things, hopes all things.

Within such a framework theology relates the twofold task of correlation and exposition. It has to relate Christ as truth to all areas of human activity, to the concerns of the religions and the secular world. But it also has to try at the same time to develop its own self-understanding in such a way as to provide a profound guide to its own reality as faith in God, creator, redeemer, reconciler. We continue to need the way of Tillich and the way of Barth, of Tracy and of Rahner.

Dialogue without fear

It becomes clear also that isolation feeds fear, and that dialogue based on confidence in our own tradition becomes increasingly important. The notion that perfect love casts out fear is central to discipleship, and to any basis for generosity. As far as inter-faith dialogue is concerned, it is hard to demonstrate concrete results in the last hundred years. Yet in the context of the history of religions, this dialogue is a very new departure, and will develop in ways which we cannot now imagine. Here is a recent example of such dialogue.

The Kagyu Samye Linh Tibetan Centre at Eskdalemuir in Scotland recently held a symposium on environmental concerns. This was admittedly not the most controversial of issues for inter-religious dialogue. But contributors from the Buddhist, Christian, Hindu, Jewish and Muslim traditions met together, agreed to respect their diversity and worked out a common statement on environmental policy as follows.

We are urgently concerned for the future welfare and integrity of the natural environment and we stress the importance of religious motivation and inspiration in making responsibility for the environment part of the daily thinking and living of people around the world. We commit ourselves to the continuing search for a deeper mutual understanding of each other's world

211

views with the aim of building up a world of growing harmony and peace in the years to come. Although the languages we use may be different, we share a concern for transcendence and we share a conviction that the love and compassion for human beings stressed by the world's religions are crucial for a viable future. (Whaling, ed., *The Samye Symposium*, Preface)

Clearly the conclusions of such a symposium have no binding force for the religious authorities of their participants. But in that they provided experience of working together and understanding through close contact the ways of thinking of other religions, they may be an invaluable preliminary to further discussion. The results of non-communication are all too clear in the history of religious conflict.

In an overview of the progress of religious dialogue in this collection Frank Whaling looks at theological views of responsibility for the world, bringing out the contrast between ecological responsibility and human selfishness in each of the major world traditions. We then have a Jewish view of Genesis from Michael Hilton, stressing the interdependence of all human beings on the planet, a Muslim view of responsibility for the world from Mohammed Mashuq Ally, showing the limits of a domination ideology, a Christian view of the created order from Michael Hare Duke and a reflection on creation myths from Alistair Hunter, recalling the importance of compassion through understanding. Concern for justice, peace and the integrity of creation is underlined by Donald McGlynn, while Rewata Dhamma examines the Buddhist understanding of the world and human responsibility in that part of the Buddhist canon known as the Abhidhamma. 'As Buddhists,' he says, 'our main task is to eliminate ignorance, attachment and self-assertion' (123). Selflessness is at the heart of Buddhism as a counter to our natural self-centredness. Khentin Tai Situpa offers a Tibetan Buddhist gloss on the theme of world responsibility. He lays weight on compassion, wisdom and respect, with reference to generosity and truth.

'Generosity means material generosity, caring for and protecting the weak and giving the gift of truth (*dharma*).' This is taken up in a rather different way in a Hindu view of God and the world by D.L. Sharma, for whom unselfishness helps to create an appropriate detachment from the world.

This is not perhaps the most weighty of inter-religious dialogue encounters. But it seems to me to be a paradigm of the need to begin in a modest but determined way to overcome some of the cultural gaps which have long been a barrier to communication, to create communities of generosity. As with most other things, without practice, there is unlikely to be great progress. It is a curious irony that in Scotland one hundred years ago James Hastings, of encyclopaedia fame, was able to take for granted a practical vision of inter-religious dialogue and build his great reference work on this principle. The whole enterprise then sank under the weight of neo-orthodoxy and has only been recovered in recent years. Yet current events, not least the tragedy of Bosnia, demonstrate the urgent necessity of dialogue as a way of life.

I have discussed Christ and truth. In order to be faithful to a Christian understanding of Christ it is not necessarily always desirable to bring Christology directly into the dialogue. The Christian understanding of Christ remains, however, at the heart of the motivation for dialogue, as an invitation to vulnerability and mutuality. It might be thought that such dialogue is only of very marginal interest to the citizens of the United Kingdom. This lack of interest is common in the churches. Yet our various local cultures have brought a legacy of deep-seated suspicion of members of other religious cultures. It takes only the approach of conflict, say in Bosnia, in Iran and Iraq, for this legacy to shape media perceptions and feed our most parochial instincts. Here again is a long-term task of great importance, in part a task of undoing the past, in part of imaginatively constructing the present and the future. In all of these areas the need to lead by example is essential. That is why the development of ecumenical relationships between the churches remains urgent, even if it is not always very effective. That is why such agreements as the Porvoo Agreement between the Church of England the Nordic and Baltic churches, and the Leuenberg Agreement between Lutheran and Reformed churches, are more important than their immediate local impact might suggest. It is also, of course, incumbent on those of us who are professional theologians to conduct our discussions in such a way that vigour in debate and candid disagreement is matched by mutual respect and appreciation. 'It is essential that faith and criticism should be allowed to operate effectively in the life of the Church, and that the tension between them should be acknowledged freely by all parties' (Basil Mitchell, *Faith and Criticism*, 167).

Dialogue by example: the Church

Precisely because of the need for outreach in dialogue, the self-understanding of the Christian community remains important. Christ himself invites us to vulnerability and mutuality. Precisely as generosity comes under pressure, there is need for renewal in faith, in doctrine and worship, in prayer integrally linked to kenosis. Without this centre there will be no motivation for outreach.

How are structures for outreach to be nurtured? This was a question which long preoccupied Karl Rahner. Rahner was not a man who spent long years walking the corridors of the Vatican. Yet he was perhaps as influential on the rethinking of the Catholic Church as almost anyone in our century. True, his influence was usually indirect. It provided a means of holding together a kind of faithful protest. But his was an important voice, which may yet have considerable implications for the future. Richard Lennan's comprehensive and careful analysis of Rahner's ecclesiology is therefore a welcome and timely contribution to contemporary theology.[3]

Though the theme is ecclesiology, Rahner's thought is never entirely inward-looking. As Lennan makes clear in the introduction, 'During his long teaching career, Rahner developed a theology characterized by its emphasis on identifying God as central to all human experience, rather than to the narrowly "religious" sphere of life' (7). He was also crucially aware of the need to change. 'Rahner's numerous publications in ecclesiology called on the church to be open to change in its doctrines, structures, in its relationship with the world, and in the relationship between different groups within the church itself' (8).

Lennan begins from Rahner's understanding of the Church in his early work as the sacrament of Christ. The Church is 'the abiding presence of that primordial sacramental word of definitive grace, which Christ is in the world, effecting what it uttered by uttering it in sign' (TI,1.83). It is both sinful and holy, offering salvation for all humanity. Rahner was seeking new categories to express the truths contained in both Scripture and tradition.

He was attempting, too, to relate Christian experience to an understanding of what it can mean to be human.

The consequences of these aims for the understanding of the constitutional Church is now spelled out. Though the Church is a social entity with a juridical constitution, it comes from divine revelation. Proclamation of the Word comes through the authorized ministers of the Church. Based on an *ius divinum*, the Church nevertheless develops and changes through the ages. The priest speaks for himself but as a messenger of the Word of God. But each local area of the Church must make its own local contribution to the whole.

The agent of change in the church is the Holy Spirit. Communication is more than the imparting of propositions. 'Knowledge in faith takes place in the power of the spirit of God, while at the same time, that spirit is the concrete reality believed' (86). Though community is important, individual freedom is also a valuable guard against 'a willingness to go with the group and an anti-individualistic diffidence' (95). It is not enough to go with the crowd. The individual, by courageous decision-making, can often provide a charismatic example for the church itself. Rahner lays stress, too, on the importance of the laity.

In part II, 'The shock of the new' the Church and the twentieth century, Rahner's call for a more positive approach to the modern world than the Church has sometimes taken is explored. We come now to the impact of Vatican II. Always much concerned for the future, Rahner saw the Council as a summons to continuing and ongoing renewal. As sacrament of salvation, the Church was there for all humanity. It was not to be withdrawn and sectarian.

The Church must not dilute the substance of the faith – that would be fatal. But it must do more than simply repeat inherited formulations. The Council was only 'the beginning of the beginning'. This meant a new assessment of faith and authority in a pluralist age. Faith is a fundamental trust in God, facilitated by participation in the Church. Pluralism will in time affect the *magisterium*, making new dialogue possible. It is not enough to insist on critical obedience (198).

The year 1971 brought a very public disagreement with Hans Küng, showing Rahner's determination to hold to a middle way between conformity and radical criticism. Yet in 1980 he supported Küng against the withdrawal of his licence to teach.

Lennan develops Rahner's later thought further in a chapter on 'The Open Church and the Future'. Christians must be free to take their own decisions and to accept the consequences of those decisions. In 1979 he strongly disapproved of Cardinal Ratzinger's decision to veto the appointment of Johann Baptist Metz to the chair of fundamental theology in Munich.

Rahner hopes that a theology of the future would be an ecumenical theology, free from preoccupation with the debates of the sixteenth century. In 1983 he was to co-author with Heinrich Fries a book entitled *The Unity of the Churches: An Actual Possibility*, which was to be much criticized by more conservative thinkers. In the future the Church and individual Christians would work together for greater social justice. Lennan sums up thus: 'In short, Rahner's position allows substantial reform, including that of the magnitude introduced by Vatican II, to be interpreted positively rather than portrayed as an abject surrender to fashion. Consequently, we ought to expect the history of the Church to be a history of change' (266). Rahner also prized continuity in the Church. But commitment to continuity called for an openness to change.

Generosity by example – the Church again

A generous view of theology is committed at least in principle to open dialogue. Does this mean, then, closure of dialogue with more conservative movements in Christianity itself? What becomes of the normative role of the Bible? It would seem rather pointless to open one dialogue only at the cost of automatically closing another.

For Christians the Bible, however interpreted, remains an indispensable guide to that purpose. Tracy aptly characterizes the relation of text to event thus: 'Christianity is a religion of a revelatory event to which certain texts bear an authoritative witness', 'Reading the Bible: A Plurality of Readers and a Possibility of a Shared Vision', from *On Naming the Present*, (120). In his biblical studies *The Open Text* and *Text, Church and World*, Francis Watson suggests that the Bible itself, centre of conservative Christian theology, is best interpreted through dialogue which is not incompatible with traditional Christian commitment. 'The open text is the biblical text as a site of a proliferation of meanings that accords with its character as a sacred text, constantly read and reread without ever being exhausted' (*The Open Text*, 4). Speaking of the work of the Spirit of God in Acts, he asks, 'Can we be satisfied with a purely textual reality, or must we assert an intratextual realism, that is, the irreducibly textual mediation of realities that nevertheless precede and transcend their textual embodiment?' (*Text, Church and World*, 287). He concludes that: 'If it wishes to engage responsibly in theological construction, biblical interpretation must therefore abandon the myth of the self-enclosed text and learn to correlate the text with the reality to which it bears witness, understanding the text as located primarily within the church which is itself located within the world' (293). In other words, we are all engaged in the task of attempting to relate social concern to ultimate concern, and we need to work at dialogue which does not constantly privilege one set of dialogue partners at the expense of another set. This is not a skill which comes easily to us, but is of the essence of the process of the civilization which Christians believe to be central to God's purpose for his creation.

We have to be self-critical in assessing our own immediate commitments. It seems to me that self-critical theology must act through examples of candid appraisal of local denominational traditions. Let me give one example.[4] Recently I was invited to give a critical response to a paper from a group of Reformed churches, 'Reflections on how the Reformed churches see themselves'. This was in fact an excellent paper. It offered a balanced and imaginative discussion of the basic issues for a Reformed self-understanding. It avoided clichés and slogans, and it was sensitive to the issues in the real world in which the churches are working.

But now a more critical reading of the document. How does the document see the future of reformed theology? What are the continuing central characteristics of a Reformed theology? We believe in the supremacy of Scripture, the Old Testament as much as the New. No Lutheran canon within the canon, no strait-jacket of a law/gospel dialectic, no centre in justification by faith alone. All of Scripture. We stress the covenant, the importance of the covenant of creation. After all, we practically invented justice, peace and the integrity of creation. We do stress the centrality of Jesus Christ, and above all our contribution relates to the role of the Spirit in society, creating freedom. We are not bound to the ecclesiological prejudices of Catholics, Orthodox and Anglicans. *Ecclesia semper reformanda.* We stress too the equality of ministers and elders in our courts, and of women. We admit all communicant members of other denominations to our eucharistic fellowship. We are the confession of true openness. Unlike all the other confessions, we are always open to being open. To be open like us is to be Reformed. Anything else is prejudice.[5]

Such an approach to systematic theology has only one disadvantage. It may produce theology so special that, once you have put it down, you are highly unlikely ever to want to take it up and read it again. The same applies to other pure denominational theologies. In a Reformed context, it would guarantee that you resolutely refuse to learn anything from theologians, exegetes and philosophers who happen to belong to other Christian denominations or none.

The report considers in turn the characteristics of Reformed theological tradition and in conclusion invites readers to consider 'the real mirror that has always been held in front of the church – the Word of God as attested for us in binding fashion in Holy Scripture and proclaimed by the church in word and deed through the centuries'.

But is this not a very Reformed sort of mirror in itself? It might be argued that the real mirror was Jesus Christ himself, his life, death and resurrection – the Word incarnate and God's sacrament for the world. Not the text but the substantial reality. If the mirror is the substantial reality of God in Jesus Christ, then one question is how faith in Jesus Christ is to be expressed in Reformed discipleship. What sort of distinctiveness in God is at issue? The distinctiveness of the God who is self-giving love, for whom to be is to give himself away for others. The character of God is the character of Jesus Christ, who identifies with the vulnerable in a world of terror and counter-terror, who is with those who are in prison, who are ill, who are outcast, who are mentally handicapped.

How is the Reformed community actively to respond to those who are in prison in Europe today? How is it to respond to health care in our world? How is it to deploy effective assistance to the outcast, to the vulnerable minorities, to those marginalized on grounds of race, sex, culture, religion or whatever? How is it to contribute constructively to the search for a deeper understanding of God? How is it to look to a future of a very different society in 500 years from now? Only by looking outwards as well as inwards can we hope, perhaps, to arrive at a new self-identity, which will always change and always be the same.

One could easily document this lack of a more open perspective from almost any other denominational project. Not all theological discussion needs to be constantly critical. But without some such capacity to engage in reappraisal of actual local traditions, it is hard to see how tangible progress can be made. If we are simply to have denominational mirrors of multinational cultures, each with its autonomous and mutually exclusive house style, then we shall probably not get far with ecumenical generosity. Such a prospect does not appear to be the sort of communitarianism to which we are invited by the gospel.

Religion, generosity and the public square

I have suggested that the need for the future will be not so much to determine whether secular discussion can be fitted into a religious framework, but where the priorities of the gospel can be brought to bear on an ongoing secular discussion. How can we effectively bring Christian values into the human dialogue about basic values, needs and priorities? In a world where there have been over a hundred minor wars in the last fifty years, in which there is still unimaginable deprivation and starvation, this remains a burning question. Christians who believe that the gospel is the key to human flourishing can hardly walk away from addressing it.

There are some useful clues to procedures here in recent American discussion about the role of religion in the public square. Michael J. Perry, in *Love and Power, the Role of Religion and Morality in American Politics*, starts from the question of whether there can ever be an entirely neutral or impartial politics, and concludes that there can't. He develops a thesis that reliance on religious premises of certain kinds can be a fitting mode of political justification and of political deliberation, even in a society as religiously and morally pluralistic as current American society. He wants to establish a 'Good-prior-to Right' justification of principles of justice, presupposing the authority of a certain range of conceptions of human good (23). Despite the importance of cultural construction, questions about human good and human rights are still important. These include concern for the well-being of the other, the stranger.

So we come to ecumenical political dialogue, which seeks to achieve in a pluralistic context a common ground that transcends local or sectarian difference, in a kind of dialogical imperative. The sharing of values serves to focus dialogic efforts. We need to embrace both fallibilism – the ideal of a self-critical rationality – and pluralism – the ideal that moral pluralism can produce deepening moral insight (100). We must aim for public intelligibility and public accessibility. We should not expect, if we value pluralism, always to agree. There needs to be an ecumenical political tolerance. We may disagree, but refrain from coercing others – there may be some groups who are incapable of dialogue because they exist to coerce others. Ecumenical politics is liberal, not as being neutral but as valuing fallibilism, pluralism, public intelligibility, importantly public accessibility and above all tolerance (138). At its worst, religion is oppressive, at its best, liberating. 'The central problem of politics for some of us, given our deepest convictions – religious convictions – about the truly, fully human way to live, is the relation of love to power' (145).

This seems to me to mesh well with our earlier discussion of the challenge of the post-modern, and especially with the thought of Richard Bernstein. On reflection we may think that this kind of open dialogical programme has been advocated in North America for a very long time, and the pluralism which has resulted has increasingly come to show less tolerance, more divisiveness. We may, however, recall that the Kingdom will always be outstanding on this earth, and that we need to continue to articulate and develop traditions which we believe to reflect the priorities of the gospel for human flourishing.[6] It is worth recalling that in the thought of Reinhold Niebuhr and those influenced by him there is a consistent attempt to relate the values of the Kingdom to the public square, to reach an approximation of the law of love, a concern continued more recently in the debates between Hauerwas and Gustafson.

Niebuhr himself was to learn from Walter Rauschenbusch, who wrote in 1907 that 'the essential purpose of Christianity was (and still should be) to transform human society into the kingdom of God by regenerating all human relations' (in *Christianity and the Social Crisis*, quoted in Harlan Beckley, *Passion for Justice*, 33). Rauschenbusch's passionate concern for social justice sat uncomfortably with the thrusting capitalist aspirations of many

American Protestants – it was scarcely surprising that he was much dismissed, and that apparently more orthodox theologies were to come as a blessed relief, allowing the Christian to have his spiritual and temporal rewards simultaneously and in full measure. These debates have become much more complex as modern management culture has appropriated for marketing purposes the whole range of human values, (though as we have seen (pp. 94–96) in Charles Handy, a Christian self-critical perspective is entirely possible and can be valuable here too).

In addition to Rauschenbusch and Niebuhr there is of course a huge mass of liberal Protestant theological tradition in the United States, in the work of William Adams Brown, Shailer Matthews and others (cf. e.g. *Contemporary American Theology*, ed. V. Ferm, in which there is an interesting essay from John Baillie's American period, 'Confessions of a Transplanted Scot'). There is also an early Catholic social theology in the work of John A. Ryan. We may recall here too that theology in South America has also been concerned for the public square in the context of liberation theology. In his *The Ethics of Human Rights*, Carlos S. Nino in Argentina has provided a rigorous philosophical analysis of the scope and range of rights and the principles underlying human rights, leading on to a concrete discussion of the justification of government, its authority and its relation to coercion. The mere presence or lack of presence of religion in the public square will not be decisive for Christian discipleship. What is required is a generous and reconciling public presence.

Actualization audit

It will be clear to any observer that creating an intellectual framework for what Perry calls ecumenical politics is not itself enough to guarantee effective actualization. Other dimensions, such as the balance between Senate and Congress, and the cycle of Presidential elections, play a crucial role in determining the art of the possible. Traditional dialogue tends too to presuppose an ability and willingness to read journals, documents and books. Here the need for education and the relief of poverty are bound to be part of the process. In a world in which a huge percentage of the population is either illiterate or semi-literate, in which most people get their information either from television, controlled by media barons, or from tabloid newspapers, often controlled from the same sources, in which there is an uneasy oscillation between populism and élitism, the conditions of the possibility of genuine dialogue are not always easily achieved. Churches and theologians have a duty to make whatever appropriate contribution they can, at any level, to facilitate constructive public dialogue and action.

Examination of the North American scene raises difficult questions about the long-term effectiveness of the churches in working towards social justice. If the application of a huge amount of energy, theology, practical involvement and financial resources could create social justice at a national level, then North America should have achieved this decades ago. But some of the strategies were undoubtedly flawed, and they have also provoked reaction on the part of other strong interests with at least as much financial and political power. The result is that there is probably more acute social inequality in America today than there has been at any time in the last fifty years. There are at least three obvious responses to this situation. The first is to conclude that the effort was misplaced and was therefore unsuccessful. The second is to conclude that the abuse does not take away the proper use, and that a much longer time-scale must be considered for what is major change. The third, perhaps related to the second, is to try to learn from the social theology of the last hundred years and produce a more self-critical and, one hopes, more effective strategy.

I want to look briefly at some recent studies of these issues. In his 1988 study *The Age of Social Responsibility: The Social Gospel in the Progressive Era, 1900-1920,* Donald K. Gorrell documented the enormous effort put into the creation of a social theology in America before and during the First World War. The year 1900 brought, as such dates usually do, resolutions for drastic change. The New York State Conference of Religion suggested that persons of various faiths could and should co-operate religiously, to promote both social reform and evangelization of individuals. Powerful figures – Washington Gladden, Lyman Abbot, Josiah Strong and Walter Rauschenbusch were among the speakers – stressed that the power of religion is necessary for democracy. F. G. Peabody produced his *Jesus Christ and the Social Question,* which was to be much reprinted. F. D. Roosevelt, a social activist in religion, became Vice-President. By 1920 the Federal Council of Churches' Commission on the Church and Social Service had prepared a comprehensive document on *The Church and Social Reconstruction*, for the post-war era. Earlier optimism was to produce a chastened mood in the 1920s, but the basic aims remained.

This is the background against which the work of Rauschenbusch and Niebuhr is to be understood. With Niebuhr there is the famous theological realism which understands corporate sin as a major force in industrial and social relationships and in church activity. Niebuhr was to have enormous influence, till the period of the Vietnam War brought a new pluralism and new radical movements, right and left. Along with liberal Christianity there is a parallel growth in conservative churchmanship. By the 1970s and 1980s issues such as abortion and capital punishment were to generate great support from the new Christian right. Immigration brought millions more Roman Catholics from Europe, at first generally conservative but later also encouraging radical protest movements. The inspiration of the Bible, moral issues and the rise of feminism created new battlegrounds.

By 1980 the main feature of American religion appeared to be radical pluralism, more radical than even before, and a great gulf between liberal and conservative Christians. The position was mirrored in Robert Bellah's classic *Habits of the Heart* (1985), in which the central role in the community of local congregations is documented. He criticized in the main-line churches the lack of a creative intellectual focus, and a 'quasi-therapeutic blandness', and underlines the traditional influence in America of self-contained sects, over against the public Church, suggesting a conflict between withdrawal into purely private spirituality and the biblical impetus to see religion as involved with the whole of life. Bellah ends with a comment on the poverty of affluence, suggesting the need for humility and outreach to those in need. 'Such a vision seeks to combine social concern with ultimate concern in a way that slights the claims of neither' (296).

A remarkably similar analysis is given in the excellent *The Restructuring of American Religion* by Robert Wuthnow (1988), whose work on the Christian future we have already considered. Wuthnow notes that 'On all sides American religion seems to be embroiled in controversy. . . .And these problems have clearly been conditioned, albeit in sometimes complex and indirect ways, by the larger changes in American society' (6). The social gospel movements appeared to have been eclipsed by right-wing religious television evangelism. 'By 1979, for example, Jim Bakker was taking in $52 million annually, Pat Robertson $46 million, Jerry Falwell $46 million, Rex Humbard $30 million and Jimmy Swaggart $20 million' (197). This at least shows the power of this movement. Wuthnow concludes that, 'As the social role of the state has expanded, American religion has been exposed to the vagaries of political life in ways far more complex than at any time in its history. And these political changes have functioned both directly and indirectly to reinforce the changes internal to the religious community that we have sought to examine' (322).

If Wuthnow is right then we might expect similar patterns to occur in other countries, with different consequences in different cultures. We might expect there to be elements of continuity with the American experience – for example, the impact of technology and of a culture heavily focused on marketing and mass media in encouraging both uniformities and particularities. If we are committed to ever-accelerating change, then it is unwise to regret this. We must rather do what we can in every particular instance, focusing on the centre of the gospel in the vulnerability of Christ, making creative use of the tradition where it is still available and attempting to look forward to a further changing future. We must see reason as communicative and community-building rather than as purely technical and neutral. We must build communities of generosity, inclusive rather than exclusive communities, and we must try to develop in every sphere a distinctive generosity of mind, which will shape perception, dialogue, policy and action, in response to the overwhelming generosity of God.

Narratives and icons of generosity

One way of considering generosity in its actualization is by looking at narratives of generosity in its absence. Generosity takes place in community, and is demonstrated in narratives of community. A striking series of narratives of lack of generosity in community is provided by Derek Phillips in *Looking Backward – a Critical Appraisal of Communitarian Thought*. Phillips argues that, contrary to the common romantic examples cited of the communitarian ideal, such communities were often anything but places of harmony and justice, but were riven by conflict and by social and economic injustice. This applies to early New England, to towns in the Middle

Ages, to classical Athens. The idea of a politics of the common good leads very often to élitism, with exclusion and persecution of those who do not agree with the policies of the ruling groups. For Phillips this underlines the need for a strong liberal emphasis on basic human rights, and the protection of every individual from communal abuse.

If we look at the Bible we can see numerous narratives of lack of generosity in community, in the treatment of Philistine neighbours, in the internal political conflicts of Israel, in the bitter tensions between Jews and Christians reflected in the gospel narratives, and between different Christian groups in the Pauline literature. We may recall what we have said about violence in the Bible. But as with violence, there are narratives too of generosity, in communal hospitality to strangers and personal friendships in the Hebrew Bible, and in the New Testament in the parables of Jesus, in the Sermon on the Mount, in Jesus' identification with marginalized groups, in the vulnerability of God on the cross.

The history of the Church, and its relations internal and external, is a history of communities of generosity and lack of generosity, from the pastoral care of the weakest to the massacre of the most defenceless. We may see positive narratives of generosity in the pastoral work done in and from medieval monasteries, in the twentieth-century community of friendship and solidarity in Bonhoeffer's illegal seminary at Finkenwalde, or in the self-sacrifice that took place within concentration camps and gulags. The narratives of pastoral outreach into all dimensions of life, in the work of such bodies as Christian Aid or more secular institutions like Oxfam, are genuine narratives of generosity. Generosity is charity in its better aspects, not as a grim or patronizing duty but as a willing and consistent response to human need. Such narratives may act as icons of generosity to illuminate and to encourage response.

The hot public square, poverty and the major religions

This public task is of course applicable in all countries. We noted that American writers, for example, in the volume edited by Don

Browning on *Habermas, Modernity and Public Theology*, have found particularly in Habermas assistance in defining the nature of creative relationality and mutuality, with his stress on the four criteria of comprehensibility, truth, rightness and sincerity involved in every act of communicative rationality. We need always to remind ourselves too that the God of all the major world religions is concerned for all humanity. It is not enough, though it is an important step, to create dialogue in the Northern Hemisphere while the Southern Hemisphere, and especially Asia and Africa, continues to suffer all the disasters, from starvation to endemic civil war, which result from mass deprivation in a world which could do more for all its citizens.

Our public priorities are reflected for example in our public expenditure.

In 1985–6 Britain spent £15 on defence for every £1 spent on the official aid programme. Defence expenditure accounted for 13.6% of central government expenditure in 1985–6 compared with 11.4 % in 1978–9. For the future, Treasury plans were for defence expenditure to rise by a further £768 million from 1985–6 to 1988–9, but for aid expenditure to rise by only £137 million ... for every extra £1 spent on foreign aid, £5.60 will be spent on defence. (*Africa's Crisis and the Church in Britain*, CTS/CAFOD, 1987, p.85.)

Since 1987 the proportion spent on aid has in fact declined. It is probably necessary in an unstable world to spend on defence, not only for self-preservation but to try to deter genocide in places like Bosnia. At the same time, the declining proportions spent on extremely poor countries tell their own tale about values and priorities.

It is clear that education is important, but it is not in itself enough. It may be that the kind of dialogue which this chapter envisages can help to suggest frameworks for real constructive encounters between strangers. The alternatives are not promising. We may reflect that most people believed firmly by 1900 that murder was always wrong. But this did not prevent at least 100 million people being murdered for political reasons in the present century.

It is especially, and perhaps inevitably, in the context of war that generosity appears to vanish most quickly. In the First World War both sides usually regarded God as their own private property, and Karl Barth, from his unique Swiss vantage point, saw in this, both rightly and wrongly, the sum and the folly of a century of theological development. In the 1939–45 war the British government chose for its own reasons to disregard the one significant contact between Christians, between Bonhoeffer and Bishop Bell, and the churches' role in reconciliation had to wait till after 1945. In the Korean and the Vietnam Wars, the conflict was to be seen from the Western side as a conflict between godless and immoral Marxism and Christianity and civilization – though the unease of the churches was to contribute to the withdrawal from Vietnam, with both positive and negative consequences for the future of global society. In the former Yugoslavia at the time of writing, there is a conflict between Christian and Muslim as well as the continuation of ancient feuds. Here the Christians are seen by most Europeans as the aggressors and perpetrators of genocide. Yet there is a reluctance to offer full support to the oppressed, and the fact that they are Muslims may not be insignificant.

Islamic fundamentalism is associated in the West with terrorism abroad and terror at home, and is perceived to be a growing force in today's world. In a study of generosity under presssure, it is an eminently appropriate subject for the conclusion of these reflections. I want to draw attention here to the excellent brief discussion of these issues in the volume *Islam, a challenge for Christianity*, ed. H. Küng and J. Moltmann. The volume opens appropriately with a piece by Smail Balic on Bosnia: 'The Challenge of a Tolerant Islam'. The suggestion is that the portrayal of Bosnian Muslims as dangerous fundamentalists is largely a creation of their Serbian opponents. John Renard stresses that Islam means not only unity but also diversity in a global tradition, the greatest diversity being of course between the Sunni and Shi'a traditions, and in different countries striking cultural and ethnic differences.

What is required amid all the differences between the religions, internal and external, would seem to be not a framework which will reduce them all to a theoretical unity, but a framework which will recognize and respect difference, but at the same time foster respect and communicative action towards mutual support. To that extent the Enlightenment project is reaffirmed and modified, modified in respect of recognition of pluralism, reaffirmed in the stress on mutual dependence and the need for communication. There is a valuable discussion on Human Rights in Islam, notably the 1981 Universal Islamic Declaration of Human Rights. This does not directly address the difficult areas of cruel corporal punishments, discrimination against women and complete freedom of religion, but it does suggest that the Shari'a should be applied in as flexible a way as possible, and is a step forward.

The collection is summed up by Hans Küng in a succinct essay on 'World Peace – World Religions – World Ethic'. There will be no new world order without a new world ethic. There cannot be a single world culture or world religion, but there are features which the religions have in common, raising basic human questions and offering ways of salvation.

Religion can prolong wars but it can also shorten them. There is need for a minimal consensus on ethics, an ethics of responsibility, exemplified by normative leading figures, notably the foci of the major religions. There is a need to become aware of what culture and religions already have in common, and to develop a culture of non-violence and interdependence. In other words, it is precisely under pressure that generosity becomes conscious of its own dimensions and is a powerful force for human good. It is up to us to keep our nerve, to lay consistent and proactive stress on reconciliation.

Beyond this we should expect not only to be able to tolerate or accept difference in religious dialogue, but to learn new ways of looking at things which will help us to develop the richness of our own traditions. So, for example, in discussing Hindu thought in *The Face of Truth*, Julius Lipner suggests how we may learn from Ramanuja's discussion of the polar tension of relationships, in their centripetal and centrifugal tendencies, to understand the relation between God self, and world in a way which has the advantages of panentheism without the disadvantages. We should not simply assume that the picture will not continually change, that it is always better to give than to receive and that there are no surprises. 'We lack the consciousness of our own relativity' (Karl Barth in *Die Woche*, 1963/4, quoted by Hans Küng in *Theology for the Third Milleunium*, 283). Tracy sees dialogue with Buddhists as helping us to move along 'the mystical-prophetic journey – where the inter-religious dialogue will become an integral part of all serious

Christian thought' ('Buddhist Christian Dialogue', in *The Christian Understanding of God Today*, 152).

Visions of a generous God

Postmodern thought has sometimes followed Marxist philosophy in criticism of presence. Not the static present but the dynamic future is important. Yet without presence the past and the future have no grounding. For Christian theology, the basic presence is the presence of God, the ultimate source and reality of the universe.

Relationships between the one and the many, the individual and the community, always remain at the centre of the issues confronting religion in society, though in ever-changing forms. Christian faith believes that both respect for individual dignity and concern for the quality of social life and social justice spring from the centre of the gospel. Inter-religious dialogue, indeed social dialogue in all its forms, depends on the same respect for individuals and effective communication and interaction between them for the benefit of humanity. How to maintain respect for the stranger, for the otherness of the other, without imposing uniformity, while strengthening mutuality in community, is rightly in the forefront of contemporary debate, notably on the merits and demerits of modernity and postmodernity. In these debates fashions change constantly. The most effective strategy for participation would seem to be to develop one's own or one's community's approach as distinctively as possible, and to offer this as a contribution to an ongoing process, while being always open to appreciate and to receive from alternative perspectives. There will be limits to the process of interaction, because there may be irreconcilable elements, for example between perceptions of good and bad. The challenge will be to maximize the benefits of dialogue for the development of the community and also of the individual.

This applies equally to such specific issues as the interpretation of Scripture or the understanding of human rights. The dialogue process stretches back to Plato and beyond. It has not prevented human disasters. Its limitations are a cause for increased and continuing effort.

I return to the theme of generosity by example. It does seem to me to be incumbent upon members of Christian communities to learn to engage in constructive dialogue among themselves, if they are to have any hope of successful, wider, inter-religious dialogue. We may accept that dialogue with those who are closest, yet divided, is sometimes the hardest of all dialogues. In these circumstances dialogues with more distant partners can actually provide a catalyst for change, and in this way inter-religious dialogue can stimulate progress in interdenominational dialogue. But it is hard to see, let us say, genuine progress between groups of liberal Christians and conservative Muslims, if we have not learned to cope with dialogue between liberal and conservative wings in Christianity. Here an appreciation of the complex links between religion and culture is important. The art of the possible will include maximization of common ground while recognizing the limits of agreement in particular areas. For all participants, religious and non-religious, the spur to progress is the hope that truth will eventually commend itself in different forms of expression and on the strength of its own credentials.

For Christian faith, engaged in the perennial dialectical task of faith seeking understanding, reflection on the relation between faith and culture leads back again to further reflection on the nature of God, whom we understand as the creator and reconciler of the cosmos and within this of human society.

The Christian future will be influenced greatly by the understanding and the vision of God which the Christian community holds. This will affect its self-understanding as much as its contribution to other religions, to culture, to society, to friends and strangers. This understanding and this vision will vary in different expressions of Christian community. It will draw on Scripture and tradition, in life and worship. It will draw on contemporary experience. In this study I have tried to draw attention to elements in this vision which I regard as important for that future.

Christians understand God as the great mystery who is the creator, sustainer and fulfiller of human life, and of the entire created order. Human beings must seek to develop their corporate self-understanding as far as they possibly can. But Christians understand life as a gift of God, who is our source and our fulfilment, and who invites us to search for a relationship with him. This searching is expressed in meditation and in worship, in formal and informal ways. This sense of wonder at the transcendent mystery of God, and of gratitude for the presence of God, is basic to human well-being as Christians understand this. We should not seek to minimize the mystery by attributing too many of our current cultural conceptions to the being of God.

At the same time, God is not a neutral or blank mystery, for God is the mystery of divine love. This love is a self-giving, creative, responsive love, characterized in the life, death and resurrection of Jesus Christ, in whom Christians believe God the creator was incarnate. Here is the focus of the relation between love and justice which is central to the Old Testament narrative and the history of the Jews. The kenosis of God, expressed in vulnerability and solidarity with the oppressed, is the essence of the divine love. God's love is his mode of action in the world, the articulation of his grace.

The action of God is understood by Christians to take place within Christian worship in Word and sacrament, and beyond the community in acts of ultimate concern. God's action, seen as a consequence of the incarnation, is envisaged as the work of the Holy Spirit, the Spirit of the crucified and risen Christ. Dying out on evil on the cross, God acts in new creation to enable human beings to participate in the consequences of reconciliation. It is this God, whose generosity creates ongoing reciprocal generosity, whom Christians seek to worship and to follow. Because creative, responsive, self-giving love is the dynamic of this cosmic action, Christian love is intended to be directed equally to strengthening and encouraging Christian community and to encouraging mutuality in individual and social dimensions in all humanity. Generosity is at the centre of discipleship.

One of the most striking aspects of the interaction of faith and culture in history is the capacity for the emergence of surprise, pleasant and unpleasant. It is possible for the most solid theological images to distort Christian discipleship, and for the Church to flourish in an imaginative way in the most unpromising of conditions. The history of human culture is one of endless subtle shifts, of constant change and interaction. In this way human development echoes that of the natural order, on a longer time-scale, within which it has evolved. The theologian, reflecting on the dialectic between faith and society, will seek to be sensitive to a changing situation, and to make suggestions. In my view the Church must continue with the exacting task of finding middle ways between exclusivism and radical pluralism. Particular strategies will vary in different situations. Christian triumphalism will not be enough, in any shape or form. Equally, accommodation of the Christian faith to any prevailing culture would not be discipleship to the God of Jesus Christ. An inclusive gospel, which has a particular shape, the shape of self-giving love, creative and responsive, and which is Evangelical, Catholic and open, continues to be in my view the central aim. It can be articulated in different styles, with different emphases in dialogue as appropriate. It remains the specific contribution which Christians bring to human interaction on the question of the human future.

The Christian understanding of God, I have suggested, will probably remain Trinitarian in shape. But it may be the sort of Trinitarian concept which has a built-in generosity and humility, which respects the mystery of God, and which does not imagine itself to have any sort of blueprint of deity. The Christian understanding of Jesus Christ will be incarnational, but will again respect the mystery. The Christian understanding of God will stress the Spirit, but will be open to dialogue with all human culture for the sake of our common human journey into the future. Understanding of catholicity and identity may be decisively widened. Worship and service are likely to remain at the centre of the passion and the challenge of faith. They will generate their own expressions in ways which we cannot imagine today.

10

A STRATEGY FOR

GENEROSITY

Conflict and consensus

Reflection on future, present and past are closely interlocked in any strategy for the Christian contribution to humanity. Without a sensitive openness to present problems it is not possible to interpret the past in relation to that present. Without appreciation of the past it is hard to gain any perspective on the dilemmas of the immediate present. Without an urgent concern for the future it is hard to engage in a serious questioning of the status quo. An excellent example of deployment of these three perspectives, not exhaustive but very stimulating, is to be seen in Hans Küng's *Christianity*. It would be highly desirable if we could lay aside internal confessional conflicts and inter-confessional rivalries in order to appreciate and take up the positive encouragement of such projects for the future. The device which Küng uses of taking the reader through the history of Christianity and illustrating paradigm shifts on a large and a small scale is effective, and hammers home the truth, if needed, that we shall not understand present and future without an intelligent appreciation of the Christian past.

It is important to do theology as a theology of human rights and of social reconstruction. An excellent example of this would be Charles Villa-Vicencio's *A Theology of Reconstruction*. But it is vital too to relate reconstruction to the centre of the gospel of the nature of God in the love of Jesus Christ. For it is this vision of God incarnate which is and will remain the driving force, constantly reappropriated, of Christian thought and action. These twin concerns may be seen as related like the law and the gospel. But law and gospel, love and justice, are integrally related in every way, and not simply in an unending dialectical pattern. Often, too, a threefold pattern may be more appropriate, exploring theology through the threefold strand of worship, service and intellectual challenge. It has been through thinking, thinking about God with all possible stringency, that Augustine, Aquinas and their successors have helped to transform faith to face the demands of cultural change. Theology which was central to the future has had to stand at the edge of the Church in the present, not outside the community but at the point of openness to development and change in human culture. Here a theology at the margins becomes an Evangelical theology, in response to Christ who chose solidarity with the marginalized rather than with the religious establishment. At the same time, it will maintain links with all Christian cultures which manifest openness and generosity, whether they be conservative, liberal or whatever.

I return to the Christian vision of God. The God of Jesus Christ does not force himself upon any of his creatures. He acts always through the Spirit of Christlikeness. He is understood in different ways at different times. But here remains, Christians believe, the force that creates the stars, and is always present to encourage love, peace and justice in a world which sometimes seems to have lost all conception of such things. We are called constantly to reimage and reimagine God. This is in large part the theologian's proper task, so that the community can focus in new ways on worship and service. In this study we have tried to reimage generosity, as a shape for the unfolding of self-giving, creative, responsive love in the contemporary world. The generosity of the resurrection of the crucified Christ is suggested as a central paradigm for the Christian life in society.

We may stretch our ability to imagine the generosity of Christ by considering concrete examples of self-giving, creative and responsive love in different situations. One obvious source of such illustration, common to Christian tradition, is the Bible itself. Christians have always believed that God uses the Bible to invite response to himself. Here we have examples of self-giving love, examples of what people have imagined to be the Word of God, but which today we may think illustrative of what is absolutely not the Word of God, and other examples somewhere between these. Obedience, Donald Mackinnon was wont to quote, is the subtlest form of temptation, and it is clear that God's love is very often a judgement on what men have thought to be the essence of obedience. It affects and judges every aspect of an action, the motive, the social, institutional, cultural, framework, the entire structure. As such it may involve severe risk for those who respond to it in love. It may be perceived as a threat precisely to the structures ordained by God, and generate anger and reaction within the Christian community itself. Moving forward may be a delicate and precarious process. We cannot expect people to have the same new insights at the same time. Love is patient.

Hans Küng sums up his programme for examining the religious situation of our time in three propositions, which are becoming well known. They are:

1. No peace among the nations without peace among the religions.
2. No peace among the religions without dialogue between the religions.
3. No dialogue between the religions without investigation of the foundation of the religions.[1]

In my view this is a highly significant programme, the importance of which will become clearer in the future. However, it obviously requires care in its application. No peace among the nations without peace among the religions. It is essential to engage in inter-religious dialogue. But it is equally important, and much less easy, to have peace between the more conservative and more progressive wings of opinion within specific religions. Otherwise we may simply have the spectacle of a small group of like-minded liberals in dialogue across the religious boundaries, facing an enormous backlash of outraged traditionalists in the major religions, creating new alienations. It requires courage, and is of vital importance, to move forward, ahead of public opinion. But it is equally important to maintain understanding and communication within specific religions, if there is to be significant interaction, and not simply the wish-fulfilment of a pressure group. Sometimes the latter is all that is possible, and may be helpful, since change takes place in haphazard ways. But it is vital to keep in view an overall strategy. Here a theology of generosity may assist us in avoiding a move from one sort of limited tribalism to another.

It is unwise to underestimate the problems in reaching agreement across the religions on basic ethical issues, as we have seen in the matter of human rights. It is equally unnecessary to despair. A good concrete example of constructive working towards ethical consensus on a specific area may be seen in the field of medical ethics, where immediate clinical necessity is sometimes the mother of invention. For example, in *Principles of Health Care Ethics*, eds Raanan Gillon and Ann Lloyd, writers from the major world religious traditions and from humanist perspectives including postmodern positions contrive to reach considerable agreement on the importance of the 'Four Principles' approach to health care ethics, centred on:

1. Beneficence (the obligation to provide benefits and balance benefits against risks).
2. Non-maleficence (the obligation to avoid the causation of harm).
3. Respect for autonomy (the obligation to respect the decision-making capacities of autonomous persons).
4. Justice (obligations of fairness in the distributions of benefits and risks).

In such a context, faith may introduce a dimension to challenge the conventional social construction of the individual case. Alastair Campbell writes (ibid. 249) that: 'Dying people are supposed to be quiet, humble, and not too assertive. Of course they are permitted to be angry, but only for a while, and only for a therapeutic end, the acceptance of the inevitable. Society seeks to put a veil of comely gloom over the features of those who have the shocking attribute of dying before their time – and many people meekly accept the assigned role.' Here the framework of transcendence may offer a catalyst of surprise and of grace. God does not have to be a local deity in order to be an effective presence at the point where it matters to human need.[2]

Christianity, it is repeated rightly, is a historical religion. Its focus is a God who has been present in history, and who accompanied humanity on its journey. Its present and its future are driven in considerable part by its past. The past is a coherent whole, not a repository for isolated bright ideas for the future. Yet it is vital, and unfortunately not common enough, to look at the past with the future very much in mind, if we are not to follow the multitudes of whom it has been justly said that they had forgotten nothing and learned nothing. Again Küng has been a pioneer. He may not have got everything right, but he invites us all to reflect for ourselves on the future of our religious past, its gifts to us for the future as well as its problems for the future. This is a particularly

236

important exercise for a theology of generosity, which seeks to integrate as well as innovate.

In this volume I have stressed the future need for an effective social theology, with mechanisms for the effective delivery of the heart of the Christian gospel to all areas of human life. I have equally stressed the need for constant reappropriation of the centre of the gospel, of the presence of God in our lives, individual and social. A theology of generosity is a theology of grace, not dominating but transforming human actuality. Generosity requires both the tradition of Christian theology, and its continuing transformation, as it has developed to meet the challenge of changed times. I want to say something about the transformation of the most internal of Christian reflections, the development of doctrine.

Christianity, Judaism and Islam go back to common roots in the religions of the Near East, and share in common much of the Old Testament narratives. The story of Abraham and his descendants, the development of their worship, legal frameworks, social customs, has been reflected on differently in the different traditions, and may in the future be a source of new religious convergence and mutual understanding. For Christianity the New Testament is the centre, with the focus on Jesus, understood increasingly as the person in whom God was incarnate, lived, died and brought life out of death. Through the Spirit the fruits of Christ's passion continue in the Church and in the whole cosmos, transforming and renewing in the midst of disaster, evil and waste.

Christians gradually came to agree on a canon of Scripture, which they increasingly regarded as a sacred text, in the manner of sacred texts in other faiths. Here was the narrative of revelation from God. Since the period of modernity many Christians have questioned this construction, and this process may yet occur in relation to the sacred texts of other world religions.

Faith gradually came to be interpreted in terms of a rule of faith, which produced conciliar decrees on the nature of God and salvation. God was to be defined as Trinity, in formulas which reached a high point at Chalcedon. Salvation was to be defined, in the West, largely in terms of substitutionary atonement. The Church was to be understood in relation to the structures of a sacred priesthood. All of these developments reflected things which were, and continue to be, of central importance to Christians. None of them could effectively claim to be directly authorized by God, but this does not diminish their importance. To preserve what is of value, and to transform what is not, remains a continuing task. Some historical Christian communities are passionate in defence of the Bible, while comparatively unconcerned about the ordained ministry, some are passionate about the doctrine of the Trinity, while less concerned for ministry and ordered worship, some focus on liturgy and are less concerned for the doctrine of God. Few Christians will be happy with the thought that all are relative and optional. Some may sympathize with Butterfield's dictum 'Hold to Christ, and for the rest be uncommitted.' Many will feel that such commitment precisely entails commitment to one or some of the other areas we have mentioned.

Troeltsch famously held that the Enlightenment rather than the Reformation was the great historical watershed. And certainly the whole approach to theological issues under the guidance of modern critical method is rather different from that of a previous era, where the biblical text was treated without historical perspective. Yet the history of theology is more important to theology than the history of medicine to medicine today. This is partly because Christians believe that reflection upon experience of God in the past may be valuable for reflection on experience of God in the future. It is also because the development of thought in the humanities still makes progress partly, though not of course entirely, by dialogue with earlier thought, e.g. in the critical reflection on Aristotle in twentieth-century philosophy. It may be precisely though historical perspective that we begin to recognize the origins of and the need for transformation in our religious structures of power, authority and influence. Part of this historical perspective will also be the unmasking of the negative sides of modernity, in its potential strengthening and sanitizing of structures of domination.

At the centre of the Christian vision stands the figure of God incarnate, tortured by the powers that be, consistently there for the vulnerable. This God is the centre, the integrating source, of theology, of ethics, of worship, life and service. This God is a Trinitarian God, in a Trinity for the understanding of which Chalcedon is the end of the beginning, an inclusive Trinity whose dynamics are fluid and remain God's mystery. This God is God in Christ, an inclusive Christology which is open to all humanity. This God is God as Spirit, creating Christlikeness within the Christian community and spreading Christlikeness as self-giving, creative, responsive love throughout the wider human community.

Reducing the negative

We have considered the task facing Christian faith of initiating dialogue on a wide range of issues, and of reinforcing this with positive examples of generosity, not least in its own internal relationships. We have looked at this project against the background of relations between religion and culture, especially in the North American context. The dialogical task is a long-term one, for people who are prepared to be patient. We have seen that it is not possible to come up with a single effective formula for managing the constant shifts in relatonship between religion and culture in particular contexts, beyond a combination of flexibility of approach and core commitment to the love of God in Jesus Christ.

It does seem, however, that the religions, and the churches in particular, have a more obviously effective role in withdrawing support from oppressive practices which only retain a cloak of public respectability through some supposed sacred sanction. A striking example is documented in Harry Potter's study, *Hanging in Judgement*, in which he shows that the Church of England's support for the practice prolonged its continuation, and that the withdrawal of that support led quickly to abolition. As he says in his introduction:

> The following chapters trace the story of hanging's long heyday, and sudden eclipse, giving special attention to the role of the churches and in particular the Church of England. Their central importance is explained by the fact that hanging was an institution which demanded, and even craved for, religious sanction. The Church by Law Established provided the intellectual and theological justification for hanging, and suggested the means by which those aspects of it which gave rise to most public outcry could be amended and thus hanging be preserved. Judicial killing was sanctioned by bishops, and its execution presided over by chaplains. Had the Church denounced it, it would have withered and died, as indeed it did quickly and without hope of resuscitation in the 1960s. Only in the 1950s, long after all other progressive religious and secular opinion

239

had ranged itself against capital punishment, did the Church of England take a firm stand in favour of abolition. Of the other arguments that sustained it – deterrence, and retribution – neither could prevail when the religious imprimatur had gone. For at least a hundred years that imprimatur preserved and sanctified the judicial taking of life. Then suddenly and totally the sanction was withdrawn, and what had been done in God's name became unconscionable.

Capital punishment is a particularly interesting topic for Christian ethics, because it raises acutely the role of sources and norms, the Bible, tradition and revelation. In fairness to the Church of England, if we ask for example what the Church of Scotland's position is, it appears that the last time it was discussed, in 1956, at the height of church membership in this century, the report presented for debate was not clearly against capital punishment. Is that then the official position? Perhaps not, because it did not go down under the Barrier Act to the presbyteries and then come back to be approved by a two thirds majority. We might ask what the Church's position on witches is? Perhaps the last recorded vote was in favour of drowning them – I don't know. What does the Bible say? It seems on any straightforward reading to be decisively in favour of capital punishment. Which is after all extremely popular today in the southern states of America, the so-called Bible Belt. Perhaps a resurgence of the Christian right will bring it back in Europe.[3]

It appears that even where the churches may not positively influence society in a general way, they can undo the damage caused by previous support for oppressive practice by supporting specific issues. This point is made from a different angle in Walter Wink, *Engaging the Powers*, e.g. 48–9:

Perhaps we can now see the gospel for what it has always been: the most powerful antidote for domination the world has ever seen. Only against a backdrop so vast do we see the world-historic significance of the liberation struggles that have come to fruition especially these past two hundred years:

- the rise and spread of democracy as a check on centralized power wielded only by a few;

- abolition of slavery;
- attempts to develop alternative economic systems;
- the women's movement;
- the non-violent movement;
- the civil rights movement;
- the human rights movement;
- the ecology movement;
- liberation theology;
- the gay rights movement (rejecting yet another way sexuality is used to disempower people and deprive them of choice).

These movements do not simply represent academic arguments for generosity. They are, as it were, areas where there are narratives of generous action, paradigms of generosity. And the list is far from exhaustive. We may think, for example, of those who have sheltered and assisted fugitives from oppression through the ages, often at the risk and even the cost of their own lives, as classic examples of generous practice. By contrast, societies which have turned away refugees fleeing from persecution can be seen as in this respect classic examples of lack of generosity.

Religion, unfortunately, has often in the past been associated with violence. Generosity is never oppressive or exploitative. Where do we find the roots of the connection between violence and religion? A classic study is Rene Girard and Ann Lloyd's *Violence and the Sacred*, one of a series of books on violence. In this book Girard begins from the study of sacrifice, to consider the origins of all myth and ritual. He develops a theory of the nature of primitive religion. To try to summarize Girard in a sentence: conflicts have arisen in humanity since the beginning, and the contestants have learned to resolve the conflicts, not by killing each other, but by killing a third party, a victim, onto whom the problem is loaded, in order to drive out the cause of dissension from the community. He says that 'There is a unity that underlies not only all mythologies and rituals but the whole of human culture, and this unity of unities depends on a single mechanism, continually functioning because perpetually misunderstood – the mechanism that assures the community's spontaneous and unanimous opposition to the surrogate victim' (299). The act which restores unity is an act of what he calls generative violence. He draws the bleak conclusion that 'In the evolution from ritual to secular institutions men gradually draw away from violence and eventually lose it, but an actual break with violence never takes place. That is why violence can always stage a stunning, catastrophic comeback' (307).

Girard's work is applied directly to biblical material in James G. Williams' book, *The Bible, Violence and the Sacred: Liberation from the Myth of Sanctioned Violence*, which includes useful summaries of Girard. He sees the Bible, especially the Old Testament, as a tale of blood and guts and God, with a redemptive line running through great darkness. He states that

> What I wish to do is to explore this revelation, this uncovering of the victimization process and the favoring of the innocent victim that the biblical heritage ascribes to the God who sides with victims. This story, the narration of a struggle against mimetic desire and for a good mimesis, God's will for nonviolent human community, will lead us through the law and the prophets to the Gospels, where we find a radical articulation of the revelation in the story of the innocent Victim. (30)

Conflict comes from a fundamental human reciprocity, people imitating one another – the mimetic, being rivals, creating conflict.

Williams discusses postmodern treatment of religion and offers here an interesting critique of Derrida on violence and metaphysics.

> Derrida seems able only to repeat in endless variations the idea of the trace, of difference, of substitution; everything for him is finally a mental operation, a substitutionary game that people play, and the worst offender is Christianity and its theology of the logos as divine presence. ... However, he in effect eliminates the oppression of Israel and its innocence. Neither the reality of historical events and circumstances nor the reality of the god of victims can have meaning except as a meaning that is continually erased or effaced. With this mode of thought one always has one's cake and eats it. (116)

Williams' narrative may remind us too that we tend to regard reciprocity, mutuality, relationship as absolutely good – we see that this too can have a profoundly negative side. We have to maximize the good and minimize the bad. We must also be careful about drawing anti-Semitic conclusions from these studies. There is no evidence that the people of Israel were any more violent than their contemporaries, and we have to recall that probably more people have been murdered in our century than in all previous world history.

Into this tale of mayhem comes Jesus as the innocent victim, the successor of innocent victims in Israel. The agent of liberation must be God and must be man. 'Very God of very God and very man of very man: that is the truth of the innocent victim that can heal us' (240). How is this truth to be expressed, Williams asks, in contemporary American society? He encourages us to notice the silent victims, to 'stand apart from the inevitable popular mythicizing of the social order, and to remember the city set on a hill, the ideal of community of those who live out of the passion' (258).

God is the God of the biblical narratives, against the biblical narratives and again for them. We do not need the god of violence, but we do need the God of forgiveness and reconciliation. We do not need the god of any sort of religion, but we do need the God of compassion. God is the God of the tradition and the Creeds, the God of incarnation and Trinity. We do not need the god of christological triumphalism. We do not need the god of destructive reciprocity. We do need the God who lead us into participation in the ultimate reality of self-giving, creative and responsive love.

Christian agonistic liberalism – after Berlin

Theologians do theology best. They are neither philosophers nor sociologists nor political theorists. They are also concerned, however, to communicate with those who may not share their basic theological beliefs. My own proposal for a theology of generosity is centrally directed to committed dialogue concerning the shape of the human future. It is of the essence that people should seek mutuality in intellectual and social communities.

I have stressed in this study the dangers of insularity among the religions and especially in the development of Christian theology. In recent times I have noted particularly the use of the work of Lindbeck and MacIntyre in forming a post-liberal sentiment, which can encourage defensive reactions in the churches. It should be said, however, that both of these writers can be read in ways which may encourage dialogue, and they cannot be held responsible for what others have made of their work. A good example of a more Catholic reading of Lindbeck is David Kelsey's essay 'Church Discourse and Public Realm', in *Theology and Dialogue* (ed. Bruce Marshall), and of MacIntyre in his own response to his critics in *After MacIntyre*, (eds J. Horton and S. Mendus). The theological discussion of the fruits of Enlightenment for theology and culture is paralleled in political theory in such volumes as *Liberals and Communitarians* (Mulhall and Swift, 1992).

MacIntyre is himself an excellent illustration of our earlier insistence on the importance of reflection on the past for the understanding of the present, and of the difficulties with which this is necessarily fraught. It seems to me for example that his brilliant *Three Rival Versions of Moral Enquiry* gives a degree of canonicity to Aquinas, the ninth edition of *Encyclopaedia Britannica* and Nietzsche which can be radically misleading. An interpretation of intellectual history centred on, say, Euripides, Origen, Duns Scotus and Goethe might produce a very different view of most of the central issues.[4]

Discussion about the commensurability of values has always been central to Christian faith, for which 'the foolishness of the cross' has always been a profound motif. I have argued that Christology could in fact create mutuality, in linking Christology to human rights. Christians believe that on the cross God does not simply illustrate the value of suffering solidarity but actually creates the reality of a new dimension of divine compassionate presence in the cosmos. Truth is there, not in logos but in pathos, in participation in the human condition. I have commended Richard Bernstein's concept of 'engaged fallibilistic pluralism' as a way of understanding the texture of debate about ultimate values.

In seeking to develop further a rationale for dialogical engagement I find much help in the writings of Sir Isaiah Berlin and reflection on these. As will emerge, Berlin seems to me to be especially helpful today in the light of the ever proliferating American discussion in this area.[5] Over many years Berlin has explored the advantages and disadvantages of liberal and communitarian arguments in relation to values, and has produced assessments which seem to me to be much better than anything else available. This may be in part because he is able to stand further back from the raw data of observation which appear to dominate much socio-political analysis, especially in North American writing. I sense that he sees, too, that no particular geographical area or historical period has a monopoly of wisdom on the subject, or is constitutive of future patterns at other times and in other places.

Theology has long engaged in dialogue with philosophy, and more recently with all the human sciences. Since the days of Troeltsch and Max Weber there has been intense dialogue with social science, and we have just been looking at the American dialogue with sociology, considering the role of theology in relation to the shape of community, Christian and civic. It would not be surprising then if illumination on theological assessment of the nature of conflicting communal values were to come from engagement with modern political theory. Isaiah Berlin, though he understands himself as Jewish, has never taken a direct professional interest in theology or in indeed in religion. Yet his view of society does allow a potential role to transcendence. I should like to explore this further.

In the introduction to *Four Essays on Liberty*, Berlin notes that 'The notion that there must exist final objective answers to normative questions, truths that can be demonstrated or objectively intuited . . . seems to me invalid, and at times to have led (and still does lead) to absurdities in theory and barbarous consequences in practice' (lvi). He goes on to observe that 'Temperaments differ, and too much enthusiasm for common norms can lead to intolerance and disregard for the inner life of man' (lviii).

Alternative views are to be found in the history of political thought. In an essay on political ideas in the twentieth century Berlin sees that 'For the first time it was now conceived that the most effective way of dealing with questions, was not by employing the tools of reason, still less those of the more mysterious capacities called insight and intuition, but by obliterating the questions themselves' (23). His comment is that 'We must submit to authority not because it is infallible, but only for strictly and openly utilitarian reasons, as a necessary expedient. Since no solution can be guaranteed against error, no disposition is final' (40).

Berlin is deeply suspicious of historical inevitability, and in an essay on that subject he says: 'Teleology is a form of faith capable of neither confirmation nor refutation by any kind of experience; the notions of evidence, proof, probability and so on are wholly inapplicable to it' (55).

These sentiments are developed classically in 'Two Concepts of Liberty'. For Berlin, negative and positive freedom (freedom from coercion and freedom to be one's own master) have both advantages and disadvantages, but accounts of positive freedom are capable of greater abuse.

> The knowledge that it is not merely in practice but in principle impossible to reach clear cut and certain answers – even in an ideal world of wholly good and rational men and wholly clear ideas – may madden those who seek for final solutions and single, all-embracing systems, guaranteed to be eternal. Nevertheless, it is a conclusion that cannot be escaped by those who, with Kant, have learned the truth that out of the crooked timber of humanity no straight thing was ever made. (170)

> Pluralism, with the measure of 'negative' liberty that it entails, seems to me a truer and more humane ideal than the goals of those who seek in the great, disciplined, authoritarian structures the ideal of 'positive' self-mastery by classes, or peoples, or the whole of mankind. It is truer, because it does, at least, recognize the fact that human goals are many, not all of them commensurable, and in perpetual rivalry with one another. (171)

Not surprisingly, Berlin has a high regard for John Stuart Mill, in discussion of whom he articulates his own philosophy. In writing on 'John Stuart Mill and the Ends of Life', he comments on Mill that 'Like Acton after him, he regarded liberty and religious toleration as the indispensable protection of all true religion, and the distinction made by the Church between spiritual and temporal realms as one of the great achievements of Christianity, inasmuch as it had made possible freedom of opinion' (204).

Berlin's mature reflections on liberalism and pluralism are beautifully illustrated in *Conversations with Isaiah Berlin* by Ramin Jahanbegloo. Only a few lines can be quoted here. 'The idea that there can be two sides to a question, that there may be two or more incompatible answers, any one of which could be accepted by honest, rational men – that is a very recent notion' (43). 'I believe in liberalism and pluralism, but they are not logically connected' (44). 'Schumpeter rightly says that people who believe that ideals have to be absolute, are idolatrous barbarians' (107). 'I myself have no sense of a reality above and beyond the life I know. I am not religious, but I place high value upon the religious experience of believers' (110). 'RB: But you don't deny human rights? IB: No, I deny a priori lists of rights. I believe passionately in human rights. This follows from a great deal else that we all accept, but it is not demonstrable a priori' (114). 'In a liberal society of a pluralist kind, there is no avoiding compromises; they are bound to be made: the very worst can be avoided by trade-offs. So much for this, so much for that. All fanatical belief in a final solution, no matter how reached, cannot but lead to suffering, misery, blood, terrible oppression.' (143) 'The bird may think that it would fly more freely in a vacuum: but it would not – it would fall. There is no society without some authority: and this limits liberty.' (150)

The power of Berlin's philosophy has been well brought out recently in John Gray's excellent *Isaiah Berlin*.

> The central claim of this book is that all of Berlin's work is ani-mated by a single idea of enormous subversive force. This is the idea, which I call value – pluralism. . . . I call the political out-look which this inspires in Berlin's work agonistic liberalism . . . By contrast with the dominant liberalisms of our time . . . Berlin's is a stoical and tragic liberalism of unavoidable conflict and irreparable loss among inherently rivalrous values. (1)

The reader may perhaps feel that there is an inherent problem in Gray's scheme: Berlin might say that even his single idea is suspect: in some contexts there may be some value in unitary systems, in others not. But nevertheless Gray's work is highly relevant to my purpose.

Berlin considers the work of Alistair MacIntyre and his analysis of Aristotle and Aquinas. 'Berlin rejects this foundational Western commitment . . . Human goods are not only often uncombinable; they are sometimes incommensurable. This is Berlin's celebrated doctrine of value pluralism. It has application at three levels' (43). Gray's thesis is that 'Berlin's political thought offers the liberal intellectual tradition a new lease of life.' The idea of freedom is central to Berlin. He cautions against 'positive' conceptions of freedom, in favour of a negative account of freedom 'in which it is conceived as the absence of constraints imposed by others' (5).

Berlin's agonistic liberalism – his liberalism of conflict among inherently rivalrous goods – grounds itself on the radical choices we must make among incommensurables, not upon rational choice. Further, it denies that the structure of liberties appropriate to a liberal society can be derived from any theory, or stated in any system of principles, since the choice among conflicting liberties is often a choice among incommensurables (8-9). (The writings of Joseph Raz are comparable in some respects.)

Negative freedom is not unimpeded pursuit of one's desires, in the style of Bentham, but 'It is rather choice among alternatives or options that is unimpeded by others' (15).
'Positive freedom ... degenerates into the fantasy of ethical rationalism, which is fatal to choice' (23). Rather 'there can be no overarching principle of liberty, and no fixed structure of fundamental rights or set of basic liberties, fixed and determinate in their content and harmonious or dovetailing in their scope' (25). 'Berlin's liberalism is significant in that its anti-perfectionism is not grounded in any Kantian idea of the priority of the right over the good of the sort that is found in the work of Rawls and Dworkin' (35).

Berlin's pluralism distinguishes his liberalism from that of John Stuart Mill. According to Berlin there are universal, or nearly universal categories of moral thought, which are not vulnerable to theoretical displacement, and which also generate incommensurabilities.

This position has consequences for Berlin's views of history and nationalism. Taking up a pluralist anthropology, Berlin's liberalism is not just Humean. There is no convergence on a single universal civilization. The human essence – if there is such a thing – is best expressed in cultural difference, in the propensity to fashion diverse forms of life with their divergent conceptions of flourishing (95). Nationalism has a limited proper role. There is a need for a common national culture. The self is best understood as the situated or embedded self (102). But the idea of membership of a single moral community is dangerous. Pluralism and conflict are integral to our identities. There is a criticism of Enlightenment uniformities in Berlin, in some respects (110). For Berlin personally, Zionism has a coherence with his liberal version of particularism. Assimilation does not guarantee escape from persecution. He is also much interested in Romanticism and the

Counter-Enlightenment – de Maistre, Hamann and Herder – as an instructive foil to Enlightenment.

Berlin's agonistic liberalism stresses liberty and value pluralism. 'All the dominant liberalisms of our time . . . have a conception of rational choice at their heart which Berlin's value-pluralism subverts' (145). Berlin quotes Joseph Schumpeter: 'To realize the relative validity of one's convictions and yet to stand for them unflinchingly, is what distinguishes a civilized man from a barbarian' (149). 'The choosing self in Berlin is never . . . an unencumbered or abstract self; it is a self whose identity is constituted by particular allegiances, cultural traditions and communal memberships, however complex and plural' (158).

'Berlin's voice is like the voice of Job, in refusing with a passion the pretence that there is peace when our lives abound in deep conflicts and hard choices. It is in its character as an anti-theodicy, and in its drawing out the implications for moral and political life of the incoherence of the very idea of perfection, that the unique and permanent achievement of Berlin's thought is to be found.'(168).

It might be thought that our long discussion of Berlin is about pluralism and morality rather than generosity. My argument is that conceptions of pluralist, liberal and multicultural values and dialogues are at the heart of any effective framework of generosity, and must be deployed in the delivery of generosity at the point of need.

The whole issue of the relationship between pluralism and moral values has been explored thoroughly again recently by John Kekes in his *The Morality of Pluralism*, in which he acknowledges the influence of Berlin. Is our morality disintegrating? Does the accelerated change in attitudes today lead only to dialogues of the deaf? For Kekes, change is not necessarily disintegration. Pluralism is a recent but important moral theory.

Kekes' view of pluralism involves six theses concerning: the pity and conditionality of values, the unavoidability of conflicts, an approach to reasonable conflict resolution, an assessment of the possibilities of life, a need for limits and the prospects for moral progress. The theses are interdependent and mutually reinforcing. Values include primary and secondary values, moral and non-moral values, overriding and conditional values. Pluralism can be discussed in relation to relativism. Pluralists believe that some conflicting values can be settled reasonably; complete relativists don't. Conflict of values is unavoidable. But the incompatibility and incommensurability of values can be discussed. Versions of monism can be identified. He makes the important point that often basic values may remain the same, e.g. about goodness, compassion, etc., even though views about specific instances, e.g. burning witches, may change.

It is possible and desirable to construct models to examine the nature of reasonable conflict resolution, to consider a pluralistic approach to conflict resolution, conventions and traditions, commitments and conceptions of a good life, the prospects for conflict resolution, concepts of integrity and reasonable commitment. It is necessary to stimulate moral imagination, to find means of increasing freedom. There is equally a need for limits. We must explore the relation between moral imagination and deep conventions. Kekes considers life as a primary value, in the context of the morality of live burial, among the Dinkas, and the claims of relativism and monism.

This leads to a reassessment of the prospects of moral progress, and the nature of shame and the forms of shame. Some moral implications of pluralism include there being some limits even to morality, reasonable immorality, pluralism beyond morality and a plea against the overridingness of morality. He considers personal implications of pluralism: innocence lost and regained, pre-reflective and reflective innocence. There are also political implications of pluralism – the conflict with liberalism, a neutrality thesis and beyond neutrality the politics of pluralism.

The effect on American society of pluralism and plural values has been well analysed by Linell E. Cady in her *Religion, Theology and American Public Life*. Reflecting on religion theology and the public realm, she offers a critique of Neuhaus, of Bellah's notion of civil religion and Marty's of public religion. What do public and private mean? For the Greeks, public did not include slaves and others. What sort of public? The Enlightenment brought an important awarenes of private selves. Today there is a sense of cultural crisis.

This leads to discussion, through Tracy, of the relation of theology to public argumentation, and to theology and jurisprudence, with reference to Gadamer and Dworkin. There are three primary forms of judicial interpretation – conventionalism, naturalism, to be called extensionalism, and instrumentalism. Extensionalism affirms continuity with a tradition.

Cady moves toward the reconfiguration of the public realm: the cultivation of a common life. There is an urgent need to overcome the sharp separation between the public and the private, as in Dworkin. She finds a focus in the symbol of God and monotheism. God relates to public life as creator, sustainer and redeemer. (There is a half-page only on Christology – one might add on Christology and human rights.) How is theology to deal with professional boundaries? There are dangers in a culture of professionalism, as in Lindbeck. The goal is to move towards the transformation of the public realm. Here Nussbaum on the fragility of goodness is helpful.

Methodological generosity

It seems to me that development of Berlin's ideas may shed light on the three issues we have been considering of the understanding of human rights across religious cultures, the debate between theorists concerning the legitimation of liberal values, and the basic theological issue of oppositions between religious doctrines. First, however, I want to take note of some further recent significant work in this area. (See the notes for further references to the voluminous literature.)

The issue of conflicting views on human rights has been usefully discussed by David Little in his volume on *Human Rights and the Conflict of Culture*, examining Western and Islamic perspectives on religious liberty. The Islamic/Christian dialogue seems to me to provide a crucial opportunity for Christian theologians to set an example of generosity, in interpreting their sacred text, the Bible, in terms of inclusiveness rather than exclusiveness in relation to other religions.

Concerning the debate about the hegemony of liberal values, and especially Western liberal values, there is an excellent clear discussion in the volume edited by Nancy Rosenblum, *Liberalism and the Moral Life–Western and Islamic Perspectives on Religious Liberty*. Seyla Benhabib compares liberal dialogue with a critical theory of discursive legitimation, and Charles Taylor, in a chapter on 'Cross Purposes', considers that the liberal/communitarian dialogue is often misconceived. Liberal, as he says, has often become simply a negative label. Relevant too is the collection by G. Outka and J. P. Reeder on *Prospects for a Common Morality*, in which

R. M. Adams comments, 'From the particular viewpoint of Christianity there is something questionable about excessive nostalgia for a religiously homogeneous society' (109). I agree with this, and with J. Raz's comment (*Multiculturalism – a Liberal Perspective*) that multiculturalism is with us to stay.

In the context of human rights, Samuel Fleischacker in *The Ethics of Culture* argues for a constructivist approach to human rights. 'It is this humanistic multiculture that I think has more to offer than the freedom story alone. We should not therefore be too easily stampeded into lamenting the absence of a single moral standard in modern society'. P. J. Ross, in his *Deprivatising Morality*, suggests that a breakdown in adherence to moral standards presupposes that there is a foundation for establishing any such standards. The point about the thesis of moral crisis or a-moral crisis is precisely that there is no such foundation, at least in modern society. Perhaps we should not exaggerate the stabilities of a golden past. There has always been conflict in society, yet miraculously there have always been prophets to pinpoint the problem and at least hint at resolutions. As Simone Weil said in her famous essay on 'The Iliad as a Poem of Force', in this bleak landscape 'only Patroklos knew how to be sweet to everybody', and she judged that 'Nothing the peoples of Europe have produced is worth the first known poem that appeared among them' (247).

In the construction of doctrinal theology too there are likely to be conflicts as the main meta-narratives clash. It may often be that the best way forward includes a pluralism which is not relativism, which holds in tension different incommensurable theories, which refuses to cut the Gordian knot by defining a final solution, but which respects the mystery as located within the dynamic interstices of discourse.[6] Thus different interpretations are *homoousios* with each other, to use the Chalcedonian model, in that they point in different ways to the same basic reality of God. But they are also *homoiousios*, in that they illuminate by respecting the different inclusive insights of different Christians. This would be in accord with Berlin's agonistic liberalism – though he himself sees Christianity as always historically offering the monochrome solution, even when in dialogue with a particular philosopher, such as Aristotle or Plato. I like a metaphor used by Michael Dummett, in an essay on the intelligibility of eucharistic doctrine. He suggests that 'Theology attempts to copy in words the thought content of religion . . . It thus constitutes crystallization, not interpretation' (Abraham and Holtzer, 231). To expand upon this rather freely, these crystals may take very different shapes in different environments, and may illuminate quite unexpected facets of reality, yet still reflect the basic reality from which they are distilled – theology as crystallography.

Agonistic pluralism may provide for doctrine a *via media* between the Scylla of foundationalism and the Charybdis of relativism. Let me illustrate with a couple of apparently diametrically opposed viewpoints on doctrinal difference from John Macquarrie and Rowan Williams (both from *The Making and Remaking of Christian Doctrine*, eds S. Coakley and D. Pailin). First Macquarrie:

> Christian faith has within itself a dynamic which is always in search of new and more adequate means of expression – not only theological but also moral, social, liturgical and so on. I do not think that there is any major difference between what Wiles affirms about Jesus Christ or what Robinson affirms or what I would want to affirm myself. If I want to retain the ancient credal formulae, it is to emphasize the continuity with the Christian community. (173)

Now Williams:

> If Jesus is finally illustrative of truths about God which are in principle independent of this particular life and death, doctrine will be above all the process of transmitting these truths. If Jesus is constitutive for Christian language about God and for the present reality of the believer's relation to God, in such a way that what is said, done and suffered is strictly unintelligible without continuing reference to Jesus in a more than historically explicatory way, doctrine will be an attempt to do justice to the way in which the narrative and the continuing presence (or presence in absence, if you want to nuance it further) of Jesus is actively held to shape present horizons, in judgement and in grace. (260)

On an agonistic liberal account, it would be recognized that these affirmations are indeed incommensurable, and that no Hegelian resolution was appropriate. Yet they could be understood to point to the cluster of affirmations which the reality of God creates for us in the mystery of his grace. Signs and examples can be understood as efficient signs, so that illustrations become more than 'mere' illustrations. Yet this whole complex is to be understood not in the construction of a master narrative but in the process of crystallization of the thought content of faith in the varieties of theology.

Berlin's views on freedom and liberty lead me to question further the kind of relationship between theology and ethics adumbrated in his three recent volumes by Alistair MacIntyre and echoed in much of the writing of Stanley Hauerwas. MacIntyre's project, as Horton and Mendus have pointed out in their excellent *After MacIntyre*, which we shall consider here, displays much pessimism about modernity. He stresses, rightly, that concepts and beliefs have to be studied historically and contextually. Modernity has produced interminable disagreements, and a basic flaw is its rejection of teleology. He stresses the importance of tradition and wishes to bring back Aristotle's theory of the good. He is in my view right to be suspicious of much in modernity. But we have stressed earlier that the abuse does not take away the proper use, and that too much cynicism may lead to fascism, as notably in the conservative critique of the Weimar Republic. He allows that rational argument is possible between traditions. It is hard to be sure whether he is happy to allow liberalism as a genuine tradition among others, or whether Thomism is the normative tradition. Charles Taylor in the same volume agrees that in modern thought it becomes increasingly problematic that one can derive ought from is, and that the powerlessness of fallen reason may indeed be a Protestant legacy, influencing Descartes. As the universalists, such as Rawls and Dworkin, debate with the communitarians, such as Waltzer and Sandel, on the nature of justice in society, the question arises sharply: what kind of society?

Janet Coleman sees liberal principles as compatible with Thomism only up to a point, since MacIntyre's Thomism remains intelligible only to a closed tradition of practitioners. We might add that the view here of MacIntyre and his critics could be held in creative tension in an agonistic liberalism, which would of course subvert the claim to absolute authority of MacIntye's Thomism, and use it only as a model among others. In this volume R. Wolker provides a useful critique of MacIntyre's picture of the Enlightenment, especially in Scotland where the academic tradition was anything but homogeneous. Wolker stresses against MacIntyre the importance of toleration in the Enlightenment. 'The moral chaos of the modern world springs not from the failure of the Enlightenment Project but from its neglect and abandonment' (126). MacIntyre's view that communities constitute the self comes in for critical scrutiny, as does his fondnesss for dichotomies and dialectics. Mulhall emphasizes that liberalism is also a genuine tradition, with a capacity for creative diversity. MacIntyre replies that liberalism is only a set of agreements to disagree, and therefore inadequate. Again, it seems to me that Berlin's reading of liberalism is much more potentially dynamic.

MacIntyre's project is eloquently developed in *Three Rival Versions of Moral Enquiry*, covering Enlightenment reason, postmodernity and relativity, and Thomism. Despite valid criticisms, in thinking of the future relationship of the gospel to human culture, there is no doubt that MacIntyre's project is a stimulating and challenging force.

We are concerned in effect with Evangelism, with the Christian contribution to communicative action in culture and society in the modern world. Here the debates of political theorists continue to be suggestive, in exploring the communication of the essential, unchanging gospel in a fast-changing world, through the vehicle of the Church as the location of Word and sacrament, of the covenanted presence of God. How is it possible to preserve Christian integrity and be faithful to incarnation in cultural change? How are we to do justice to Christian concern for the dignity of the individual and the call to mutuality as the essence of discipleship? Here I find Stephen Mulhall and Adam Swift's *Liberals and Communitarians* helpful in reminding us of the dimensions of community. They examine recent critiques of liberal and communitarian theories in the work of Sandel, MacIntyre, Taylor and Waltzer, defining their use of terms, of person, individualism, universalism, subjectivism and objectivism, anti-perfectionalism and neutrality. They consider Rawls' responses to his critics and his changing views, and the case for and against political liberalism. They look at liberalism, politics and perfection in Rorty and Raz, and conclude that liberalism has in Raz the resources to accommodate the communitarian critique.

A religion of incarnation is forced to pay attention to secular theories of social interaction and of the common good, for it is concerned with the salvation of all humanity, and with dialogue in the public square. What I hope to have shown in this section is that the rhetoric of monochrome ideologies will always break down when it comes to the illumination of specific details of concepts and issues. There is no master narrative, either humanly created or divinely given. There is no historical inevitability, and as Berlin constantly reminds us, no coercive theory worth dying for, or more likely, killing others for. There is not even a Christian theory of everything. That sort of infallibility, whether enshrined in *magisterium* or sacred script, is not the certainty of faith. The last temptation is the greatest treason. Christians believe that it is only in the vulnerability of God in cross and resurrection that we are enabled, not to possess the tree of knowledge, but to participate in the divine mystery of the life of God. In inter-faith dialogue and in discussion of human rights, this is communicated as the authority of self-giving, creative and responsive love. As love it is always opposed to exploitation, of individuals or social groups. It has a priority for the poor and the marginalized. It is responsive, listening to learn from the stranger as well as to give.

Because God loves in vulnerability he does not seek to dominate or coerce. This is the reality at the heart of the universe, which theology seeks to reflect upon, though not to reflect in any sort of mirror image. Karl Barth was right to emphasize the transcendence of God over against human institutions and systems of thought. The presence of God is a mystery even in its nearness in Word and sacrament. God's presence is not tied to any of our interpretations of Word and sacrament. Therefore our theologies always remain human theologies, as our ethics and search for justice remain human ethics and a human search for justice, and we are not given any architectonic key from above. Here unfortunately Barth's own model of revelation was itself too much of an architectonic principle, which could become a means of excluding all perspectives but his own. But we are invited to think on a human level as precisely as we can about the mystery of faith, the experience of participation in the presence of God.

To this state of affairs corresponds in my view Berlin's insight that the massive monist philosophical systems from Plato to Hegel are fatally flawed, even though an immense amount has been learned from the process of their development. There is no theory of everything. For Berlin there is no sense of divine presence, though equally the search for and respect for values of transcendence is basic to humanity and civilization. For Christians the gospel is the promise of the mystery of the presence of the divine love in the vulnerability of Jesus Christ. This is not a key in the world of human keys to knowledge, for it is not a system but an invitation to participate in vulnerability. In this sense it is compatible in my view with Berlin's insight into true freedom. God is the one who loves in vulnerable freedom. At the same time, a theology of agonistic liberalism offers the possibility of a human theology for human beings, because it denies the hubris of assertion of a Christological key to all things, which has been shown often to be a form of domination and of idolatry.

This seems to me to be the direction in which reflection on the vulnerability of the incarnate God in the context of a public theology for Church and society is likely to take us. I find confirmation of this in a different context in William Placher's recent and excellent *Narratives of a Vulnerable God*.

> Many who are anxiously fighting rearguard actions to preserve power and privilege and delay justice and equality adopt the slogans of 'Biblical Christianity' or claim to speak in the name of Jesus . . . Little wonder that many women, to say nothing of gays and lesbians, hear appeals to the Bible or to christological doctrines as instruments of their oppression, (xiv) . . . God is the one who loves in freedom, and in that free love God is vulnerable, willing to risk suffering (xv).

Placher affirms that 'Vulnerability . . . is a perfection of loving freedom' (19) and relates this to God as Trinity, with reference to Richard of St Victor (67f). He considers the vulnerability of biblical narratives. 'Why is this scripture so unclear?' Ludwig Wittgenstein once asked (*Culture and Value*, ed. G. H. Wright, 32e) (90). 'Only if we refuse to let any single narrative overpower the diversity of these texts can we authentically encounter the vulnerable one who turned away from misuse of power . . . '(104). In reflecting on 'The Savior and the Vulnerable' he notes, as we have done, the themes of Girard. Placher too underlines the importance of holding different views in constructive tension. 'There can be honest disagreement in religious dialogue' (122).

Discipleship means risking vulnerability. In a chapter on 'Christian Faith in Academy and Society' he notes that 'problems arise only when a Christian voice tries to dominate (165). How then is the Church to relate to the academy? Bellah saw dangers of individualism and decline of sense of the common good. But there is a danger of dilution, addressed by Hauerwas, in his concern for Church as Church. We need a practice of vulnerability (178), which goes beyond traditional liberalism – this is spelled out in a good discussion of Rawls (180–1).

I agree with much of this, except that I think Hauerwas' model of Church avoids individualism only to fall into corporatism, where the market brand of the denomination resembles the modern multinational corporation in its stress on company culture and corporate image. A more inclusive, less exclusive, vulnerable and responsive tradition in the denominations might correspond more closely to the New Testament call to unity, not indeed to monochrome unity but to constructive diversity.[7]

Cross, resurrection and human rights

How does God point to the universal significance of kenotic love in all areas of human society? I suggest that he does this through the particularity of identification with the oppressed on the cross. Here we may be single-minded but not narrow-minded. Christ crucified is Christ consummator, transformative of all layers of culture.

How does this relate to traditional Christology and doctrine? Traditional approaches clarify, but need to be embedded in the culture of past, remote and near, and present. Let's look at a recent reappraisal of the traditional problematic of classical systematic Christology (eds R. Feenstra and A. Platinga). In the collection, *Trinity, Incarnation and Atonement* (ed. T.V. Morris) the editor examines the metaphysics of God incarnate (110ff). He regards as definitive the Chalcedonian two-natures doctrine, and safeguards the unity of Christ with a view of two minds in Christ.

R.J. Feenstra, in the chapter, 'Reconsidering Kenotic Christology' (128f), proceeds somewhat as Rahner, but his picture is more static. There is little sense of self-giving, responsive love, or of the reality of the tension between cross and resurrection. It is a little like an old fashioned X-ray of the skeletal structure alone, compared with modern NMR scans and the like. He makes a crucial distinction between incarnation and kenosis. The incarnation is simply the Son's taking on human nature. The kenosis only continues through the period of Christ's being human: his incarnation continues even when his kenosis ceases. This answers some questions, but leaves other layers of the problem unresolved. This sort of Christology can be done with no impact on society. Being becomes. The relation to love and justice needs to be filled in as substantive content of formal structure. This is rather like the mathematics of Christology. We need also the sociology, the political, economic and other dimensions, and so on.

We are led back to the cross and human rights. The basic reality is not the reality of being, nor even of Word, but of real presence in creation and reconciliation in our world. The Spirit of Christlikeness in darkness acts as Trinitarian participation into which we are drawn, not by mathematics but by the shared experience of grace. It may be thought, however, that there is an urgent need to analyse further the historical grounds of our ecclesial failures, and to challenge the plausibility criteria of a world often alienated from itself.

If we ask ourselves why the sort of radical interpretation of Christology and human rights expounded by Moltmann and Sobrino did not come to the fore in earlier sections of the tradition, part of the answer will presumably be that medieval society was in important respects a closed and totalitarian society, in which freedom of expression for social critique was almost non-existent. Romantic enthusiasm for the Middle Ages and for the Reformation churches should not blind us to what we owe to the modern democratic process. Even in the nineteenth century, dissent from the status quo often had painful social consequences. Recent freedoms are easily taken for granted.

This does not make the christological tradition irrelevant. On the contrary, the social dimensions of Christology need to be spelled out, and then supplemented by the spiritual dimensions, not least in the areas of prayer, liturgy and literature. The richness of the tradition is essential to encourage and sustain devotion. To be emancipated from discrimination is not only to be given rights but to be given responsibilities, to be empowered to share in the fullness of the devotional life of the Christian community.

Christology, one might consider, reflects the paradox that the person of Jesus Christ is at the heart of the Christian understanding of God as creator and sustainer as well as reconciler of the cosmos. The particularity of the man Jesus is itself a clue to transcending particularity in mutuality of relationship. This is indicated in the relationship-centred life of Jesus, in the cosmic significance of his crucifixion and resurrection, and in the relationality which Christians see in the essence of God as relational, Father and Son. It is developed further in the keynote of mystery signalled in language of the Spirit, of God as dwelling in new creation through the Spirit of Christlikeness. An effective contemporary theology must bring together the emancipatory authority of Jesus as the Christ with the shape of the concept of a God for whom to be is truly to be self-giving, and in doing so give fresh meaning to the understanding of life in the Spirit. None of this is new to the tradition of the gospel. But it does need to be spelled out in language to fire the imagination in each new generation.

I want to make a further connection here of cross, resurrection and human rights.

First, concern for human rights is a point at which the pain of God is disclosed, and the cosmic significance of the cross and resurrection for the new creation is underscored. Through the particularity of identification with the oppressed on the cross, God points to the universal significance of kenotic love in all areas of human society. This is a challenge to deepen both Evangelical and Catholic dimensions of the faith.

Second, it is often thought that modern theology reduces the claims of traditional Christology. I suggest the opposite. The tradition often reduced the impact of Christology to rescue from individual sin. Concern for incarnation as radically transforming every sphere of society makes an infinitely larger claim. Self-giving love is the sustaining source of all that is. Human rights and Christology may be mutually illuminating concerns. By thinking of human rights we think of the shape of the human in God's self-giving purpose. In Christology we consider being as creating authenticity and capacity for self-giving in mutuality.

The elements of human rights include: (i) the right to live, (ii) the right to enjoy and maintain a cultural identity, (iii) the right to participate in decision-making, (iv) the right to dissent, (v) the right to personal dignity, (vi) the right to choose freely a religion or belief. 'Suffered under Pontius Pilate' is central to faith. God has characterized his nature as both committed to identification with oppressed humanity, and as bringing a universal new creation out of that particularity. We are called to be a pressure group for the oppressed, but not to become trapped in a culture of marginality.

Christ crucified is *Christus Transformator*, transformation of the wider layers of culture. The cross may be a catalyst for opposition to oppression. God, as the pressure of self-giving love, invites us to respond to his active presence in the widest possible perspective. Incarnation is a standing provocation in history to attend to human rights, as God seeks to humanise us further.

At the centre of the Christian vision stands the figure of God incarnate, tortured by the powers that be, consistently there for the vulnerable. This God is the centre, the integrating source, of theology, ethics, worship, life and service. This God is a trinitarian God, in a Trinity for the understanding of which Chalcedon is the end of the beginning, an inclusive Trinity whose dynamics are fluid and remain God's mystery. This God is God in Christ, an inclusive Christology which is open to all humanity. This God is God as Spirit, creating Christlikeness within the Christian community and spreading Christlikeness as self-giving, creative, responsive love throughout the wider human community.[8]

Conclusion – unconditional generosity

It is not perhaps surprising that this study of the Christian future should focus on generosity as the capacity most desirable for negotiating the potential tensions of the world of the future. It should not be surprising, either, that the generosity of God in Christ is related to human rights. Rudolf Bultmann was much criticized for reducing theology to anthropology. There is of course an important cosmic dimension to theology. God is the creator and reconciler of the entire universe, and we have to learn to respect that environment. Yet we cannot do this without sensitive attention to our human condition, and especially to those manifestations of it which are most near to the vulnerability of God – those people who are vulnerable, who are put at risk by our inability to respond to God's humanity in Christ.

The relation of the generous love of God to humanity is not simply an intellectual problem, as the emancipatory theologians have told us, it is first and foremost a human problem about the quality of our generosity to one another on this planet. Human rights, or the lack of them, are where the problem often becomes acute. The unwillingness of governments to take generous decisions in these matters, often in cases of asylum seekers, is notorious.

The lessons of the 1930s, where many Jews in Europe were turned back to be sent to the death camps (not least from Britain), have clearly not been learned. On the cross God showed that vulnerable generosity was of the essence of his nature, and that solidarity with the tortured and the persecuted was at the very heart of the gospel. Generations since have found this an inconvenient gospel and have found innumerable ways of masking its impact. It seems to me that this unique generosity of God is a microcosm of the need for development of generosity across the chasms and divides of society at all times, and not least in the present.

Generosity is especially germane to the intense current debate about the nature of modernity, and the relation between religion and public reason. Charles Taylor has argued recently that modernity is not that form of life to which all cultures converge as they discard beliefs that held our forefathers back (acultural theories). Rather, it is a movement from one constellation of background understandings to another, which repositions the self in relation to others and the good. (*Hastings Center Report* 25/2 1995, 24ff). Modernity involves the coming to be of new kinds of public space. 'We cannot be without *some* sense of our moral situation, *some* sense of our connectedness to others.' In that case, the development, or not, of a sense of generosity in response to the situation of others should make a considerable difference to our own selfhood, as individuals and in community.

James Buchanan has taken this issue further (*Soundings* 78.1, Spring 1995), in questioning the givenness of the tradition of hypergoods which Taylor wants to commend. What about other, non-Western traditions?

> Among the most pressing moral issues with which the world is faced are competing cross-cultural claims about goods and hypergoods, each connected with the deeply held feelings of communities, particularly of ethnic hatred for other communities. This hatred is almost always described by the others in moral terms and tones and is even raised to the level of hypergoods within those communities.

Here is a case where Berlin's notion of the negotiation of incommensurables through agonistic liberalism might again help us.

In the recent Harvard Symposium (Spring 1995) on *Political Liberalism – Religion and Public Reason*, centred around John Rawls' limited permission for religious discourse in public policy debate, Cornel West voices a similar concern: 'There is no doubt in our minds that among us we have such levels of irrationality and superstition that it is hard to explain how any liberal society stays afloat. Oklahoma City was a reminder of just how fragile liberal societies are. In Bosnia, Guatemala and elsewhere, just trying to get a liberal project off the ground is so very difficult' (7). There was a need expressed for effective liberal Christian voices on public issues, so that the discussion should not be left to fundamentalists. It is worth recalling that Rawls has gone a long way towards seeking to accommodate criticism of *A Theory of Justice* as élitist in the more pluralist approaches of *Political Liberalism*, though this has not satisfied all the critics.[9]

One might note here that Habermas, a prominent critic of religion, has recently also allowed that religion may have a limited place in the communicative action of public discourse, Reason cannot console. But it is basically a matter for private rather than public life. This argument is part of Habermas' basic suspicion of metaphysics and religion's metaphysical framework. It may be, however, that religion does not require the kind of foundationalism about which Habermas is justifiably anxious. I have suggested, from a Christology of vulnerable generosity and from Berlin, that there is a middle way here. I have been impressed by some recent comments by Bruce McCormack on transfoundationalism (cf. too, W.J. Meyer in *Journal of Religion* 1995, 370f). It may be that beyond consolation there are other fields in which the stress on reason alone of Rawls and Habermas needs to be supplemented and where religion may help, e.g. moral indignation, (cf. R.M. Adams, 'Moral Horror and the Sacred', *Journal of Religious Ethics*). A rather different defence of theology against Habermas in the sevice of pluralism in public discourse has been made by Michael Welker 'On Pluralism and the Promise of the Spirit': 'What is becoming recognizable is a fragile and variously endangered societal form, on which the quality of democratic politics and of a free and human life together depends' (51). How may the Church strengthen this fragile form? For Welker the Spirit brings about

a transition from an abstract and pretentious ethic of sameness (in which doubtless there might be the greatest advantages) to a dynamic ethics of equality which is sensitive to differences, that is not satisfied with formal protestations of equality and with only partial honoring of the same. Without dissolving or suspending the different languages, the different loyalties and historical customs, a differentiated, differentiation-protecting experience of community is established. (59-60)

A theology of generosity will recognize Welker's proposal as a valuable exegetical and theological encouragement.

The role of religion in public discourse, to which theologians may attribute Evangelical, missiological and dialogical dimensions, is central to the debates centred on the work of Stanley Hauerwas, developing the positions of Alistair MacIntyre. Christopher Beem has well summarized Hauerwas' basic positions as follows (*Journal of Religious Ethics*, Spring 1995). Contemporary liberalism is morally bankrupt, and American society reflects this pathology. His epistemology denies the possibility of substantive moral discourse between narratives, and thereby effectively rejects the possibility of politics in a pluralistic world. To this he contrasts Martin Luther King's plea for 'a liberalism which is truly liberal', which is committed to defending what it believes to be true. In response Hauerwas has underlined the failure of liberal rhetoric to deliver on promises, not least on racism. With this I can only agree, yet still reflect that the abuse does not take away the proper use, and that apocalyptic is no substitute for patient engagement in a pluralist society. It can be said in Hauerwas' favour that he can be as critical of right-wing political rhetoric as of the left. 'When Fascism comes to America, it will come with a friendly face . . . "Family values," it turns out, is how Americans talk about "blood and soil" ', (*Dispatches from the Front*). But we shall not avoid fascism, of the right or of the left, by retreating to the sanctuary and pulling up the drawbridge. (For a devastating though one-sided critique of Hauerwas, as a supporter of *Theos* without *Logos*, see Max Stackhouse in *Christian Century*, Oct. 18th 1995.)

I return to the specific instance which I regard as a kind of litmus test of the effectiveness of the gospel in a pluralistic culture, the relation of theology and Church as understood and engaged with in practical commitment to human rights.

In his excellent 1982 essay *Defining Human Rights: a Revision of the Liberal Tradition* John Langan, SJ reconsiders the meaning of a human right. 'First, it is a right that a human person has simply by virtue of being a human person, irrespective of his or her social status, cultural accomplishments, moral merits, religious beliefs, class memberships or contractual relationships' (*Human Rights in the Americas: The Struggle for Consensus*, eds A. Henelly, SJ and J. Langan SJ, 71). There may be conflicts between rights. 'The problem is to understand respect for rights in such a way that rights are not absolutized, but that at the same time rights are indeed taken seriously' (75). However, some rights, e.g. not to be tortured, may be absolute. This brings us back to the negotiation of incommensurables, and the need not to be bound by systems, positive or negative. Hence the value of liberalism. Liberalism, in its classic eighteenth-century form, sets fences around individuals to protect them against certain things that governments or social groups or other individuals might want to do to them'.This requirement is a standing challenge to governments. There is here a way of relating individuals to community 'For to acknowledge the rights of others is to enter into a form of community with them. Acknowledging the needs, the liberty and the worth of other individuals in this view is not a retreat into selfishness but a step to a just ordering of the world' (99).

What has this fundamental consideration of humanity as humanity with a right to dignity and basic requirements for subsistence to do with the generosity of God? It was in opposition to the inhumane, to the violence which distorts creation, that God's incarnation led specifically to the place of the vulnerability of the cross. It is of course possible to trace the Christian contribution to respect for human rights to a doctrine of creation, to the existence of a universal moral law created by God, to the understanding of the image of God, even to the Reformation understanding of common grace. Max Stackhouse does this in a useful paper on *Public Theology, Human Rights and Missions*. He sees Western patterns of human rights as greatly indebted to this tradition. I would agree, though I think the residual classic tradition also played an important part, in Christian humanism. Then theology tended to become fideist. Public theology developed out of Catholic concern for the common good and liberation theology, which was, however, sectarian. A truly public theology can be both Catholic and Evangelical.

I am happy to share Stackhouse's concern for public theology and for human rights as a central area of public engagement. It seems to me, however, that the kind of foundational framework which he seeks in the universal moral law is unlikely to be retrieved, at least in the substantial sense in which he wants this, though it may prove to be a provocative imaginative construct. Theologies of orders of creation and mandates have proved in our century to have more disadvantages than advantages. However, I do think that Christology, more precisely the kenotic, vulnerable, generous Christ who is the incarnation of the self-giving, creative, responsive love of God, is a basis for public theology, which is also open to dialogue with all humanity, religious or non-religious. As the basis of new creation through the Spirit a Christology of generosity has cosmological implications for our understanding of theology and the natural sciences as well as the human sciences. A Christology of vulnerable generosity should also be able to contribute to dialogue with Judaism, on the face of it one of the most difficult areas, because it is a statement of identification with radical suffering, with powerlessness and with marginalization.

Generosity cannot immediately relieve radical suffering, which may repeat violence suffered in violence inflicted. But it may create the conditions of the possibility of forgiveness, which may lead to reconciliation and so to a weakening in the cycle of violence. The dynamics of forgiveness have been eloquently explored recently in relation to sin by Marjorie Suchocki and in relation to public polity by Don Shriver. It begins with a recognition of the full weight of oppression which ungenerous action thrusts upon its victims, memorably described in a specific instance by Jacquelyn Grant.

> The multi-dimensional nature of black women's oppression means that trouble is always in the way. . . . It is literally impossible to hide. Being neither among the dominant culture nor the privileged class, black women and other non-white women, because of their triple jeopardy, are three times removed from the image of Jesus and the image of God' (M. Stevens, ed., *Reconstructing the Christ Symbol*, 56, 65).

Triple jeopardy is a phrase easily dismissed as overblown rhetoric. Yet it describes a condition which any view of the vulnerable generosity of God must take full account of. The Trinitarian God is identified not only with triune glory but with triple jeopardy.

Generosity may not produce instant results, and indeed in the short-term it may lead to disappointment. Yet one of the main fruits of love in St Paul's characterization is patience. The generosity of God is patient, and waits for the consummation of the fruits of the Spirit in the future of the Kingdom. Given that this is the shape of the future in God's purpose, it may be possible for us to learn a long-term strategy of patience as part of our understanding of discipleship. It has been well said that 'Faith in a steadfast love that endures for ever in a dominion of resurrection that is confessed to have no end looks upon no situation as hopeless' (Christopher Morse, *Not Every Spirit*, 345). It is this hope in the future as God's future for us that makes generosity a possibility in the face of impossibility, the generosity of the great 'nevertheless' which has always been at the centre of faith, and which is aware of participation in a deeper generosity which is always there before us. But the future is anticipated in the presence of the vulnerable generosity of God in crucifixion and resurrection. God is in time, before time and after time. The Christian future, which is God's future for all humanity, is the generosity of God in Jesus Christ, in his eternal self-giving and responsive love. Participation in this community of generosity is a human right delivered through grace to all humanity.

Generosity, I have suggested, is central to faith, and is likely to be a vital element in resolving the tasks of reconciliation and development in the multicultural society of the future. Human history is full of imitations and examples of generosity, and these may be developed to help us face the future. We may look at many aspects of our past and learn by evaluating our story from a perspective of generosity. We may develop a generous reading of our Christian heritage, of the Church, of the Bible, of pastoral care and public service within the wider world. Generosity may become the tone which underlies all Christian thought and action.

Generosity as I conceive it has a basic liberal dimension, being concerned with the welfare of every individual as a child of God. It also has a community dimension, for we grow through our interpersonal relationships. A generous community founded on the generosity of God will always be an open community, not privileging élites or excluding minorities. It will always be aware of the dangers of exclusive ideologies. It will not encourage ungenerous conduct, but will seek always to promote wider generosity. It will be open to continuing change, believing that the human future is not simply the freezing of present structures as they are, but rather a moving forward through trust in the promise of God's future, a future of the establishment of God's reign of vulnerable love, the overflow of divine generosity. For creation itself is God's first act of generosity, and reconciliation is the ultimate unconditional squandering of God's love for the new creation.

NOTES

Introduction

1. *Generositas* in Latin suggests excellence or goodness (Pliny). The more obvious equivalent of our contemporary understanding of generosity is perhaps *liberalitas*. Cicero, (*Officiisc.*), Plato (*Republic* 402C) and Aristotle (*Eth.Nic.* 1119b2) speak of *eleutheriotes*, generosity, and in the Fathers the word is used by Basil and Gregory of Nyssa. Cf. E. Pybus, *Human Goodness-generosity and Courage*, Harvester, London 1990 on Aristotle's understanding of liberality. She offers the following definition (47): 'As a virtue, generosity will be a willingness on the part of a person to respond to needs, to be willing to judge that a need arises (i.e. a willingness to recognise needs), and to act when they judge it necessary to do so, giving up something if necessary, but not minding the sacrifice more than is possible.' A. A. Long outlines Cicero's critical discussion of generosity in *De Officiis*, where he notes that apparently generous acts may spring not from natural benevolence but from 'a kind of glory' (*Justice and Generosity*, Cambridge, CUP, 1995). We may recall Luther's critique of a 'Theology of Glory'.

   It soon becomes clear in considering concepts of generosity and vulnerability, which appear often in these pages, that in both cases a critical assessment is important. Not any sort of generosity or vulnerability will do. In communities legal rights and formal recognition are much more important than pious but empty expressions of brotherly love. A rhetoric of generosity may conceal a silent apartheid and a system of glass ceilings. Lack of generosity over a period may create an atmosphere of genuine fear and hatred in ordinary people – classically illustrated in Daniel Goldhagen's overstated but sobering *Hitler's Willing Executioners*. The attempt has to be made to create communities where love banishes fear, but working carefully at conflict limitation, e.g. in eradicating inequalities.

2. Effective generosity cannot be naive, for this leads to disaster. Likewise vulnerability in a Christian context is the vulnerability of goodness. Vulnerable people may themselves create destruction, e.g. murderers are usually highly vulnerable people. Hospitality is important, but may lead to betrayal. In the Gospels Judas shares in the Last Supper.

   Descartes reflected on generosity in *The Passion of the Soul. Generosité.* preface xvii cf. Susan James' essay in J. Tully ed., *Philosophy in an Age of Pluralism*, 15ff. Generosity, which consists in both a person's 'knowing that nothing truly belongs to him but (the) freedom to carry out whatever he judges to be best' and in 'a firm and constant resolution to carry out whatever he judges to be best' (*The Passion of the Soul*, 153), Descartes tells us, 'as it were the key to all the other virtues. Because they esteem nothing more highly than doing good and disregarding their own self-interest, they are always perfectly courteous, gracious and obliging to everyone' (156). Therefore Descartes' self is not quite the disengaged self for which Taylor argues. Charles Taylor replies that. 'Generosity is a turning inwards in its seventeenth century sense.' 'The focus of moral awe and admiration is turning inward' (216). The generosity with which this study will be concerned is more a turning outwards, towards the generosity of Christ.

1 Faith and the human future

1. Reflections on the future are not a monopoly of the twentieth century. People have always wondered, and worried, about what was to come. We may think of the apocalyptic and prophetic traditions of the Bible and the ancient Near East, the oracular traditions at Delphi and elsewhere, the *sortes Vergilianae*. Important too was the Christian expectation, which we shall consider later, that the world would come to an end soon, to be replaced often by a belief in progress. The twentieth century saw the development of an industry of futurology, from Jules Verne and George Orwell to science fiction. Alvin Toffler's *Future Shock* was a landmark of prediction of a technological future. Biblical eschatology was secularized in Marxist hope, and then returned in theologies of hope and apocalyptic.
2. See especially Gilles Kepel, the *Revenge of God*, and Martin Marty and R. S. Appleby, *The Fundamentalism Project*.
3. For useful and very different reflections on revelation see R.F. Thiemann, *Revelation and Theology*, and N. Wolterstorff, *Divine Discourse*.
4. To take full account of discussion of the postmodern would require a book in itself. I am inclined to regard the postmodern as a subset of the modern, and to doubt the value of either affirming or rejecting the postmodern, or indeed the modern, as a whole. I have much sympathy with Charles Taylor's essay, *Two Theories of Modernity*. For a full-scale theological assessment of the postmodern (with which I have some reservations) see J. Milbank, *Theology and the Social Sciences*. cf. too, Mark Kline Taylor's challenging *Remembering Esperanza*.
5. Bernstein's approach comes close to Berlin's agonistic liberalism, which will be discussed in Part II.
6. Reference may be made here to two very useful articles on the postmodern in *JAAR* Winter 1993 LXI/4: 'The Postpositivist Choice:

Tracy or Lindbeck?' by Richard Lints, and 'Hermeneutics in Theology and the Theology of Hermeneutics', by Stephen L. Stell. Lints distinguishes between 'a rejection of an Enlightenment (and positivist) inspired vision of objectivity or a rejection of an Enlightenment (and positivist) inspired vision of public rationality' (657). The first is postmodern and the second postliberal. Stell wants to bring together the insights of both. 'From this perspective of Christ's unfolding identity and the triune reality of God, does not the context for Christian understanding necessarily consist in the mutual interplay of traditional experience of the living God and the experienced tradition of the narrative framework?' (695). This leads Stell to recommend the centrality of a Trinitarian structure for theology.

2 Faith at Vatican X

1. It would in some ways be easier to think of a council in fifty years' time, rather than in 500, because by then there will probably be changes quite unimaginable to us today. But I think it important to bear in mind that theology, Church and society in our time is only part of a very long term picture. As I shall argue, it may be that we are only at the beginning of important developments.

2. I pursue this narrative further, in order to try to underline the transience of the present, and the fact that the issues on which we often express so much certainty today will undoubtedly be discussed and written about in different ways in the future. New technological and scientific discoveries will themselves inevitably contribute to a new climate of discussion. In the face of such change, it seems right that we should take a fairly modest view of the finality of our present perspectives.

3 The future of our religious past

1. I am grateful to Gustav Adolf Benrath for a fascinating Alexander Robertson Lecture in the University of Glasgow on historical perceptions of church history.

2. Leighton and Campbell in Scotland provide fascinating affinities and contrasts. Both were concerned for their theological convictions – Leighton on the need for peace between ecclesiastical factions, Campbell for an understanding of the suffering of God in atonement, against opposition from parties to the right and the left. Campbell's theology, later almost universally accepted, was no defence against party interests. Leighton's writings rarely mention the public arena. But his spirituality gave him insight into the fatal divisions within it –

a good example of the important complementarity between Christian worship and public engagement.

3. On Liberalism and liberal theology, see Stephen Holmes, *The Anatomy of Antiliberalism*, xi: 'In the century of Hitler and Stalin, wise professors still brand liberalism as the great enemy'. On pluralism, liberalism and multiculturalism see also Chapter 10. There is a good discussion of issues related to pluralism in W. Jeanrond and J. Rike, eds, *Radical Pluralism and Truth – David Tracy and the Hermeneutics of Religion*, John Macquarrie relates pluralism to Christology: 'If there is a sense in which God was in Christ, this is something so stupendous that we could only destroy it by trying to package it too neatly.' Hans Küng relates pluralism to 'dialogibility': 'Dialogibility is therefore a deeply democratic virtue which can only survive under the umbrella of a positive intellectual, cultural and religious pluralism, under the reign of liberty, equality and fraternity' (238).

4. Cf. *Barth and Schleiermacher, Beyond the Impasse*, ed Streetman and Dukes. While there were of course important differences between Barth and Schleiermacher, there were also important continuities, in part deriving from Calvin. Much of the controversy of the Schleiermacher debate in recent decades has been particularly sterile.

5. The Schleiermacher Seminar at the AAR, and the work of Brian Gerrish, have been a valuable stimulus to a new critical appreciation of his work. Brian Gerrish reminds me of Schleiermacher's continuing interest in biblical exegesis as integral to theology, illuminating the divine presence in Christ.

6. W.P. Alston, *'Religion'*, *Encyclopaedia of Philosophy*, (ed. P. Edwards). London Macmillan, 1967.

7. M.E. Marty and R.S. Appleby *The Fundamentalism Project* vol. I, pp. 821f , offer a list of characteristics of fundamentalisms in their conclusion. Fundamentalism

1. includes religious idealism;
2. provides an irreducible basis for communal and personal identity;
3. is intentionally scandalous;
4. shows extremism – poses a litmus test for separating true believers from outsiders;
5. offers dramatic eschatologies;
6. seizes upon particular historical moments matched to sacred texts and traditions;
7. names, dramatizes and even mythologizes their opponents;
8. sets boundaries, protecting the group from contamination, and preserves purity;
9. comes to prominence in times of crisis, actual or perceived – crisis of identity;

10. seeks to replace existing structures with a comprehensive system;
11. has proved itself selectively traditional and selectively modern;
12. lifts old doctrines from original contexts, then uses them as ideological weapons against a hostile world;
13. tends to use charismatic and authoritarian male leaders;
14. shows closer affinity to modernism than traditionalism;
15. takes advantage of the openness of secular democracies;
16. repudiates separation of religion from politics;
17. has mass appeal.

In their recent *The Glory and the Power*, Marty and Appleby suggest that fundamentalism should never be underestimated or overestimated: 'So long as there are threats to their identities, people will claim their God as agent of the formation of their groups and as one who would bless them uniquely and charge them to act particularly' (201).

8. Cf. Part II below. Taylor is, as it were, a communitarian of a higher order, whose views often overlap with liberal perceptions (cf. the areas of agreement suggested by Mulhall and Swift below chapter 10). Cf. again James Tully, ed., *Philosophy in an Age of Pluralism*. In this volume Richard Tuck, 'Rights and Pluralism', 159ff, offers a good discussion of rights: 'Taylor has always been both fascinated and appalled by programmes of moral or cultural unification' (160). Patricia Benner, in *The Role of Articulation in Critical Care Medicine*, provides a striking correlation between theory and clinical practice.

Common or shared meanings do not mean that everyone agrees with one another or even that they always get the correct understanding of the situation. But common meanings, concerns, habits, do make it possible for one embodied human being to understand another's situation and plight . . . claim here is that caring and caring practices must be located in a community, in a shared world of members and participants. I take this to be the communitarian stance articulated by Taylor (143-4).

Charles Taylor's work provides the vision and example for examining notions of the good embedded in narratives and observations of actual practice (154).

Taylor's reply, *Pluralism*, 213f., includes an interesting appreciation of Isaiah Berlin. 'Berlin has tirelessly pointed out the irreconcilable conflict that we frequently face between different goods which we cannot help subscribing to. . . . I still believe that we can and should struggle for a "transvaluation" (to borrow Nietzsche's term *Umwertung*) which could open the way to a mode of life, individual and social, in which these demands could be reconciled.' We shall notice other ways of attempting to bridge this tension, in Edward Farley's balance between the foundational and the non-foundational, in Bruce McCormack's transfoundationalism, and in my own appeal to the vulnerability of Christ. Taylor is unhappy with the term 'communitarianism' (250): 'I just want to say that single principle neutral liberalism can't suffice.' This is in my view close to Berlin's own position.

Taylor's understanding of the self in relation to community is a central theme of many of his writings, for example in *The Ethics of Authenticity* and *Philosophical Arguments*. *The Ethics of Authenticity* contains carefully differentiated discussions of such controversial themes as individualism and instrumental reason and political liberty. Taylor seeks to commend self-authenticating freedom as a source of authenticity, to consider the forms of equal recognition, and coming together on a mutual recognition of difference, and at the same time the need to avoid fragmentation in society. He concludes 'As Pascal said about human beings, modernity is characterized by grandeur as well as by misery. Only a view that embraces both can give us the undistorted insight into our era that we need to rise to its greatest challenge' (121). This theme of 'both/and', not dissimilar to the tension which we will later explore in Isaiah Berlin, is the theme of the essays 'Cross-Purposes: The Liberal-Communitarian Debate' and 'Invoking Civil Society', in *Philosophical Arguments*. The relation of individual to community is of course of perennial interest. For example the Baillie Commission of 1944 noted with approval 'the returning spirit of community after the long reign of individualism' (quoted by Ron Ferguson in *George MacLeod*, 201). A good example of a community of generosity is documented in R. Ferguson, *Geoff, The Life of the Revd Geoffrey Shaw*, Famedram, Gartocharn, 1979.

4 Faith and theological pluralism

1. Wall and Heim, *How My Mind has Changed*. It seems to me that American theology is especially productive at the present and worthy of special attention in looking to the future. At the same time I shall argue that other perspectives may cast light on some of the impasses of the American debate.
2. Cf. below on John Kekes, *The Morality of Pluralism*.
3. Cf. good discussions of Frei in Garrett Green, ed., 'Scriptural Authority and Narrative Interpretation', in D. Ford, *JTS*, October 1995, in Gerard Loughlin's *Telling God's Story*, Cambridge 1995, and more critically in J. F. Kay, *Rudolf Bultmann*.
4. There is a heroic synthesis of scientific and theological reflection in the

treatment of creation in Pannenberg's *Systematic Theology* II. Though I find the connections made here in some ways too much of a coincidence, it is clear that such attempts are necessary and valuable accounts of the state of the art at a particular time. I agree that R. J. Russell and his team make a particularly valuable contribution to this area at the present. Cf. Russell, Stoeger and Coyne, *Physics, Philosphy and Theology*.

5. I am grateful to Robert Wuthnow of Princeton University and to Don Shriver in Union Theological Seminary for extremely helpful discussions of the role of religion and theological education in public life in America today. There is a useful snapshot and bibliography of mainstream Protestantism in America in 1996 in Coalter, Mulder and Weeks, *Vital Signs*.

6. The effect of a strong management culture emanating largely from America on societies elsewhere should not be underestimated. Here there is obviously much to be welcomed, provided that management techniques are not used to exploit people and to diminish human dignity.

5 Faith and transformation

1. Generosity by example will only be possible when the churches are seen to work effectively together, within a framework of reconciled diversity. Ecclesiastical tensions in the recent Bosnian conflict demonstrate the fragility of ecumenical understanding to date.

2. Despite the fierce criticisms which his specific proposals have drawn, it is clear that John Hick has given an enormous stimulus to inter-religious dialogue.

3. Dialogue between Christianity and Judaism is complicated by the terrible fact of the Holocaust and also by the important denominational differences within the two faiths themselves. Continuing proselytism does nothing to improve relations.

4. It seems to me that a liberal theology which is also determinedly pluralist is more likely to learn from alternative proposals than a purely liberal stance would be. Taking account of objections may strengthen a proposal, stimulate criticism and perhaps even encourage a measure of humility. There are illuminating discussions of Edward Farley's 'Good and Evil' in *Theology and the Interhuman*, ed. R. R. Williams, and by Walter Lowe in *Religious Studies Review* for July 1995. Williams notes that for Farley 'freedom' (virtue) is a power to exist in the face of tragic vulnerability *vis-a-vis* a specific dimension of human reality' (91). (Many refs in index to vulnerability).'Being -founded' is a historical freedom that is not a release from vulnerability and the tragic, but a way of existing as vulnerable and tragic' (93). Cf. Nancy Ramsey

on Farley: 'Primacy lies with the interhuman sphere because it is in relationships that we recognise a deep summons to transcend self-preoccupation and move towards a sense of compassionate obligation for one another in our fragility' (208). The central themes of good and evil are well brought out in the article by Walter Lowe (*Religious Studies Review* 21/3 1995:202f.).

5. Cf. too, chapter nine. On the relation between theology and justice, I have learned much from Duncan Forrester's *Christian Justice and Public Policy*: Cambridge, CUP, 1997, which I was privileged to read in draft. The argument is along these lines. Underlying the whole discussion is the question as to the Christian voice in the public realm, and how best it might be articulated. What is justice? Is Fairness enough? (Rawls), Justice and the Market (Hayek), Community and communicative action, (Habermas). Forrester explores the connections poverty-social, justice-criminal justice, then justice and beyond – love, justice and justification, justice and community, the hope of justice. Rawls and Hayek are too narrow – no priority for the poor. 'For Habermas philosophy can give an account of what justice is, but cannot spell out the demands of justice' (in press). He examines the work of such writers as Eliott, Hayek, Garland, Bottoms and Lebacqz, plus the feminists – Gilligan, Okin and Benhabib. Where does religion affect the issues? For Habermas – the ideal speech community is the just community. Religion has no role: 'the solidarity on which discourse ethics builds remains within the bounds of earthly justice'. In response, Peukert sees Habermas's theory as incoherent except within a theological horizon. What of the dead? There is a need for eschatological hope.

Forrester affirms that 'My own conviction is that all serious theology must be public theology, and that the most serious and probing theology is also the most publicly relevant', quoting Karl Barth, *Church Dogmatics i.i xvi*, on the real needs of the day. But there is not the Christian theory of justice, or of punishment. He recalls Kierkegaard's suspicion of systems, which mask unpalatable realities, e.g. theory of rehabilitation can conceal brutalizing practices. People have to learn to rise above their illusions. Kierkegaard was deliberately unsystematic. We have only fragments. 'And when a fragment is recognized as true, there should be an interest in its provenance, in its embeddedness in a broader truth. In this sense the kind of approach I am advocating could well be a modest way of confessing the faith in public'.

6. Despite fierce criticism, it should be noted that the churches have produced some valuable reports on marriage and human sexuality in recent years, which show a consensus in willingness to re-examine traditional assumptions, and to distinguish between the challenge of

the gospel and the cultural constructions of different ages. Cf., in Britain, *The Church of Scotland, reports of the Panel on Doctrine*, 1993,94, 95, the Church of England, Board of Social Responsibility in 1995, The Methodist Church and the URC, in America PCUSA and UCC in the 1990s, the Churches in the Netherlands 1990-95. It ought to be possible both to affirm the importance for society of families (cf. Don Browning's multi-volumed project sponsored by the Lilly Foundation) and to affirm those whose family ties are not only those of the traditional nuclear family, in this way strengthening the whole fabric of a multicultural society.

7. There is an excellent discussion of the issues in the 1996 Princeton collection ed. C. L. Seow, *Homosexuality and Christian Community*, WJK. J.D. Hunter in *Culture Wars*, New York, Harper 1991, makes the point that progress on social issues often involves hard decisions and a willingness to bear costs. 'A tremendous amount of money, people and resources, therefore, would disappear if homosexuality were sanctioned even more than it is now' (194). There are interesting similarities (and also differences) between the various modern emancipatory theologies; cf. e.g. James H. Cone, *God of the Oppressed*, New York Seabury 1975.

8. I have discussed these issues in relation to the theology of Eberhard Jüngel in J. Webster, ed. *The Possibilities of Theology*, Edinburgh, T & T Clark 1994.

6 Faith, theology and community

1. William Placher writes of an *Unapologetic Theology* in his book of that name. This seems to be to be the sort of approach that is likely to be productive in the future.

2. A theology of Word and sacrament might be expected to take up the strengths of both Catholic and Protestant theology in a way which still remains to be done.

3. Cf. esp. J. Grant, *White Women's Christ, Black Women's Jesus*, and the writings of James Cone and Alan Boesak, also C. West, *Contextual Theology*.

4. On the christological dimension cf. Julie M. Hopkins, *Towards a Feminist Christology* (Grand Rapids, Eerdmans 1994); Maryanne Stevens, *Reconstructing the Christ Symbol* (New York, Paulist Press 1993); Ellen K. Wondra, *Humanity has been a Holy Thing*. Women who are disabled, like black women, often suffer from a double discrimination, cf. Nancy L. Eiesland, The *Disabled God: Towards a Liberatory Theology of Disability*. (Nashville, Abingdon Press 1994).

5. On the different dimensions of poverty cf. Jeremy Seabrook, *Landscapes of Poverty*.

7 Generosity in the Christian future

1. Baillie's American experience was important for the development of his particular understanding of a liberal theology. Though influenced by Barth, especially in the 1930s, he was often to return to the quest for an authentic liberal theology which would overcome the standard criticisms. I hope to document this search, which I regard potentially fruitful for the theological future, in an intellectual biography of John and Donald Baillie. For John and Donald Baillie, cf. D. Fergusson, ed., *Christ, Church and Society*, Edinburgh T. & T. Clark 1993.
2. Bonhoeffer was strikingly generous in his personal relationships. See E. Bethge, *Friendship and Resistance*, WCC/Eerdmans, 1995.
3. There is a huge and highly controversial literature on rights and human rights, produced by philosophers, political theorists, sociologists, lawyers, theologians and others. L. W. Sumner in *The Moral Foundation of Rights* observes that 'Like the arms race the escalation of rights rhetoric is out of control.' He distinguishes conventional rights, such as legal rights and institutional rights, from natural rights, contractarian or moral rights, and consequentialist rights. Sumner stresses that 'the concept of a right does not lock us into an individualist social/political theory' – it is also possible to consider collective rights, and to honour both individual and communitarian values (210).

   Alan Gewirth among others has argued that, though freedom may on occasion be justifiably denied on utilitarian grounds, like driving on the wrong side of the road, there may be some absolute rights. 'All innocent persons have an absolute right not to be made the intended victims of a homicidal project' (*Human Rights*, 233).
4. On Marxism and theology. cf. esp. Peter Scott, *Theology, Ideology and Liberation*.

8 Generosity through the tradition

1. I do not think that we shall contribute to the Christian future by neglecting the traditional centres of doctrine. What we need is a continuing reappropriation and application of the centre of faith.
2. In a period in which churches experience increasing polarization between radical and conservative, it must be possible to learn from both traditional and radical theologies. One advantage of David Tracy's description of theology as both prophetic and mystical is that it may facilitate such an appropriation. Formulations of doctrine are important, but God is a real presence, not a formulation incarnate.
3. Now that slavery has gone (though not in all parts of the world), we find it hard to imagine that Jefferson continued to own slaves and that slavery was taken entirely for granted till comparatively recently.

If the churches were to be persuaded that Jesus Christ is the generosity of God incarnate, as the ecclesial reality, this would have a radically transforming effect on Christianity in the public realm.

4. If we believe that the life and action of Jesus is the engagement of the generosity of God with human life at a particular time and place, then the historical dimensions of Jesus' life are always central to a doctrine of God, especially a doctrine of God as Trinity.

5. Balance between fundamental theology, worship and social justice was fundamental to the thought of Bonhoeffer, who might have gone on to develop such a theology in detail.

6. The whole project of a Christian humanism, from Erasmus to modern thinkers such as Baillie, Lampe and Tillich, has perhaps not yet come to full fruition, not least because it does not always fit easily with the immediate interests of ecclesiastical structures. It is not of course incompatible with devotion to the Church, but it is especially concerned with outreach.

7. Though it is only mentioned here, we may expect the Christian Gospel to continue to have a deeply challenging, subversive and fortunately unpredictable effect on the arts.

8. D. Tracy, *On Naming the Present*, 14–15 in Ralph Harper's *On Presence*, (TPI, 1991). This is a good discussion of presence, for which I am grateful to David Tracy.

9. The interpretation of the Bible is as important for Catholic as for Protestant Christianity, if only because much that is enshrined in the tradition is based on particular historical readings of the biblical text, e.g. on the ordination of women as priests. Ecclesial communities need to learn to work together on the basis of different understandings of Scripture within each community, a difficult but crucial negotiation. Cf. F. H. Borsch, (ed.) *The Bible's Authority in Today's Church*, Philadelphia, TPI 1993; W. Brueggeman, *Interpretation and Obedience*, Minneapolis, Fortress 1991; R. P. Carroll, *Wolf in the Sheepfold*, London, SPCK 1994.

10. The whole notion of a sacramental understanding of the universe is one which Protestants sometimes find hard to appreciate – Karl Barth was notoriously unable to do much with the concept of sacrament. Yet it is an implicit correlate to the role of language and the Word as bearer of reality.

9 Generosity under pressure – heresy, reconciliation and the Christian future

1. Stephen Katz, *The Holocaust in Historical Context*, I. On issues of interfaith dialogue see too, H. Vroom, ed., *Religions and the Truth*, and *No Other Gods*.

2. Christ is the truth. More will be said in chapter 10 on the relation of truth claims to pluralism. The suggestion is that Christ is the truth of consistent generosity and vulnerability, creating being in others through self giving and response.

3. Rahner and Küng represent two different ways of progress, both valuable: need for radical action, and need to carry a majority of those who may be persuaded by more moderate advocacy.

4. Word and sacrament, Bible and Eucharist, continuing development of Church. I have chosen an example from the Reformed tradition with which I am directly involved in Scotland, while being associated also with the Episcopal Church. It is all too easy for non-Roman Catholics to see the abuse of power as a papal problem, anti-Semitism as a Lutheran problem, etc. and to support such scholars as Hans Küng and Karl Barth as champions against wickedness abroad. It is incumbent on us to start with a realistic critical assessment of the communions with which we are most closely involved.

There are good illustrations of generosity by example in Christian community in Dick Simpson, *The Politics of Compassion and Transformation*. 'Compassionate and transformative politics is based upon a theology of compassion' (93). 'Both conservative and radical evangelical Christians conclude that Christianity requires compassion in the form of service to the hungry, the poor and the wretched' (100). Chapter 6, 'Compassionate Action', looks at Chicago today. Wellington Avenue United Church of Christ formally becomes a 'sanctuary' for illegal immigrants in 1982 – refugees from El Salvador. Programmes of care for the hungry and the homeless are set up. The scale of poverty is formidable. 'One-third of the dog food sold in grocery stores in the low income areas of the United States is eaten by humans' (3) (Simpson p.3).

5. Much is made in recent discussion of the dangers of individualism, often characterized as a peculiarly liberal vice and a concomitant of the role of market forces in society. It does not appear to have been noticed that much denominationalism, often seen as a good thing because based on community, may be seen as equally an echo of market forces, in which denominations develop a house style, company culture and image which is exactly like the practice of modern multinational companies. On the current debate between liberals and conservatives in America, J.D. Hunter's *Culture Wars* is particularly clear. 'Clearly then, within each of these opposing public philosophies, the words "freedom and justice" carry enormous symbolic meaning. Where cultural conservatives tend to define freedom economically (as individual economic initiative) and justice socially (as righteous living), progressives tend to define freedom socially (as individual rights) and justice economically (as equity)' (115).

6. Some of the debate between liberals and communitarians, and between liberal Protestants and traditional Catholics especially, on the status of human goods has the rather artificial tone of much discussion of free will and determinism. Clearly there is much to be said on both sides. Absolutizations of natural law positions or conventionalism may be clear but often removed from practical reality, and a balance between conflicting considerations may be the best available solution. From a liberal perspective cf. esp. Stephen Holmes, *The Anatomy of Antiliberalism*.

For the development of a liberal multiculturalism Joseph Raz and Will Kymlicka are excellent. Cf. Joseph Raz, *Ethics in the Public Domain*, ch.3, pp.45ff for a good discussion of Rawls and esp ch.7 'Multiculturalism, a liberal perspective', 154ff. He defines liberal multiculturalism in this way (174):

Liberal multiculturalism, as I called it, as a normative principle affirms that, in the circumstances of contemporary industrialist or post-industrialist societies, a political attitude of fostering and encouraging the prosperity, cultural and material, of cultural groups within a society, and respecting their identity, is justified by considerations of freedom and human dignity . . . While incorporating policies of non-discrimination, liberal multiculturalism transcends the individual approach which they tend to incorporate, and recognizes the importance of unimpeded membership in a respected and flourishing cultural group for individual well-being.'

Liberal multiculturalism leads not to the abandonment of a common culture, but to the emergence of a common culture which is respectful towards all the groups of the country and hospitable to their prosperity (176).

Will Kymlicka, *Multicultural Citizenship. A Liberal View of Minority Rights*, examines the importance of cultural membership (105f.): 'I have tried to show that liberals should recognize the importance of people's membership in their own societal culture, because of the role it plays in enabling meaningful individual choice and in supporting self-identity. While the members of a (liberalized) nation no longer share moral values or traditional ways of life, they still have a deep attachment to their own language and culture.' On tolerance he makes the point that 'What distinguishes liberal tolerance is precisely its commitment to autonomy – that is, to the idea that individuals should be free to assess and potentially revise their existing ends' (158). Cf. Susan Mendus, *Toleration and the Limits of Liberalism*. In James Tully's *Philosophy in an Age of Pluralism*, 159f.; Richard Tuck, in his essay on rights and pluralism, makes useful comments on Kymlicka: 'Cultural membership is therefore, according to Kymlicka, a primary good just as vital as more traditional ones such as individual freedom and material well-being' (179).

10 A strategy for generosity

1. It is scarcely surprising that Küng has attracted endless criticism for his theological work. He does indeed sometimes appear stressed, embattled and too sharp in his formulations. This is perhaps inevitable, given the radical nature of his work. It does seem to me that he will eventually be seen as one of the great Christian figures of our time.

2. It is such discoveries of divine presence which create hope in what is often a rather bleak landscape of religious retrenchment.

3. Richard Holloway has called for liberal Christians to stand up and be counted, in order to be effective in countering an increasing conservatism within the churches. I think this is crucial, and the most important aspect is for liberal Christians to learn at last to work together.

4. It is a tribute to MacIntyre's scholarship that even his critics have largely allowed him to set the agenda for debate. I hope to suggest alternative perspectives for understanding the theological tradition in a study of the legacy of the Baillie brothers.

5. Perhaps strangely, there is almost no mention of Berlin in the transatlantic debate. Yet his incisive reasoning, allied to a deep knowledge of the European tradition, enables him to gain a perspective which seems to me to be uniquely illuminating in the discussion of liberalism and pluralism. The issues debated here are issues which I regard as part of the infrastructure of generosity, and central to the struggle for negotiated progress on human rights.

6. Again it seems to me that theologians will only become credible dialogue partners in the public realm when they are seen to be credible and responsible dialogue partners in their own guilds.

7. It may seem that the stress on pluralism has been overdone. In my view theology, churches and denominations have maintained triumphalist and monopolistic stances for so long that the habit has become ingrained – a characteristic ecclesial 'habit of the heart' – which has to change. On the nature of mission in the modern world cf. David J. Bosch, *Transforming Mission*.

8. In *An Ethic for Enemies – Forgiveness in Politics*, Don Shriver provides a reminder, if such is needed, that forgiveness, like generosity, is a complex and multidimensional concept. This is a book about forgiveness, forgiveness not simply in the area of personal relationships but in the field of secular politics, and it is absolutely germane to our theme of generosity. The introduction contains a quotation from Robert Frost which sums up the agenda – 'to be social is to be forgiving'. In this book Don Shriver traces the history of forgiveness and its opposite,

revenge, from Aeschylus to Jesus – the discoverer of 'social' forgiveness – and beyond. The centre of the book is an analysis of political ethics as moral memory – against the background of recent American relations with Gemany and Japan, in the continuing domestic problem of racism and in the Civil Rights Movement in the present. Forgiveness is a complex and multidimensional concept, not easy to actualize, but vital to the future of the human race. Forgiveness involves memory and moral judgement. In a political context it includes the fourfold strand of moral truth, forbearance, empathy and commitment. It seeks to repair fractured human relationships.

Chapters 1 and 2 consider forgiveness in the sources of European and American culture, in Aeschylus and Thucydides, in the Hebrew Bible, in the New Testament and the Church. The *Oresteia* unfolds to show how individual and collective acts of vengeance inevitably lead to political disaster. It is high time to learn from the past and join in common friendship. Thucydides documents a similar circle of violence and revenge, and appeals for a certain trust and mutual recognition. In the Hebrew Bible the stories of Cain and Joseph tell of crime, fear, revenge, the difficulty of reconciliation. Justice is not simple, but requires careful deliberation.

The ministry of Jesus took place in a specific political and social context. Forgiveness is linked to healing, prayer and community discipline. In church history forgiveness tended to be restricted to the personal sphere in the sacrament of penance or obscured in a Kantian sense of duty. Chapter 3 examines the conditions of the possibility of agreement on ethical standards in a modern pluralistic culture. More people, over 100 million, have been killed in wars in our century than in the wars of the previous 5,000 years. How can nations learn to remember, repent and forgive?

Chapters 4 to 6 seek an answer to this question – dealing with Germany, Japan and African Americans. Shriver considers first Germans and Americans, and the effects of Nazism. Germans found confession of guilt difficult, Americans found forgiveness hard. President Reagan's visit to the Bitburg cemetery, with its SS graves, is examined. 'Stunning' courage is seen in President von Weizsäcker's speech of public repentance.

The relationship between the United States and Japan remains more difficult. Attitudes were coloured by racism throughout the war, on both sides. There were atrocities on both sides. To empathize, the two nations have to learn to appropriate each other's memories, Pearl Harbor and Hiroshima, the interned on both sides. Otherwise self-righteousness will generate new hostilities. The realization of equal citizenship for African Americans seems paradoxically to be the hardest of the three tasks. Shriver quotes Cornel West: 'Either we learn a new language of empathy and compassion, or the fire this time will consume us all' (170). Justice here includes above all economic justice.

The conclusion seeks to identify pointers to a human future of forgiveness. There is a place for apology and for restitution in national life and public record. Democratic pluralism is central to this future. 'And once we have learned the discipline of forgiveness for the harms we do inflict, we will experience, with our enemies, a new increment of hope that neither strangeness nor enmity is forever' (233). This is an outstanding study on a theme which is right at the centre of Christian faith and witness. It has implications both for internal relationships within the churches and for the role of the churches in the public square. Shriver's insistence that Christian presence must be a forgiving and reconciling presence, a generous presence, if it is to be authentic Christian presence, is clearly a message that cries out to be heard and acted on with a measure of urgency, and not just on the other side of the Atlantic.

9. Cf. Leif Wenar, 'Political Liberalism, an internal critique', in *Ethics* 106, October 1995, 36-62.

References

Adams, R.M., 'Moral Horror and the Sacred', *Journal of Religious Ethics* 23/2, Summer 1995, 201ff

Alston, W.P., *Religion, Encyclopedia of Philosophy*, (ed. P. Edwards). London Macmillan, 1987

Baillie, J., *The Sense of the Presence of God*. Oxford, OUP, 1962

Bellah, R.N., ed. *Habits of the Heart*, Berkeley, University of California Press 1985

Berlin, I., *Four Essays on Liberty*. Oxford, OUP 1969

Bernhardt, R., *Christianity without Absolutes*. London SCM Press, 1994

Bernstein, R., *The New Constellation: The Ethical-political Horizons of Modernity/Postmodernity*. Oxford, Polity 1991

Borg, M., *Jesus in Contemporary Scholarship*. Pennsylvania, TPI 1994

Braaten, C., *No Other Gospel*. Minneapolis, Fortress 1992

Browning, D., *A Strategic Practical Theology*. Minneapolis, Fortress 1991

Browning, D. and Fiorenza, F., *Habermas, Modernity and Public Theology*. NewYork, Crossroad 1992

Brummer, V., *The Model of Love*. Cambridge, CUP 1994

Buchanan, J.C., 'Taylor and the Communitarians'. *Soundings* 78.1. Spring 1995, p.143

Bultmann, R., *Retrospect and Prospect*. ed. E.C. Hobbs (Harvard Theol St), Philadelphia, Fortress 1985

Byrne, J.M., ed., *The Christian Understanding of God Today*. Dublin, Columba Press 1993

Cady, L.E., *Religion, Theology and American Public Life*. New York, SUNY 1993

Chadwick, O., *The Secularisation of the European Mind*. Cambridge, CUP 1976

Coakley, S. and Pailin, D., eds, *The Making and Remaking of Christian Doctrine*. Oxford, OUP 1993

'Conflict, Community – arts' in *Int. Encl. of Soc. Sci.* New York, 1968

Cook, M., *The Open Circle*. Minneapolis, Fortress 1991

Cousins, E., *Christ of the 21st century*. Dorset, Element 1992

Coyle, A., *Inside – Rethinking Scotland's Prisons*. Edinburgh, Scottish Child 1991

Cronin, K., *Rights and Christian Ethics*. Cambridge, CUP 1994

Cupitt, D., *After All – Religion without Alienation*. London, SCM Press 1994

Dalferth, I., *Der auferweckte Gekreuzigte*. Tübingen, Mohr 1994

Davis, C., *Religion and the Making of Society*. Cambridge, CUP 1994

Del Colle, R., *Christ and the Spirit – Spirit Christology in Trinitarian Perspective*. Oxford, OUP 1994

Drewermann, E., *Kleriker*. Munich, DTV 1989

Duke, J.O. and Streetman, R.F., *Barth and Schleiermacher, Beyond the Impasse*. Philadelphia, Fortress 1988

Edwards, D., *Religion and Change*. London, Hodder 1969

Edwards, D., *The Futures of Christianity*. London, Hodder 1987

Eide, A. and Hagtvet, B., *Human Rights in Perspective*. Oxford, OUP 1992

Elliott, C., *Praying the Kingdom*. London, DLT 1985

Falconer, A.D., ed., *Understanding Human Rights*. Dublin, Irish School of Ecumenics 1980

Farley, E., *Good and Evil – Interpreting a Human Condition*. Philadelphia, Fortress 1990

Feenstra, R. and Plantinga, A., *Trinity, Incarnation and Atonement*. Notre Dame, Indiana, University of Notre Dame Press 1989

Ferm, V., ed., *Contemporary American Theology*, New York 1993

Fiorenza, E.S., *In Memory of Her*. London, SCM Press 1983

Fleischacker, S., *The Ethics of Culture*. Ithaca and London, Cornel University Press 1994

Frei, H., *The Unity of the Churches: An Actual Possibility*, New York 1985

Frei, H., *Types of Christian Theology*. Yale, Yale University Press 1992

Frei, H., *Theology and Narrative*. Oxford, OUP 1993

Gadamer, H.-G., *Truth and Method*

Galtung, J., *Human Rights in Another Key*. Cambridge, CUP 1994

Geertz, C., *Local Knowledge*. New York, Harper 1984

Gellner, E., *Postmodernism, Reason and Religion*. London, Routledge 1992

Gerrish, B.A, *Continuing the Reformation*. Chicago, University of Chicago Press 1993

Gillon, R. and Lloyd, A., eds, *Principles of Health Care Ethics*. Chichester, John Wiley 1994

Girard, R. *Violence and the Sacred*. Baltimore, Johns Hopkins University Press 1977

Gorrell, D.K., *The Age of Social Responsibility: The Social Gospel in the Progressive Era, 1900–1920*. Macon, Georgia, Mercer UP 1988

Gray, J., *Isaiah Berlin*. Oxford, OUP 1995

Gudorf, C., *Victimization, Examining Christian Complicity*. Philadelphia TPI 1992

Gunton, C., *The One, the Three and the Many*. Cambridge, CUP 1993

Gutierrez, G., *A Theology of Liberation*. London, SCM Press 1974

Haight, J., *Mystery and Promise, A Theology of Revelation*. Liturgical Press, Minnesota, 1993

Handy, C., *The Age of Unreason*. London, Hutchison 1990

Handy, C., *The Empty Raincoat*. London, Hutchison 1994

Harvey, D., *The Condition of Postmodernity*. Oxford, Blackwell 1990

Hauerwas, S., *Dispatches from the Front*. North Carolina, Duke UP 1994

Hauerwas, S., 'Response to C. Beem'. *Journal of Religious Ethics* 1995, 135f

Hauerwas, S. and MacIntyre, A., *Revisions: Changing Perspectives in Moral Philosophy*. Notre Dame, Indiana, University of Notre Dame Press 1983

Hick, J., ed., *The Myth of God Incarnate*. London, SCM Press 1977

Hick, J., *An Interpretation of Religion*. London, Macmillan 1989

Hick, J., *The Metaphor of God Incarnate*. London, SCM Press 1993

Hodgson, P., *Winds of the Spirit*. London, SCM Press 1994

Honore, D. ed., *Trevor Huddleston. Essays*. Oxford, OUP 1988

Horsley, R., *Sociology and the Jesus Movement*. New York, Continuum 1994

Horton, J. and Mendus, S., *After MacIntyre*. Oxford, Polity 1994

Jahanbegloo, R., *Conversations with Isaiah Berlin*. London, Phoenix 1992

Jeanrond, W., *Theological Hermeneutics*. New York, Crossroad 1991

Jones, G., *Critical Theology*. Oxford, Blackwell 1995

Joyce, J., *The New Politics of Human Rights*. London 1978

Katz, S., *The Holocaust in Historical Context, I*. Oxford, OUP 1994

Kaufman, G., *In Face of Mystery*. Cambridge, Mass., Harvard University Press 1993

Kee, A.C., *Knowing the Truth: A Sociological Approach to New Testament Interpretation*. Minneapolis, Fortress 1989

Kekes, J., *The Morality of Pluralism*. Princeton, Princeton University Press 1993

Küng, H., *Christianity*. London, SCM Press 1995

Küng, H., *Theology for the Third Millennium*. London, SCM Press 1991

Küng, H. and Moltmann, J., *Islam, a challenge for Christianity*.

Kymlicka, W., *Multiculturalism and Citizenship*. Oxford, OUP 1995

Lacugna, C., *God for Us*. San Francisco, Harper Collins 1991

Leech, K., *The Eye of the Storm: Spiritual Resources for the Pursuit of Justice*. London, DLT, 1982

Lindbeck, G., *The Nature of Doctrine*. London, SPCK 1984

Lipner, J., *The Face of Truth*. London, Macmillan 1986

Lissner, J. and Slovik, A. eds, *A Lutheran Reader on Human Rights*. Geneva, LWF 1978

Little, D., *Human Rights and the Conflict of Culture – Western and Islamic Perspectives on Religious Liberty*. Columbia, University of South Carolina Press 1988

Long, A., *Justice and Generosity*. Cambridge, CUP 1995

MacIntyre, A., *Three Rival Versions of Moral Enquiry*. London, Duckworth 1990

Markham, I., *Plurality and Christian Ethics*. Cambridge, CUP 1993

Marshall, B., ed., *Theology and Dialogue*. Notre Dame, Indiana, University of Notre Dame Press 1990

Marty, M.E. and Appleby, R.S., *The Fundamentalism Project I – IV.* Chicago, University of Chicago Press 1994

Miller, D., *The Case for Liberal Christianity.* London, SCM Press 1981

Mitchell, B., *Faith and Criticism.* Oxford, Clarendon 1994

Moltmann, J., *On Human Dignity.* London, SCM Press 1984

Moltmann, J., *The Spirit of Life – A Universal Affirmation.* London, SCM Press 1992

Morse, C., *Not Every Spirit.* Pennsylvania, TPI 1995

Mulhall, S. and Swift, A., *Liberals and Communitarians.* Oxford, Blackwell 1992

Neuhaus, R. *The Naked Public Square.* Grand Rapids, Eerdmans 1984

Niebuhr, R., *The Nature and Destiny of Man,* I and II. London, Nisbet 1941-3

Nino, C.S., *The Ethics of Human Rights.* Oxford, Clarendon 1991

O'Collins, G., *Christology.* Oxford, OUP 1995

Outka, G. and Reeder, J.P., *Prospects for a Common Morality.* Princeton 1993

Pagels, E., *On Human Dignity, the Internationalization of Human Rights.* New York 1979

Peacocke, A.R , *Theology for a Scientific Age.* 2nd edn, London, SCM Press 1993

Perry, M., *Love and Power, the Role of Religion and Morality in American Politics.* Oxford, OUP 1991

Phillips, D., *Looking Backward – a Critical Appraisal of Communitarian Thought* Princeton, Princeton UP 1993

Placher, W., *Unapologetic Theology.* Kentucky, WJK 1989

Polkinghorne, J., *Science and Providence.* London, SPCK 1989

Polkinghorne, J., *Reason and Reality.* London, SPCK 1991

Polkinghorne, J., *Science and Christian Belief – Theological Reflections of a Bottom-up Thinker.* London, SPCK 1994

Potter, H., *Hanging in Judgement.* London, SCM Press 1993

Pybus, E. *Human Goodness – generosity and courage.* London, Harvester 1990

Rowland, C., *Radical Christianity.* Oxford, Blackwell 1988

Rowland, C., *Reflections on the Politics of the Gospel*

Rubin, B. and Spiro, E., eds., *Are Human Rights Universal?*

Schillebeeckx, E., *Christ.* London, SCM Press 1980

Schleiermacher, F., *The Christian Faith,* eds H.R. Macintosh and J.S. Stewart. Edinburgh, T.&T. Clark 1928

Scott, P., *Theology, Ideology and Liberation.* Cambridge, CUP 1994

Stackhouse, M., *Public Theology, Human Rights and Missions.* Boston Theol. Inst. 1990

Stevens, M., *Reconstructing the Christ Symbol.* New York, Paulist Press 1993

Stocker, M., *Plural and Conflicting Values.* Oxford, OUP 1990

Suchocki, M., *The Fall to Violence.* New York, Continuum Press 1994

REFERENCES

Taylor, C., *Sources of the Self – The Making of Modern Identity*. Cambridge, CUP 1989

Taylor, C., 'Two Theories of Modernity'. *Hastings Center Report*, 25/2 March 1995, 24ff

Tracy, D., *Plurality and Ambiguity*. London, SCM Press 1988

Tracy, D., *On Naming the Present*. London, SCM Press 1994

Villa-Vicencio, C., *A Theology of Reconstruction*. Cambridge, CUP 1994

Ward, K., *Religion and Revelation*. Oxford, OUP 1994

Watson, F., *The Open Text*. London SCM Press 1993

Watson, F., *Text, Church and World*. Edinburgh, T. & T. Clark 1994

Weil, S., *The Iliad or the Poem of Force*, in *Revisions* (eds S. Hauerwas and A. MacIntyre). Notre Dame, University of Notre Dame Press 1983

Whaling, F., ed., *The Samye Symposium*. Dumfriesshire, Langholm 1994 Oxford 1995

Wink, W., *Engaging the Powers*. Minneapolis, Fortress 1992

Wuthnow, R., *The Restructuring of American Religion*. Princeton, Princeton University Press 1988

Wuthnow, R., *Acts of Compassion*. Princeton, Princeton UP 1991

Wuthnow, R., *Christianity in the 21st Century – Reflections on the Challenges Ahead*. Oxford, OUP 1993

Further Reading

Abraham, W. J. and Holtzer, S.W. ed., *The Rationality of Religious Belief.* Oxford, OUP 1987

An-Na'im, A., Gort, J., Jansen H. and Vroom, H. *Human Rights and Religious Values.* Grand Rapids, Eerdmans 1995

Barbour R.S. ed., *The Kingdom of God and Human Society.* Edinburgh, T. & T. Clark 1993

Barr, J., *Fundamentalism.* London, SCM Press 1981

Barry, B., *Justice and Impartiality.* Oxford, OUP 1995

Barth, K., *Church Dogmatics.* Edinburgh, T. & T. Clark 1936-69

Barton, J., *What is the Bible?* London, Triangle 1991

Battin, M.P., *Ethics in the Sanctuary.* Yale University Press, New Haven 1990

Bauckham, R., *The Bible in Politics.* London, SPCK 1989

Baumann, Z., *Postmodern Ethics.* Oxford, Blackwell 1993

Beckley, H., *Passion for Justice.* Kentucky, WJKP 1992

Beem, C., 'American Liberalism v the Christian Church', *Journal. of Religious Ethics,* 1995, p.119

Beiner, R., *What's the Matter with Liberalism?* Berkley, University of California Press, 1992

Benne, R., *The Paradoxical Vision: Public Theology for the 21st Century.* Minneapolis, Fortress 1995

Berry, P., and Wernick A., eds, *Shadow of Spirit, Postmodernism and Religion.* London, Routledge 1992

Betz, H.D., ed., *The Bible as a Document of the University.* Chico, Scholars Press, 1981

Board of Social Responsibility, Church of England, *Something to Celebrate.* London, Church House 1995

Boesak, A., *Black and Reformed.,* New York, Orbis 1986

Bonhoeffer, D., *Meditating on the Word.* Boston, Cowley 1986

Bosch, D., *Transforming Mission.* New York, Orbis 1994

Braybrooke, M., ed., *Stepping Stones to a Global Ethics.* London, SCM Press 1992

Brown, S.J., Responses to the Great War in the Scottish Presbyterian Churches'. JEH 94/1

Browning, D., The Lilly Family Project. *Christian Century,* Jan. 31, 1996

Cady, L.E., *Theology in Politics and Society.* Cambridge, CUP 1980

Casey. J., *Pagan Virtue.* Oxford, OUP 1990

Clements, K., *The Theology of Ronald Gregor Smith.* Leiden, Brill 1986

Coakley, S., *Christ without Absolutes.* Oxford, OUP 1988

Coalter, M., Mulder, J. and Weeks, L., *Vital Signs – The Promise of Mainstream Protestantism*. Grand Rapids, Eerdmans1996

Cone, J.H., *God of the Oppressed*. Seabury, New York, 1975

Davaney, S., *Theology at the end of Modernity*. Philadelphia, TPI 1991

Davie, W., *Shattered Dream*. Pennsylvania, TPI 1994

Delaney, C.F., ed., *The Liberal-Communitarian Debate*. New York, Rowanfield 1994

Etzioni, A., *The Spirit of Community*. London, Fontana 1995

Evans, R. J., *Rituals of Retribution. Capital Punishment in Germany 1600–1987*. Oxford, OUP 1996

Ewing, K.D., *Human Rights and Labour Law*. Mansell, Dorset, 1992

Galipeau, C., *Isaiah Berlin's Liberalism*. Oxford, Clarendon 1994

Gatrell, V.A.C., *The Hanging Tree*. Oxford, OUP 1994

Geertz, C., *The Interpretation of Cultures*. London, Fontana 1975

Gewirth, A., *Human Rights*. Chicago, University of Chicago Press 1982

Gewirth, A., *The Community of Rights*. Chicago, University of Chicago Press 1996

Giddens, A., *The Consequences of Modernity*. Stanford, Stanford University Press 1990

Gilligan, C., *In a Different Voice*. Cambridge, Mass., Harvard University Press 1983

Goldhagen, D., *Hitler's Willing Executioners*. New York, Knopf 1996

Gombrich, R., *Precepts and Praxis*. Oxford, OUP 1971

Goodin, R.E., *Motivating Political Morality*. Oxford, Blackwell 1992

Greeley, A., *The Denominational Society*. Illinois, Scott, Foresmann and Co. 1972

Gostin, L., *Civil Liberties in Conflict*. London, Routledge 1988

Gould, W., *The Generosity of Christian Love*. London 1676

Grant, J., *White Women's Christ, Black Women's Jesus*

Green, G., *Scriptural Authority and Narrative Interpretation*. Philadelphia, Fortress 1987

Hardy, H., *Concepts and Categories. Essays for Isaiah Berlin*. London, Hogarth Press 1978

Harper, R., *On Presence*. Philadelphia, TPI 1991

Harris, D.A., ed., *Multiculturalism from the Margins*. Westport, Conn., Bergin & Garvey 1995

Hauerwas, S. and Matzko, D., 'The Sources of Charles Taylor'. *Religious Studies Review*, October 1992

Hebblethwaite, B.L., 'The Varieties of Goodness', in Runzo, J., ed., *Ethics, Religion and the Good Society*. Louisville, Kentucky, WJK 1992

Hennelly, A. and Langan, J., eds, *Human Rights in the Americas: The Struggle for Consensus*. Washington, DC, Georgetown University Press 1982

Hilton, B., *The Age of Atonement*. Oxford, OUP 1988

Hollinger, D.A., *Postethnic America – beyond Multiculturalism*. New York, Harper 1996

Holmes, S.P., *Passions and Constraints – on the Theory of Liberal Democracy*. Chicago, University of Chicago Press 1996

Holmes, S., *The Anatomy of Antiliberalism*. Cambridge, Mass., Harvard University Press 1993

Houlden, J., ed., *The Interpretation of the Bible*. London, SCM Press 1995

Hourani, A., *Arabic Thought in the Liberal Age 1798 – 1939*. Cambridge, CUP 1962

Hunter, J.D., *Culture Wars*. New York, Harper 1991

Hutchison, W.R., ed., *Between the Times, the Travail of the Protestant Establishment in America*. Cambridge, CUP 1989

Jeanrond, W. and Rike, J., eds, *Radical Pluralism and Truth – David Tracy and the Hermeneutics of Religion*. New York, Crossroad 1991

Kellenberg, J., *Inter-religious Models and Criteria*. London, MacMillan 1993

Kelsey, D., *Between Athens and Berlin*. Grand Rapids, Eerdmans 1993

Kepel, G., *The Revenge of God*. Oxford, Polity 1995

Kuitert, H.M., *I have my Doubts*. London, SCM Press 1993

Kymlicka, W., *Multicultural Citizenship. A Liberal View of Minority Rights*. Oxford, Clarendon 1995

Lacey, M.J., ed., *Religion in 20th Century American Intellectual Life*. Cambridge, CUP 1989

Larmore, C., *Patterns of Moral Complexity*. Cambridge, CUP 1987

Lawrence, B., *Defenders of God*. London, Tauris 1990

Lebacqz, K., *Six Theories of Justice*. Minneapolis, Augsburg Press 1986

Lennan, R., *Karl Rahner's Ecclesiology*. Oxford, OUP 1994

Lomasky, L.E., *Persons, Rights and the Moral Community*. New York, OUP 1987

Lovin, R. ed., *Religion and American Public Life*. New York, Paulist Press 1986

Lucas, J., *Responsibility*. Oxford, OUP 1993

MacIntyre, A., *After Virtue*. London, Duckworth 1981

Macintyre, A., *Whose Justice? Which Rationality?* London, Duckworth 1990

Mackey, J., *Power and Christian Ethics*. Cambridge, CUP 1994

Marsden, G., *Fundamentalism and American Culture*. Oxford, OUP 1980

Marsden, G., *The Soul of the American University*. New York, OUP 1994

Martin, R., *A System of Rights*. Oxford, OUP 1992

Marty, M., *Modern American Religion*, 1893-1919. Chicago, University of Chicago Press 1986

Marty, M., *Religion and American Politics*. Chicago, University of Chicago Press 1990Marty, M. and Appleby, B., *The Glory and the Power*. Chicago, University of Chicago Press 1992

Marx, K., *Critique of Hegel's Philosophy of Right* (ed. J. O'Malley). Cambridge, CUP 1970

Matilal, B., *Perception*. Oxford, OUP 1986

Mendus, S., *Toleration and the Limits of Liberalism*. Basingstoke, MacMillan 1989

Meyer, W., 'Habermas' Changing View of Religion'. *Journal of Religion*. 1995, 371f

Migliore, D., 'Christology in Context'. *Interpretation*, July 1995, 242f

Milbank, J. *Theology and Social Theory*. Oxford, Blackwell 1990

Miller, D., *Social Justice*. Oxford, OUP 1976

Mudge, L., *The Sense of a People – Towards a Church for the 21st Century*. Philadelphia, TPI 1992

Newlands, G., *God in Christian Perspective*. Edinburgh, T. & T. Clark 1994

Newman, J., *Foundations of Religious Tolerance*. Toronto, University of Toronto Press 1982

Nussbaum, M., *The Fragility of Goodness*. Cambridge, CUP 1986

Odendahl, T.J., *Generosity begins at Home – Generosity and Self-interest among the Philanthropic Elite*. New York, Foundation Center 1990

Odugoye, M.A., 'The Church of the Future, its Mission and Theology'. *Theology Today*, 1995, pp.494–505.

Outka, G. and Reeder, J.P., *Religion and Morality*. New York 1973

Placher, W., *Narratives of a Vulnerable God*. Kentucky, WJK 1994

Poling, J.N., *The Abuse of Power – a Theological Problem*. Nashville, Abingdon 1991

Pontifical Biblical Commission, *The Interpretation of the Bible in the Church*. St Paul, Boston 1993

Rasmussen, L., *Moral Fragments and Moral Community*. Minneapolis, Fortress 1993

Rawls, J., *Political Liberalism*. New York, Columbia University Press 1993

Rawls, J. *et al.*, Political Liberalism. (*Harvard Divinity Bulletin*) 3.4, Columbia University Press 1995

Raz, J., *The Morality of Freedom*. Oxford, OUP 1986

Raz, J., *Ethics in the Public Domain*. Oxford, OUP 1994

Reynolds, C.H. and Norman, R., *Community in America*. 1988

Rorty, R., *Contingency, Irony and Solidarity*. Cambridge, CUP 1989

Rosenblum, N., ed., *Liberalism and the Moral Life*. Cambridge Mass., Harvard University press 1989

Ross, P.J., *Deprivatising Morality*

Russell, R.J., Stoeger, W.R. and Coyne, G.V., eds, *Physics, Philosophy and Theology: a Common Quest for Understanding*. Vatican City State, Vatican Observatory 1988.

Ryan, A., ed., *The Idea of Freedom*. Oxford, OUP 1979

Sandel, M., *Liberalism and the Limits of Justice*. Cambridge, CUP 1982

Sandel, M., *Democracy's Discontents: America in Search of a Public Philosophy*. Cambridge Mass., Harvard University Press 1996

Schillebeeckx, E., *Jesus*. London, SCM Press 1979

Schweiker, W., *Responsibility and Christian Ethics*. Cambridge, CUP 1995

Seabrook, J., *Landscapes of Poverty* . Oxford, Blackwell 1985

Shapiro, I., *The Evolution of Rights in Liberal Theory*. Cambridge, CUP 1986

Shriver, D., *An Ethic for Enemies – Forgiveness in Politics*. New York, OUP 1995

Simpson, D., *The Politics of Compassion and Transformation*. Swallow, Ohio UP 1989.

Stackhouse, M., 'Alasdair MacIntyre, an Overview'. *Rel. Stud. Rev.*, July 1992

Stackhouse, M., Creeds, *Society and Human Rights*. Grand Rapids, Eerdmans 1984

Stackhouse, M., *Creeds, Theology and Human Rights*. Grand Rapids, Eerdmans, 1988

Stackhouse, M., 'Review of Hauerwas', *Dispatches Christian Century*. October 18 1995, 962ff

Steiner, H., *An Essay on Rights*. Oxford, OUP 1994

Stewart, M.A., and Wright, J.P., *Hume and Hume's Connections*. Edinburgh, EUP 1994

Stone, R.H., *Professor Reinhold Niebuhr*. Louisville, Kentucky, WJKP 1992

Stout, J., *Ethics after Babel*. Boston, Beacon 1988

Sullivan, W.M., *Reconstructing Public Philosophy*. Berkeley, University of California Press 1982

Sumner, L.W., *The Moral Foundation of Rights*. Oxford, OUP 1987

Taylor, C. *The Ethics of Authenticity*. Cambridge Mass., Harvard University Press 1991

Taylor, C., *Philosophical Arguments*. Cambridge Mass., Harvard University Press 1995

Taylor, M.K., *Remembering Esperanza*. New York, Orbis 1990

Thiel, J.E., *Nonfoundationalism*. Minneapolis, Fortress 1994

Thistleton, A., *New Horizons in Hermeneutics*. London, Harper Collins 1992

Thomson, J.J., *The Realm of Rights*. Cambridge Mass., Harvard University Press 1990

Tracy, D., *Catholicism and Liberalism*. 1994

Tracy, D. and Küng, H., *Towards Vatican III*. Dublin 1978

Tulloch, J., *Movements of Religious Thought*. London 1885

Tully, J., ed., *Philosophy in an Age of Pluralism*. Cambridge, CUP 1995.

Vroom, H., ed., *Religions and the Truth*. Grand Rapids, Eerdmans 1989

Vroom, H., *No Other Gods*. Grand Rapids, Eerdmans 1996

Waldron, J., *Theories of Rights*. Oxford, OUP 1984

Wall, J. and Heim, D., eds, *How my Mind has Changed*. Grand Rapids, Eerdmans 1991

Waltzer, *Spheres of Justice*. Oxford, OUP 1983

Welker, M., 'On Pluralism and the Promise of the Spirit', *Soundings* 78.1, 1995, 49ff

Wenar, L., 'Critique of Rawls', *Political Liberalism Ethics* 1995, 32ff

Williams, B., *Moral Luck*. Cambridge, CUP 1981

Williams, J.G., *The Bible, Violence and the Sacred: Liberation from the Myth of Sanctioned Violence*. San Francisco, Harper 1989

Williams, R.R., *Theology and the Interhuman. Essays in Honour of E. Farley*, Pennsylvania, TPI 1995

Wolpert, J., *Patterns of Generosity in America*. Washington DC, Twentieth Century Fund Press 1993.

Wolterstorff, N., *Divine Discourse*. Cambridge, CUP 1995

Wondra, E., *Humanity has been a Holy Thing*. New York, UPA 1994

Wright, C., *Realism, Meaning and Truth*. Oxford, OUP 1993

Wuthnow, R., *God and Mammon in America*. New York, Free Press 1994

Wuthnow, R., *I Came Away Stronger*. Grand Rapids, Eerdmans 1994

Wuthnow, R., *Sharing the Journey*. New York, Free Press 1994

Young, P.D., *Christ in a Postchristian World*. Minneapolis, Fortress 1995.

Young-Bruehl, E., *The Anatomy of Prejudice*. Cambridge Mass., Harvard University Press 1996

INDEX